The Frontier
and
The American West

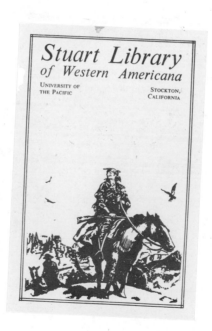

GOLDENTREE BIBLIOGRAPHIES
In American History
under the series editorship of
Arthur S. Link

The Frontier
and
The American West

compiled by

Rodman W. Paul
California Institute of Technology

and

Richard W. Etulain
Idaho State University

Copyright © 1977

AHM PUBLISHING CORPORATION

All rights reserved

ISBN: 0-88295-542X, paper
ISBN: 0-88295-5659, cloth

Library of Congress Card Number: 76-11622

PRINTED IN THE UNITED STATES OF AMERICA
787

Contents

Editor's Foreword ix

Preface xi

Abbreviations xv

I. Bibliographical Guides and Selected Reference Works . . 1
   1. General Accounts, General Interpretations,
         and Series 1
   2. Selected Reference Works 2
   3. State and Regional Histories 3
   4. Bibliographies of the West, the Frontier, and the
         Individual Western States 5

II. The Frontier Hypothesis and
         Frederick Jackson Turner 7

III. Frontiers East of the Missouri: the Earliest "Wests" . . 12

IV. Indians 16
   1. Reference Materials and Documentary Collections . . 16
   2. A Selection of Books and Articles 18

V. The Fur Trade and the Trappers 25

VI. Manifest Destiny: Diplomacy and Wars of Westward
         Expansion 30

VII. The Army in the Nineteenth-Century West 34

VIII. Explorers and Scientists in the Nineteenth-Century
         West 39

IX. The Spanish-Speaking Peoples in the West 42
   1. Before 1900: the Pioneer and Transitional Eras and
         Herbert Eugene Bolton 42
   2. Since 1900: the Era of Large-Scale Immigration . . 44

X. The Mormons 47

XI. Mining and Miners 52

CONTENTS

XII. Cattle and Sheep 58
    1. Cattlemen and Cowboys 58
    2. Sheep and Wool 62

XIII. Agriculture 64

XIV. Irrigation, Reclamation, and Water Supply 70

XV. Land and Land Policy in the West 73

XVI. Lumbering and Forestry in the West 77

XVII. Oil in the West 82

XVIII. Transportation and Communication 85
    1. The Great Trails 85
    2. Pre-Railroad: Teamsters, Stagecoaches, Express
               Companies, Pony Express, Wagon Roads,
               and Steamboats 86
    3. Railroads, Interurban Lines, and Highways 89
    4. Mail and Telegraph 92

XIX. Western Cities and Towns 92

XX. Merchants, Investors, Speculators, and the Economy . 96

XXI. Labor in the West 99

XXII. Chinese and Japanese Immigrants, Their Descendants,
            and Treatment of Them 103

XXIII. Black Americans in the West 107

XXIV. European Ethnic Groups 110

XXV. Racism, Nativism, and Ethnicity 112

XXVI. Vigilantism, Violence, and Extra-Legal
           Government 114

XXVII. State and Territorial Government and Politics in the
            Nineteenth Century 117

XXVIII. Western Politics and Reform Movements
           since 1890 121

XXIX. Conservation and Concern for the Environment; the
           National Parks and the Wilderness . . . 126

XXX. Women, the Family, and Women's Rights
           in the West 130

CONTENTS

XXXI. Western Literature and Literature about the West . 134

XXXII. The Visual and Performing Arts 138
    1. Art and Artists 138
    2. Architecture 139
    3. Drama , ... 140
    4. Music . . . . , , 141

XXXIII. Education 142

XXXIV. Journalism 143

XXXV. Religion 144

XXXVI. Western Characteristics 146

Index 149
Notes 169

Editor's Foreword

Goldentree Bibliographies in American History are designed to provide students, teachers, and librarians with ready and reliable guides to the literature of American history in all its remarkable scope and variety. Volumes in the series cover comprehensively the major periods in American history, while additional volumes are devoted to all important subjects.

Goldentree Bibliographies attempt to steer a middle course between the brief list of references provided in the average textbook and the long bibliography in which significant items are often lost in the sheer number of titles listed. Each bibliography is, therefore, selective, with the sole criterion for choice being the significance—and not the age—of any particular work. The result is bibliographies of all works, including journal articles and doctoral dissertations, that are still useful, without bias in favor of any particular historiographical school.

Each compiler is a scholar long associated, both in research and teaching, with the period or subject of his volume. All compilers have not only striven to accomplish the objective of this series but have also cheerfully adhered to a general style and format. However, each compiler has been free to define his field, make his own selections, and work out internal organization as the unique demands of his period or subject have seemed to dictate.

The single great objective of *Goldentree Bibliographies in American History* will have been achieved if these volumes help researchers and students to find their way to the significant literature of American history.

Arthur S. Link

Preface

This bibliography should be approached through the table of contents. There the reader will note that the bibliography has been organized into fifty-four categories and subdivisions of categories. Under the heading for each category are listed the principal books, articles, and doctoral dissertations bearing on that particular topic. Included are any useful bibliographies that the compilers have been able to discover. The number of items under any one heading or subheading has been restricted to a maximum of about one hundred, even though this has made it necessary to omit many deserving references. The compilers have faced difficult choices in deciding what to include and what to omit. Our operations have been influenced not only by the relative significance of one topic as compared to another, but also by the relative amount that has been written about each, and by the quality or lack of quality of that output. Where a subject has inspired an abundance of good books and articles, it is hard to refuse extensive representation.

Since most of the books and articles contain their own footnotes and bibliographies, we have conceived of the present volume as not only guiding the reader directly to the references printed here, but as also steering the inquirer to the much larger range of offerings cited in the individual volumes and essays. We have made an especial attempt to include under each heading some recent publications that both reflect the latest interpretations and also contain citations that will lead the reader into the wealth of material that has become available recently. Anyone who compiles a volume of this kind is bound to be impressed by both the extraordinary outpouring of the past twenty years and the heartening rise in quality. Professionalism without stuffiness has characterized much of this recent output.

To stay within our limit of a hundred entries per category, we have adopted several practices that require explanation. Where an author who has published articles on a subject subsequently incorporates the substance of those articles into a book, we have listed only the book. But since a dissertation is not always quickly or easily available, we have thought it desirable to list a published essay by the same student when it is one that includes at least a part of his thesis. Where a periodical centers an entire issue around articles dealing with a common topic, we have, in most cases, confined ourselves to a single reference that cites the periodical by name, date, and volume and describes it as "special issue devoted to. . . ."

An original intent to have a separate category of biographies and autobiographies has been abandoned in favor of listing personal narratives only under the "functional" heading most closely associated with the individual's career. In the case of the Indians, a special scheme and a disproportionately large selection have been unavoidable if the scholar is to be given access to both the unusual body of strictly reference material that is now available and to a reasonable representation of the flood of modern publishing and reprinting.

Cross-referencing has been used to cope with such obvious questions as whether to list a mining labor dispute under "Mining" or "Labor" or whether a study of timber lands belongs under "Lumbering and Forestry" or "Land and Land Policy." The index is a guide only to the authors of the works cited here; it is not a subject index.

Geographically and chronologically this volume devotes most of its attention, respectively, to lands west of the 98th meridian (the approximate location of the line of semiaridity) and to the period from the 1840s to the present day. Whenever the beginnings of a topic lie farther back in space or time the compilers felt free to select accordingly, and, as the table of contents indicates, headings II–VI and IX, part 1, have been designed to offer coverage for the Turnerian approach, with its stress on the "frontier era" of what is now the East and Middle West, and for the Bolton approach concerning California and the Southwest. When the western phase of an industry such as oil or lumber or railroads is inextricably bound up with the national history of that activity, the compilers have included materials that are national in scope. This includes Alaska, but, regretfully, does not extend to Hawaii, whose history involves a whole new set of problems.

As a convenience to users, we have indicated reprintings or new editions wherever we have had evidence that a book has been reissued, but because of the immense amount of republishing in western history in recent years, it has not been practicable to attempt completeness in this respect. The entire list, however, has been checked against the latest edition of *Paperbound Books in Print,* and books available in that form have been marked with a dagger.

Finally, it should be remembered that this is one of the series of *Goldentree Bibliographies.* Therefore we have in several cases, such as

Western Literature, given enough references to get the reader well started, but have left to other volumes in the series the task of going deeper.

We wish to thank the staffs of the Henry E. Huntington Library, San Marino, California, where much of the work on this bibliography was done, and of the Millikan Library at the California Institute of Technology, Pasadena, and the Idaho State University Library at Pocatello, Idaho. Numerous scholarly friends interrupted their own work to answer queries or to give advice—especially Ray A. Billington, David J. Weber, Ted C. Hinckley, Doyce Nunis, W. Sherman Savage, and Maxine McCloskey.

At Pocatello Marilyn Samore cheerfully handled a dull assignment. At Caltech Margaret Noonan Foutch checked the whole list for paperback availabilities. Joy Hansen of the Division of the Humanities and Social Sciences at Caltech took on the burden of making finished copy out of 3,000 bibliography cards, and she also made the revisions and final corrections before the final version went to the printer. For the imaginative and graceful resourcefulness with which she handled these exacting tasks, our deepest thanks.

Rodman W. Paul
Richard W. Etulain
December 1976

Abbreviations

Ag Hist	*Agricultural History*
AHA News	*American Historical Association Newsletter*
Alas Rev	*Alaska Review*
Am Her	*American Heritage*
Am Hist Rev	*American Historical Review*
Am J Soc	*American Journal of Sociology*
Am Jew Arch	*American Jewish Archives*
Am Jew Hist Q	*American Jewish Historical Quarterly*
Am Pol Sci Rev	*American Political Science Review*
Am Q	*American Quarterly*
Am Sch	*American Scholar*
Am W	*The American West*
Ann Ass Am Geog	*Annals of the Association of American Geographers*
Ann Rep Am Hist Assoc	*Annual Report, American Historical Association*
Ann Wyo	*Annals of Wyoming*
Ant Rev	*Antioch Review*
Ariz	*Arizoniana*
Ariz Hist Rev	*Arizona Historical Review*
Ariz Q	*Arizona Quarterly*
Ariz W	*Arizona and the West*
Ark Hist Q	*Arkansas Historical Quarterly*
Brig You Univ Stud	*Brigham Young University Studies*
Brit Col Hist Q	*British Columbia Historical Quarterly*
Buck Rev	*Bucknell Review*
Bus Hist Rev	*Business History Review*
Calif Geog	*California Geography*
Calif Hist Q	*California Historical Quarterly*
Calif Hist Soc Q	*California Historical Society Quarterly*
Can Hist Rev	*Canadian Historical Review*
Chicago Rev	*Chicago Review*
Chron Okla	*Chronicles of Oklahoma*
Church Hist	*Church History*
Civil War Hist	*Civil War History*
Col Soc Mass Trans	*Transactions, Colonial Society of Massachusetts*
Colo Mag	*Colorado Magazine*
Comp Stud Soc Hist	*Comparative Studies in Society and History*
Curr Anth	*Current Anthropology*

ABBREVIATIONS

Dialogue	*Dialogue: A Journal of Mormon Thought*
Econ Geog	*Economic Geography*
Econ Hist Rev	*Economic Historical Review*
For Hist	*Forest History*
Great Plains J	*Great Plains Journal*
Harp	*Harper's Magazine*
His-Am Hist Rev	*Hispanic-American Historical Review*
Hist	*The Historian*
Hist Stud: Aust New Zea	*Historical Studies (Australia and New Zealand)*
Hunt Lib Q	*Huntington Library Quarterly*
Idaho Yes	*Idaho Yesterdays*
Ind Hist	*Indian Historian*
Ind Mag Hist	*Indiana Magazine of History*
J Am Hist	*Journal of American History*
J Am Stud	*Journal of American Studies*
J Ariz Hist	*Journal of Arizona History*
J Econ Bus Hist	*Journal of Economics and Business History*
J Econ Hist	*Journal of Economic History*
J Eth Stud	*Journal of Ethnic Studies*
J Farm Econ	*Journal of Farm Economics*
J For Hist	*Journal of Forest History*
J Geog	*Journal of Geography*
J Hist Ideas	*Journal of the History of Ideas*
J Land and Public Utility Econ	*Journal of Land and Public Utility Economics*
J Mex-Am Hist	*Journal of Mexican-American History*
J Neg Hist	*The Journal of Negro History*
J Pol Econ	*Journal of Political Economy*
J Pop Cult	*Journal of Popular Culture*
J S Hist	*The Journal of Southern History*
J W	*Journal of the West*
Kan Hist Q	*Kansas Historical Quarterly*
Labor Hist	*Labor History*
Land Econ	*Land Economics*
Lat Am Res Rev	*Latin American Research Review*
Mass Hist Soc Proc	*Massachusetts Historical Society Proceedings*
Mid-Am	*Mid-America*
Mil Aff	*Military Affairs*
Mil Engin	*Military Engineer*
Minn Hist	*Minnesota History*
Miss Val Hist Rev	*The Mississippi Valley Historical Review*
Mo Hist Rev	*Missouri Historical Review*
Mo Hist Soc Bull	*Bulletin, Missouri Historical Society*
Mont: Mag W Hist	*Montana: The Magazine of Western History*
Monthly Labor Rev	*Monthly Labor Review*
N D Hist Q	*North Dakota Historical Quarterly*
N Eng Q	*New England Quarterly*

ABBREVIATIONS

N M Hist Rev	The New Mexico Historical Review
Neb Hist	Nebraska History
Neg Hist Bull	Negro History Bulletin
Nev Hist Soc Q	Nevada Historical Society Quarterly
Ore Hist Q	Oregon Historical Quarterly
Pa Hist	Pennsylvania History
Pa Mag Hist Biog	The Pennsylvania Magazine of History and Biography
Pac Hist Rev	Pacific Historical Review
Pac N W Q	The Pacific Northwest Quarterly
Per Am Hist	Perspectives in American History
Pol Sci Q	Political Science Quarterly
Proc Am Philos Soc	Proceedings, the American Philosophical Society
Q J Econ	Quarterly Journal of Economics
Q Ore Hist Soc	Quarterly of the Oregon Historical Society
Roc Mt Soc Sci J	Rocky Mountain Social Science Journal
Rural Soc	Rural Sociology
S Atl Q	South Atlantic Quarterly
S Calif Q	Southern California Quarterly
S D Hist Coll	South Dakota Historical Collections
S D Rev	South Dakota Review
S Sp Com J	Southern Speech Communications Journal
S W Am Lit	Southwestern American Literature
S W Hist Q	Southwestern Historical Quarterly
S W Rev	Southwest Review
S W Soc Sci Q	Southwestern Social Science Quarterly
S W Stud	Southwestern Studies
Sierra Club Bull	Sierra Club Bulletin
Smoke Sig	The Smoke Signal
Soc Sci	Social Science
Soc Sci Q	Social Science Quarterly
Sov Rev	Soviet Review
Tex	Texana
U Kan City Rev	The University of Kansas City Review
Utah Hist Q	Utah Historical Quarterly
Va Mag Hist Biog	Virginia Magazine of History and Biography
Wash Hist Q	Washington Historical Quarterly
Wash Univ Stud	Washington University Studies (Humanistic Series)
W Am Lit	Western American Literature
W Econ J	Western Economics Journal
W Folk	Western Folklore
W Hist Q	The Western Historical Quarterly
W Hum Rev	Western Humanities Review
W Pol Q	Western Political Quarterly
W Pol Sci Q	Western Political Science Quarterly
W States Jew Hist Q	Western States Jewish Historical Quarterly

ABBREVIATIONS

W Tex Hist Assn Yrbk	*West Texas Historical Association Yearbook*
Wis Mag Hist	*Wisconsin Magazine of History*
Wm Mar Q	*William and Mary Quarterly*
Yale Rev	*Yale Review*

NOTE: The publisher and compiler invite suggestions for additions to future editions of the bibliography.

I. Bibliographical Guides and Selected Reference Works

1. General Accounts, General Interpretations, and Series

1 BANCROFT, Hubert H. *The Works of Hubert Howe Bancroft.* 39 vols. San Francisco, 1882–1890.

2 BIEBER, Ralph P., and LeRoy R. HAFEN, eds. *The Southwest Historical Series: Historical Documents, Hitherto Unpublished, or Inaccessible, Depicting Social and Economic Conditions in the Southwest during the Nineteenth Century.* 12 vols. Glendale, Calif., 1931–1943.

3 BILLINGTON, Ray A. *The Far Western Frontier, 1830–1860.* New York, 1956. †

4 BILLINGTON, Ray A. *Westward Expansion: A History of the American Frontier.* 4th ed. New York, 1974.

5 BILLINGTON, Ray A., and Howard R. LAMAR, eds. *Histories of the American Frontier Series.* New York, 1963–1971; Albuquerque, N.M., 1974–

6 CARTER, Clarence E., and John Porter BLOOM, eds. *The Territorial Papers of the United States.* Washington, D.C., 1934–

7 CAUGHEY, John W. *The American West: Frontier and Region: Interpretations.* ed. Norris Hundley, Jr., and John A. Schutz. Los Angeles, 1969.

8 CAUGHEY, John W. "The Insignificance of the Frontier in American History, or 'Once Upon a Time There Was an American West.'" *W Hist Q,* V (1974), 5–16.

9 DAVIS, W. N., Jr. "Will the West Survive as a Field in American History?" *Miss Val Hist Rev,* L (1964), 672–685.

10 GUTHRIE, A. B., Jr., ed. *The American Trail Series.* New York, 1962–

11 HAFEN, LeRoy R., and Ann W. HAFEN, eds. *The Far West and the Rockies Historical Series, 1820–1875.* 15 vols. Glendale, Calif., 1954–1961.

12 LAMAR, Howard R. "Persistent Frontier: The West in the Twentieth Century." *W Hist Q,* IV (1973), 5–25. Includes good bibliographical notes.

13 MEINIG, D. W. "American Wests: Preface to a Geographical Introduction." *Ann Ass Am Geog,* LXII (1972), 159–184.

14 MORGAN, Neil. *Westward Tilt: The American West Today.* New York, 1963.

15 NASH, Gerald D. *The American West in the Twentieth Century: A Short History of an Urban Oasis.* Englewood Cliffs, N.J., 1973. †

16 PAXSON, Frederic L. *History of the American Frontier, 1763–1893.* Boston, 1924.

17 POMEROY, Earl. "The Changing West." *The Reconstruction of American History.* Ed. John Higham. New York, 1962. †

18 POMEROY, Earl. "Old Lamps for New: The Cultural Lag in Pacific Coast Historiography." *Ariz W,* II (1960), 107–126.

19 POMEROY, Earl. "Toward a Reorientation of Western History: Continuity and Environment." *Miss Val Hist Rev,* XLI (1955), 579–600.

20 THWAITES, Reuben G., ed. *Early Western Travels, 1784–1846.* 32 vols. Cleveland, Ohio, 1904–1907. Repr. New York, n.d.

21 TURNER, Frederick Jackson. See section on "Turner and the Frontier Hypothesis."

21A VANDIVER, Frank E. *The Southwest: South or West?* College Station, Tex., 1975.

22 WEBB, Walter Prescott. *The Great Frontier.* Boston, 1952.

2. Selected Reference Works

23 ADAMS, James T. *Dictionary of American History.* 5 vols. and Index. New York, 1940. Vol. VI (Supplement One), ed. J. G. E. Hopkins and Wayne Andrews. New York, 1961.

24 ADAMS, James T., and Roy V. COLEMAN, eds. *Atlas of American History.* New York, 1943.

25 ADAMS, Ramon F. *Western Words: A Dictionary of the American West.* Rev. ed. Norman, Okla., 1968.

26 ANDRIOT, John L., comp. *Guide to U.S. Government Statistics.* 4th ed. McLean, Va., 1973.

27 ATWOOD, Wallace W. *The Physiographic Provinces of North America.* Boston, New York, etc., 1940.

28 JAMES, Edward T., Janet W. JAMES, and Paul S. BOYER, eds. *Notable American Women, 1607–1950: A Biographical Dictionary.* 3 vols. Cambridge, Mass., 1971.

29 JOHNSON, Allen, and Dumas MALONE, eds. *Dictionary of American Biography.* 20 vols. and Index. New York, 1928–1936. Supplements I-III, covering 1935–1945. New York, 1944, 1958, 1973.

30 KAGAN, Hilde H., ed. *The American Heritage Pictorial Atlas of United States History.* New York, 1966.

31 LAMAR, Howard R., ed. *The Readers' Encyclopedia of the American West.* To be published, New York, 1977.

32 MORRIS, Richard B., ed. *Encyclopedia of American History.* Enl. and updated. New York, 1970.

33 *The National Cyclopaedia of American Biography.* 55 vols. plus current, index, and conspectus vols. New York, 1898–1974.

34 PAULLIN, Charles O. *Atlas of the Historical Geography of the United States.* Washington, D.C., 1932.

35 POULTON, Helen J. *The Historian's Handbook: A Descriptive Guide to Reference Works.* Norman, Okla., 1972. †

36 STEWART, George R. *American Place-Names: A Concise and Selective Dictionary for the Continental United States of America.* New York, 1970.

37 U.S. Bureau of the Census. *Historical Statistics of the United States: Colonial Times to 1970.* Washington, D.C., 1975.

38 U.S. Geological Survey. *The National Atlas of the United States of America.* Washington, D.C., 1970. Shows physical resources, history including Indian tribes, economic and social factors, governmental activities.

39 VAN ZANDT, Franklin K., comp. *Boundaries of the United States and the Several States.* (U.S. Geol. Surv. Bull. 1212). Washington, D.C., 1966. Reprints and revises five earlier editions by Henry Gannett, Edward M. Douglas.

3. State and Regional Histories

40 ATHEARN, Robert G. *High Country Empire: The High Plains and Rockies.* New York, 1960. Repr. Lincoln, Neb., 1965. †

41 BEAL, Merrill D., and Merle W. WELLS. *History of Idaho.* 3 vols. New York, 1959.

42 BEAN, Walton. *California: An Interpretive History.* New York, 1968.

43 BECK, Warren A. *New Mexico: A History of Four Centuries.* Norman, Okla., 1962.

44 BRIGGS, Harold E. *Frontiers of the Northwest: A History of the Upper Missouri Valley.* New York, 1940.

45 BURLINGAME, Merrill G., and K. Ross TOOLE. *A History of Montana.* 3 vols. New York, 1957.

46 CAUGHEY, John W. *California: A Remarkable State's Life History.* 3d ed. Englewood Cliffs, N.J., 1970.

47 CONNOR, Seymour V. *Texas: A History.* New York, 1971.

48 ELLIOTT, Russell R. *History of Nevada.* Lincoln, Neb., 1973.

49 ELLSWORTH, S. George. *Utah's Heritage.* Santa Barbara, Calif., and Salt Lake City, Utah, 1972.

50 FAULK, Odie B. *Arizona: A Short History.* Norman, Okla., 1970. †

51 FEDOROVA, Svetlana. *The Russian Population in Alaska and California, Late 18th Century – 1867.* Trans. and ed. by Richard A. Pierce and Alton S. Donnelly. Kingston, Ontario, 1973. Alaska before acquisition by the United States.

52 GOODWYN, Frank. *Lone-Star Land: Twentieth-Century Texas in Perspective.* New York, 1955.

53 GRUENING, Ernest. *The State of Alaska.* New York, 1954.

54 HINCKLEY, Ted C. *The Americanization of Alaska, 1867–1897.* Palo Alto, Calif., 1972. A comprehensive history of the first thirty years under the American flag.

55 HOLLON, W. Eugene. *The Southwest: Old and New.* New York, 1961. †

56 HORGAN, Paul. *Great River: The Rio Grande in North American History.* 2 vols. New York, 1954. †

57 HOWARD, Joseph K. *Montana: High, Wide, and Handsome.* New Haven, Conn., 1943.

58 JOHANSEN, Dorothy O., and Charles M. GATES. *Empire of the Columbia: A History of the Pacific Northwest.* 2d ed. New York, 1967.

59 KRAENZEL, Carl F. *The Great Plains in Transition.* Norman, Okla., 1955. †

60 LARSON, T. A. *History of Wyoming.* Lincoln, Neb., 1965.

60A LAVENDER, David. *California: A Bicentennial History.* New York and Nashville, Tenn., 1976.

61 LAVENDER, David. *Land of Giants: The Drive to the Pacific Northwest, 1750–1950.* Garden City, N.Y., 1958.

62 LAVENDER, David. *The Rockies.* New York, 1968.

63 MCREYNOLDS, Edwin C. *Oklahoma: A History of the Sooner State.* Rev. ed. Norman, Okla., 1969.

63A MALONE, Michael P., and Richard B. ROEDER. *Montana: A History of Two Centuries.* Seattle, Wash., 1976.

64 MEINIG, D. W. *The Great Columbia Plain: A Historical Geography, 1805–1910.* Seattle, Wash., 1968.

64A MEINIG, D. W. *Imperial Texas: An Interpretive Essay in Cultural Geography.* Austin, Tex., 1969. †

65 MEINIG, D. W. *Southwest: Three Peoples in Geographical Change, 1600–1970.* New York, 1971. †

66 MOORE, R. Laurence. "The Continuing Search for a Southwest: A Study in Regional Interpretation." *Ariz W,* VI (1964), 275–288.

67 OLSON, James C. *History of Nebraska.* Rev. ed. Lincoln, Neb., 1966, 1974. †

68 OSTRANDER, Gilman M. *Nevada: The Great Rotten Borough, 1859–1964.* New York, 1966.

69 PERRIGO, Lynn. *The American Southwest: Its Peoples and Cultures.* New York, 1971.

69A PETERSON, F. Ross. *Idaho: A Bicentennial History.* New York and Nashville, Tenn., 1976.

70 PEYTON, Green. *America's Heartland: The Southwest.* Norman, Okla., 1948.

71 POMEROY, Earl. *The Pacific Slope: A History of California, Oregon, Washington, Idaho, Utah, and Nevada.* New York, 1965. †

72 ROBINSON, Elwyn B. *History of North Dakota.* Lincoln, Neb., 1966.

73 ROLLE, Andrew F. *California: A History.* 2d ed. New York, 1969. †

74 SAGE, Leland L. *A History of Iowa.* Ames, Iowa, 1974.

75 SCHELL, Herbert S. *History of South Dakota.* 3d ed. Lincoln, Neb., 1975 †

76 SHARP, Paul F. *Whoop-Up Country: The Canadian-American West, 1865–1885.* Minneapolis, Minn., 1955. Repr. Norman, Okla., 1973.

77 SHERWOOD, Morgan B., ed. *Alaska and Its History.* Seattle, Wash., 1967.

77A SPRAGUE, Marshall. *Colorado: A Bicentennial History.* New York and Nashville, Tenn., 1976.

78 TOOLE, K. Ross. *Montana: An Uncommon Land.* Norman, Okla., 1959.

79 TOOLE, K. Ross. *Twentieth-Century Montana: A State of Extremes.* Norman, Okla., 1972.

80 UBBELOHDE, Carl, Maxine BENSON, and Duane A. SMITH. *A Colorado History.* 3d ed. Boulder, Colo., 1972. †

81 WARREN, Sidney. *Farthest Frontier: The Pacific Northwest.* New York, 1949.

82 WEBB, Walter Prescott. *The Great Plains.* Boston, 1931. † See also Fred A. Shannon, *Critiques of Research in the Social Sciences: III An Appraisal of . . . Webb's The Great Plains . . .* (New York, 1940); and Gregory M. Tobin, *The Making of a History: Walter Prescott Webb and "The Great Plains"* (Austin, Tex., 1976).

83 WINTHER, Oscar O. *The Great Northwest: A History.* 2d ed., rev. and enl. New York, 1964.

84 WYLLYS, Rufus K. *Arizona: The History of a Frontier State.* Phoenix, Ariz., 1950.

4. *Bibliographies of the West, the Frontier, and the Individual Western States*

85 ADAMS, Ramon F. *Burs Under the Saddle: A Second Look at Books and Histories of the West.* Norman, Okla., 1964.

86 APPLETON, John B., comp. *The Pacific Northwest: A Selected Bibliography . . . 1930–1939.* Portland, Ore., 1939.

87 BILLINGTON, Ray A. "Bibliography." *Westward Expansion: A History of the American Frontier.* 4th ed. New York, 1974, 663–805. The best and most comprehensive bibliography of western history as a whole.

88 BOEHM, Eric, ed. *America: History and Life: A Guide to Periodical Literature.* Santa Barbara, Calif., 1964–

89 CARROLL, John A. "Broader Approaches to the History of the West: A Descriptive Bibliography." *Ariz W,* I (1959), 217–231.

90 COOLEY, Everett L., comp. *Utah: A Students' Guide to Localized History.* New York, 1968. †

91 COWAN, Robert E., and Robert G. COWAN, comps. *A Bibliography of the History of California, 1510–1930.* 4 vols. San Francisco, 1933–1964.

92 DOBIE, J. Frank, comp. *Guide to Life and Literature of the Southwest.* Rev. ed. Dallas, Tex., 1952. †

93 ELLIOTT, Russell R., and Helen J. POULTON, comps. *Writings on Nevada: A Selected Bibliography.* Reno, Nev., 1963.

94 *The Emerging Minorities in America: A Resource Guide for Teachers.* Santa Barbara, Calif., 1972.

95 ETULAIN, Richard W., and Merwin SWANSON, comps. *Idaho History: A Bibliography.* Pocatello, Idaho [1974].

96 FINGERHUT, Eugene R., comp. *The Fingerhut Guide: Sources in American History.* Santa Barbara, Calif., 1973. †

97 FREIDEL, Frank, ed. *Harvard Guide to American History.* 2 vols. Rev. ed. Cambridge, Mass., 1974.

98 GIBSON, Arrell M. *Oklahoma: A Students' Guide to Localized History.* New York, 1965. †

99 *Guide to the National Archives of the United States.* Washington, D.C., 1974.

100 HOMSHER, Lola M., comp. *Wyoming: A Students' Guide to Localized History.* New York, 1966. †

101 JUDD, Gerrit P., comp. *Hawaii: A Students' Guide to Localized History.* New York, 1966 †

102 KAPLAN, Louis, *et al.,* comps. *A Bibliography of American Autobiographies.* Madison, Wis., 1961.

103 KUEHL, Warren F., comp. *Dissertations in History: An Index to Dissertations Completed in History Departments of United States and Canadian Universities 1873–1960.* Lexington, Ken., 1965 . . . *1961–June 1970.* 1972.

104 MALONE, Rose Mary, comp. *Wyomingana: Two Bibliographies.* Denver, Colo., 1950.

105 MILLER, Nyle H., comp. *Kansas: A Students' Guide to Localized History.* New York, 1965. †

106 MUGRIDGE, Donald H., and Blanche P. MCCRUM, comps. *A Guide to the Study of the United States of America: Representative Books Reflecting the Development of American Life and Thought.* Washington, D.C., 1960. Well annotated. By subject and geographical area.

107 POWELL, Donald M., comp. *Arizona Gathering II, 1950–1969: An Annotated Bibliography.* Tucson, Ariz., 1973.

108 ROCQ, Margaret M., comp. *California Local History: A Bibliography and Union List of Library Holdings.* 2d ed., rev. and enl. Stanford, Calif., 1970.

109 RUNDELL, Walter, Jr. "Interpretations of the American West: A Descriptive Bibliography." *Ariz W,* III (1961), 69–88, 148–168.

110 SAUNDERS, Lyle, comp. *A Guide to Materials Bearing on Cultural Relations in New Mexico.* Albuquerque, N.M., 1944.

111 SMITH, Charles W., comp. *Pacific Northwest Americana: A Check List of Books and Pamphlets Relating to the History of the Pacific Northwest.* 3d ed., rev. and enl. Portland, Ore., 1950. †

112 SMITH, Dwight L. "The Periodical Literature on Western History." *Roc Mt Soc Sci J,* X (1973), 71–77.

113 "Sources and Literature for Western American History: A List of Dissertations." *W Hist Q,* 1970–1977. Published annually in the July issue of the journal.

114 "Sources and Literature for Western American History: A Selection of Basic Works." *W Hist Q,* II (1971), 55–60.

115 "Sources and Literature for Western American History: State Histories and Bibliographies." *W Hist Q,* II (1971), 171–194.

116 STREETER, Thomas W., comp. *Bibliography of Texas: 1795–1845.* 5 vols. Cambridge, Mass., 1955–1960.

117 SWADESH, Frances L., comp. *20,000 Years of History: A New Mexico Bibliography.* Santa Fe, N.M., 1973.

118 TOURVILLE, Elsie A., comp. *Alaska: A Bibliography 1570–1970 with Subject Index.* Boston, 1974.

119 WAGNER, Henry R., comp. *The Plains and the Rockies: A Bibliography of Original Narratives of Travel and Adventure, 1800–1865.* San Francisco, 1921. Rev. and enl. by Charles L. CAMP, San Francisco, 1937. 3d ed., by Camp, Columbus, Ohio, 1953. 4th ed., by Camp, now in preparation. Usually referred to as "Wagner-Camp." An extensively annotated basic catalog of narratives of westward travel.

120 WALLACE, William S., comp. *Bibliography of Published Bibliographies on the History of the Eleven Western States, 1941–1947: A Partial Supplement to the Writings on American History.* Albuquerque, N.M., 1954.

121 WEBER, Francis J., comp. *A Select Bibliographical Guide to California History, 1863–1972.* Los Angeles, 1972.

122 WILCOX, Virginia L., comp. *Colorado: A Selected Bibliography of Its Literature 1858–1952.* Denver, Colo., 1954.

123 WINTHER, Oscar O., and Richard A. VAN ORMAN, comps. *A Classified Bibliography of the Periodical Literature of the Trans-Mississippi West (1811–1967).* Bloomington, Ind., 1961, 1970. Repr. Westport, Conn., 1972.

II. The Frontier Hypothesis and Frederick Jackson Turner

124 ALLEN, Harry C. "F. J. Turner and the Frontier in American History." *British Essays in American History.* Ed. Harry C. Allen and C. P. Hill. London, 1957.

125 ANDERSON, Jack. "Frederick Jackson Turner and Urbanization." *J Pop Cult,* II (1968), 292–298.

126 ANDERSON, Per Sveaas. *Westward is the Course of Empires: A Study of the Shaping of an American Idea: Frederick Jackson Turner's Frontier.* Oslo, Norway, 1956.

127 BARTLETT, Richard A. "Freedom and the Frontier: A Pertinent Re-Examination." *Mid-Am,* XL (1958), 131–138.

128 BECKER, Carl. "Frederick Jackson Turner." *American Masters of Social Science.* Ed. Howard W. Odum. New York, 1927.

129 BECKMAN, Alan C. "Hidden Themes in the Frontier Thesis: An Application of Psychoanalysis to Historiography." *Comp Stud Soc Hist,* VIII (1966), 361–382.

130 BENSON, Lee A. "Achille Loria's Influence on American Thought, Including His Contributions to the Frontier Hypothesis." *Ag Hist,* XXIV (1950), 182–199.

131 BENSON, Lee A. "The Historian as Mythmaker: Turner and the Closed Frontier." *The Frontier in American Development: Essays in Honor of Paul Wallace Gates.* Ed. David M. Ellis. Ithaca, N.Y., 1969.

132 BENSON, Lee A. "The Historical Background of Turner's Frontier Essay." *Ag Hist,* XXV (1951), 59–82.

133 BERKHOFER, Robert F., Jr. "Space, Time, Culture and the New Frontier." *Ag Hist,* XXXVIII (1964), 21–30.

134 BILLINGTON, Ray A. *The American Frontier Thesis: Attack and Defense.* Washington, D.C., 1971. † Analysis and bibliography.

135 BILLINGTON, Ray A. *America's Frontier Heritage.* New York, 1966. † A careful analysis of the frontier and its effect on American life.

136 BILLINGTON, Ray A. "Frederick Jackson Turner and the Closing of the Frontier." *Essays in Western History in Honor of T. A. Larson.* Ed. Roger Daniels. Laramie, Wyo., 1971.

137 BILLINGTON, Ray A. "Frederick Jackson Turner Comes to Harvard." *Mass Hist Soc Proc,* LXXIV (1962), 51–83.

138 BILLINGTON, Ray A. *Frederick Jackson Turner: Historian, Scholar, Teacher.* New York, 1973. A distinguished biography that gives thoughtful treatment to every aspect of Turner's life.

139 BILLINGTON, Ray A., ed. *Frontier and Section: Selected Essays of Frederick Jackson Turner.* Englewood Cliffs, N.J., 1961. Contains Turner's principal essays on the frontier, the West, and sections.

140 BILLINGTON, Ray A. "The Frontier in American Thought and Character." *The New World Looks at Its History.* Ed. Archibald R. Lewis and Thomas F. McGann. Austin, Tex., 1963.

141 BILLINGTON, Ray A. "Frontiers." *The Comparative Approach to American History.* Ed. C. Vann Woodward. New York, 1968. † Distinctive American traits.

142 BILLINGTON, Ray A. *The Genesis of the Frontier Thesis: A Study in Historical Creativity.* San Marino, Calif., 1971.

143 BILLINGTON, Ray A. "Why Some Historians Rarely Write History: A Case Study of Frederick Jackson Turner." *Miss Val Hist Rev,* L (1963), 3–27.

144 BILLINGTON, Ray A., ed., with collaboration of Walter Muir Whitehill. *"Dear Lady": The Letters of Frederick Jackson Turner and Alice Forbes Perkins Hooper, 1910–1932.* San Marino, Calif., 1970. Important insights.

145 BOLKHOVITINOV, N. N. "The Role of the 'Frontier' in the History of the USA: A Critical Analysis of the Views of F. J. Turner." *Sov Rev,* V (1964), 22–38.

146 BURNETTE, O. Lawrence, Jr., comp. *Wisconsin Witness to Frederick Jackson Turner: A Collection of Essays on the Historian and the Thesis.* Madison, Wis., 1961. Includes Merle Curti's biographical sketch and essays by Schafer, Pierson, Craven, Nettels, Burkhart.

147 CARPENTER, Ronald H. "The Rhetorical Genesis of Style in the 'Frontier Hypothesis' of Frederick Jackson Turner." *S Sp Com J,* XXXVII (1972), 233–248.

148 COLEMAN, William. "Science and Symbol in the Turner Frontier Hypothesis." *Am Hist Rev,* LXXII (1966), 22–49.

149 CRAVEN, Avery. "Frederick Jackson Turner." *Marcus W. Jernegan Essays in American Historiography.* Ed. William T. Hutchinson. Chicago, 1937.

150 CRAVEN, Avery. "Frederick Jackson Turner and the Frontier Approach." *U Kan City Rev,* XVIII (1951), 3–17.

151 CRAVEN, Avery. "Frederick Jackson Turner, Historian." *Wis Mag Hist,* XXV (1942), 408–424.

152 CURTI, Merle. "The Section and the Frontier in American History: The Methodological Concepts of Frederick Jackson Turner." *Methods in Social Science: A Case Book.* Ed. Stuart A. Rice. Chicago, 1931.

153 DALE, Edward E. "Memories of Frederick Jackson Turner." *Miss Val Hist Rev,* XXX (1943), 339–358.

154 DAVIS, Ronald L. "Culture on the Frontier." *S W Rev,* LIII (1968), 383–403.

155 EDWARDS, Everett E., comp. "Bibliography of the Writings of Frederick Jackson Turner." *Early Writings of Frederick Jackson Turner.* Madison, Wis., 1938.

156 ELKINS, Stanley, and Eric MCKITRICK. "A Meaning for Turner's Frontier." *Pol Sci Q,* LXIX (1954), 321–353, 565–602.

157 ELKINS, Stanley, and Eric MCKITRICK. "Institutions in Motion." *Am Q,* XII (1960), 188–197.

158 FORBES, Jack D. "Frontiers in American History." *J W,* I (1962), 63–73. A protest against narrowness of concept.

159 FREUND, Rudolph. "Turner's Theory of Social Evolution." *Ag Hist,* XIX (1945), 78–87.

160 GOODRICH, Carter, and Sol DAVISON. "The Frontier as Safety Valve: A Rejoinder." *Pol Sci Q,* LIII (1938), 268–271.

161 GOODRICH, Carter, and Sol DAVISON. "The Wage-Earner in the Western Movement." *Pol Sci Q,* L (1935), 161–185; LI (1936), 61–116.

162 GRESSLEY, Gene M. "The Turner Thesis—A Problem in Historiography." *Ag Hist,* XXXII (1958), 227–249.

163 HARPER, Norman D. "Frontier and Section: a Turner 'Myth'?" *Hist Stud: Aust New Zea,* XVIII (1952), 1–19.

164 HARPER, Norman D. "Turner the Historian: 'Hypothesis' or 'Process'?" *U Kan City Rev,* XVIII (1951), 76–86.

165 HAYES, Carlton J. H. "The American Frontier—Frontier of What?" *Am Hist Rev,* LI (1946), 199–216. A demand for a more cosmopolitan point of view.

166 HOFSTADTER, Richard. *The Progressive Historians: Turner, Beard, Parrington.* New York, 1968. †

167 HOFSTADTER, Richard. "Turner and the Frontier Myth." *Am Sch,* XVIII (1949), 433–443.

168 JACOBS, Wilbur R. "Colonial Origins of the United States: The Turnerean View." *Pac Hist Rev,* XL (1971), 21–37.

169 JACOBS, Wilbur R. *Frederick Jackson Turner's Legacy: Unpublished Writings in American History.* San Marino, Calif., 1965. Reprinted with new title *America's Great Frontiers and Sections.* Lincoln, Neb., 1969.

170 JACOBS, Wilbur R. "The Many-Sided Frederick Jackson Turner." *W Hist Q,* I (1970) 363–372.

171 JACOBS, Wilbur R. "Turner's Methodology: Multiple Working Hypothesis or Ruling Theory." *J Am Hist,* LIV (1968), 853–863.

172 JURICEK, John T. "American Usage of the Word 'Frontier' from Colonial Times to Frederick Jackson Turner." *Proc Am Philos Soc,* CX (1966), 10–34.

173 KANE, Murray. "Some Considerations on the Frontier Concept of Frederick Jackson Turner." *Miss Val Hist Rev,* XXVII (1940), 379–400.

174 KAPLAN, L. S. "Frederick Jackson Turner and Imperialism." *Soc Sci,* XXVII (1952), 12–16.

175 KERNEK, Sterling. "Pierson versus Turner: A Commentary on the Frontier Controversy." *Hist Stud,* XV (1969), 3–18.

176 KESSELMAN, Steven. "The Frontier Thesis and the Great Depression." *J Hist Ideas,* XXIX (1968), 253–268.

177 LAMAR, Howard R. "Frederick Jackson Turner." *Pastmasters: Some Essays on American Historians.* Ed. Marcus Cunliffe and Robin W. Winks. New York, 1969. Includes application of the Turner thesis to the Dakotas and New Mexico. †

178 LEE, Everett S. "The Turner Thesis Re-Examined." *Am Q,* XIII (1961), 77–83. Stresses mobility as a factor.

179 LERNER, Robert E. "Turner and the Revolt against E. A. Freeman." *Ariz W,* V (1963), 101–108.

180 LEWIS, Merrill E. "The Art of Frederick Jackson Turner: The Histories." *Hunt Lib Q,* XXXV (1972), 241–255.

181 LITTLEFIELD, Henry M. "Textbooks, Determinism and Turner: The Westward Movement in Secondary School History and Geography Textbooks, 1830–1960." Doctoral dissertation, Columbia University, 1967.

182 LYON, William H. "The Third Generation and the Frontier Hypothesis." *Ariz W,* IV (1962), 45–50. Time for a new appraisal?

183 MAGINNIS, Paul M. "The Social Philosophy of Frederick Jackson Turner." Doctoral dissertation, University of Arizona, 1969.

184 MOOD, Fulmer. "The Development of Frederick Jackson Turner as a Historical Thinker." *Col Soc Mass Trans,* XXXIV (1939), 283–352.

185 MOOD, Fulmer. "Turner's Formative Period." *The Early Writings of Frederick Jackson Turner.* Madison, Wis., 1938.

186 MURPHY, George G. S., and Arnold ZELLNER. "Sequential Growth, the Labor-Safety-Valve Doctrine and the Development of American Unionism." *J Econ Hist,* XIX (1959), 402–421.

187 NARDROFF, Ellen von. "The American Frontier as Safety Valve—The Life, Death, Reincarnation and Justification of a Theory." *Ag Hist,* XXXVI (1962), 123–142.

188 NETTELS, Curtis. "Frederick Jackson Turner and the New Deal." *Wis Mag Hist,* XVII (1934), 257–265.

189 NIXON, Herman C. "The Precursors of Turner in the Interpretation of the American Frontier." *S Atl Q,* XXVIII (1929), 83–89.

189A NORDSTROM, Carl. *Frontier Elements in a Hudson River Village.* Port Washington, N.Y., 1973.

190 OSTRANDER, Gilman M. "Turner and the Germ Theory." *Ag Hist,* XXXII (1958), 258–261.

191 PAXSON, Frederic L. "A Generation of the Frontier Hypothesis, 1893–1932." *Pac Hist Rev,* II (1933), 34–51.

192 PEARCE, T. M. "The 'Other' Frontiers of the American West." *Ariz W,* IV (1962), 105–112. Other frontiers than the Anglo-American, as revealed in literature.

193 PETERSON, Richard H. "The Frontier Thesis and Social Mobility on the Mining Frontier." *Pac Hist Rev,* XLIV (1975), 52–67.

194 PIERSON, George W. "American Historians and the Frontier Hypothesis in 1941." *Wis Mag Hist*, XXVI (1942), 36–60, 170–185.

195 PIERSON, George W. "The Frontier and American Institutions: A Criticism of the Turner Theory." *N Eng Q*, XV (1942), 224–255.

196 PIERSON, George W. "The Frontier and Frontiersmen of Turner's Essays." *Pa Mag Hist Biog*, LXIV (1940), 449–478.

196A PUTNAM, Jackson K. "The Turner Thesis and the Westward Movement: A Reappraisal." *W Hist Q*, VII (1976), 377–404

197 RUNDELL, Walter, Jr. "Concepts of the 'Frontier' and the 'West'." *Ariz W*, I (1959), 13–41.

198 SCHAFER, Joseph. "The Author of the Frontier Hypothesis." *Wis Mag Hist*, XV (1931), 86–103.

199 SCHAFER, Joseph. "Turner's America." *Wis Mag Hist*, XVII (1934), 447–465.

200 SCHEIBER, Harry N. "Turner's Legacy and the Search for a Reorientation of Western History: A Review Essay." *N M Hist Rev*, XLIV (1969), 231–248.

201 SHANNON, Fred A. "A Post Mortem on the Labor-Safety-Valve Theory." *Ag Hist*, XIX (1945), 31–37.

202 SIMLER, Norman J. "The Safety-Valve Doctrine Re-Evaluated." *Ag Hist*, XXXII (1958), 250–257.

203 SIMONSON, Harold P. "Frederick Jackson Turner: Frontier History as Art." *Ant Rev*, XXIV (1964), 201–211.

204 STRICKLAND, Rex W. *The Turner Thesis and the Dry World*. El Paso, Tex., 1960.

205 SUSMAN, Warren I. "The Useless Past: American Intellectuals and the Frontier Thesis, 1910–1930." *Buck Rev*, XI (1963), 1–20.

206 TOLL, William. "W. E. B. Du Bois and Frederick Jackson Turner: The Unveiling and Preemption of America's 'Inner History'." *Pac N W Q*, LXV (1974), 66–78. Neglect of the role of Blacks.

207 TURNER, Frederick Jackson. *The Early Writings of Frederick Jackson Turner*. Madison, Wis., 1938.

208 TURNER, Frederick Jackson. *The Frontier in American History*. New York, 1920 † Collected essays.

209 WELTER, Rush. "The Frontier West as Image of American Society: Conservative Attitudes before the Civil War." *Miss Val Hist Rev*, XLVI (1960), 593–614.

210 WELTER, Rush. "The Frontier West as Image of American Society, 1776–1860." *Pac N W Q*, LII (1961), 1–6.

211 WILLIAMS, William A. "The Frontier Thesis and American Foreign Policy." *Pac Hist Rev*, XXIV (1955), 379–395.

212 WOOLFOLK George R. "Turner's Safety Valve and Free Negro Westward Migration." *Pac N W Q*, LVI (1965), 125–130; same article, *J Neg Hist*, L (1965), 185–197.

213 WRIGHT Benjamin F., Jr. "American Democracy and the Frontier." *Yale Rev*, XX (1930), 349–365.

214 WRIGHT, Benjamin F., Jr. "Political Institutions and the Frontier." *Sources of Culture in the Middle West*. Ed. Dixon R. Fox. New York, 1934.

215 WYMAN, Walker D. and Clifton B. KROEBER, eds. *The Frontier in Perspective.* Madison, Wis., 1957. †

III. Frontiers East of the Missouri: the Earliest "Wests"

See also: Indians; The Army

216 ABERNETHY, Thomas P. *From Frontier to Plantation in Tennessee: A Study in Frontier Democracy.* Chapel Hill, N.C., 1932.

217 ABERNETHY, Thomas P. "The Southern Frontier, an Interpretation." *The Frontier in Perspective.* Eds. Walker D. Wyman and Clifton B. Kroeber. Madison, Wis., 1957, 1965. †

218 ABERNETHY, Thomas P. *Three Virginia Frontiers.* University, La., 1940.

219 ABERNETHY, Thomas P. *Western Lands and the American Revolution.* New York, 1937.

220 ALDEN, John R. *John Stuart and the Southern Colonial Frontier: A Study of Indian Relations, War, Trade, and Land Problems in the Southern Wilderness, 1754–1775.* Ann Arbor, Mich., 1944.

221 ALVORD, Clarence W. *The Illinois Country, 1673–1818.* Springfield, Ill., 1920; Chicago, 1922.

222 ALVORD, Clarence W. *The Mississippi Valley in British Politics: A Study of the Trade, Land Speculation, and Experiments in Imperialism Culminating in the American Revolution.* 2 vols. Cleveland, Ohio, 1917.

223 ANDREWS, Charles M. *The Colonial Period of American History.* 4 vols. New Haven, Conn., 1934–38. Repr. 1964.

224 BAILEY, Kenneth. *The Ohio Company of Virginia and the Westward Movement, 1748–1792.* Glendale, Calif., 1939.

225 BAKELESS, John E. *Daniel Boone.* New York, 1939.

226 BARBER, William D. "The West in National Politics, 1784–1804." Doctoral dissertation, University of Wisconsin, 1961.

227 BARNHART, John D. *Valley of Democracy: The Frontier vs. the Plantation in the Ohio Valley, 1775–1818.* Bloomington, Ind., 1953. †

228 BOND, Beverly W., Jr. *The Civilization of the Old Northwest: A Study of Political, Social, and Economic Development, 1788–1812.* New York, 1934. Repr. New York, 1969; St. Clair Shores, Mich., 1971.

229 BREBNER, John B. *The Explorers of North America, 1492–1806.* New York, 1933; Garden City, N.Y., 1955. Repr. Cleveland, O., 1964.

230 BREWSTER, William. *The Pennsylvania and New York Frontier: History of from 1720 to the Close of the Revolution.* Philadelphia, Pa., 1954.

231 BRIDENBAUGH, Carl. *Myths and Realities: Societies of the Colonial South.* Baton Rouge, La., 1952. Lecture III: "The Back Settlements." †

232 BUCK, Solon J., and Elizabeth H. BUCK. *The Planting of Civilization in Western Pennsylvania.* Pittsburgh, Pa., 1939. †

233 BULEY, R. C. *The Old Northwest: Pioneer Period, 1815–1840.* 2 vols. Indianapolis, Ind., 1950, 1951.

234 BUTLER, Lindley S. "The Early Settlement of Carolina: Virginia's Southern Frontier." *Va Mag Hist Biog,* LXXIX (1971), 20–28.

235 CARROLL, Peter N. *Puritanism and the Wilderness: The Intellectual Significance of the New England Frontier, 1629–1700.* New York, 1969.

236 CARUSO, John A. *The Appalachian Frontier: America's First Surge Westward.* Indianapolis, Ind., 1959.

237 CARUSO, John A. *The Great Lakes Frontier: An Epic of the Old Northwest.* Indianapolis, Ind., 1961.

238 CARUSO, John A. *The Mississippi Valley Frontier: The Age of French Exploration and Settlement.* Indianapolis, Ind., 1966.

239 CARUSO, John A. *The Southern Frontier.* Indianapolis, Ind., 1963.

240 CLARK, Charles E. *The Eastern Frontier: The Settlement of Northern New England, 1610–1763.* New York, 1970.

241 CLARK, Thomas D. *The Rampaging Frontier: Manners and Humors of Pioneering Days in the South and Middle West.* Indianapolis, Ind., 1939.

242 CRANE, Verner W. *The Southern Frontier, 1670–1732.* Durham, N.C., 1928. Repr. Ann Arbor, Mich., 1956.

243 CRAVEN, Wesley F. *The Colonies in Transition, 1660–1713.* New York, 1967, 1968. †

244 CRAVEN, Wesley F. *The Southern Colonies in the Seventeenth Century, 1607–1689.* Baton Rouge, La., 1949; 2d ed., 1970. †

245 DAVIS, James E. "Demographic Characteristics of the American Frontier, 1800–1840." Doctoral dissertation, University of Michigan, 1971.

246 DE VOTO, Bernard. *The Course of Empire.* Boston, 1952. †

247 DICK, Everett. *The Dixie Frontier: A Social History of the Southern Frontier from the First Transmontane Beginnings to the Civil War.* New York, 1948.

248 DOWNES, Randolph C. *Frontier Ohio, 1788–1803.* Columbus, Ohio, 1935.

249 ECCLES, W. J. *The Canadian Frontier, 1534–1760.* New York, 1969. †

250 ECCLES, W. J. *France in America.* New York, 1972. †

251 ELAZAR, Daniel J. *Cities of the Prairie: The Metropolitan Frontier and American Politics.* New York, 1970.

252 ELLIS, David M., ed. *The Frontier in American Development: Essays in Honor of Paul Wallace Gates.* Ithaca, N.Y., 1969.

253 FLINT, Timothy. *Recollections of the Last Ten Years . . . in the Valley of the Mississippi, from Pittsburgh and the Missouri to the Gulf of Mexico, and from Florida to the Spanish Frontier.* Boston, 1826. Ed. with intro. by C. Hartley Grattan. New York, 1932.

254 FOLMER, Henry. *Franco-Spanish Rivalry in North America, 1542–1763.* Glendale, Calif., 1953.

255 FOX, Dixon R., ed. *Sources of Culture in the Middle West: Backgrounds versus Frontier.* New York, 1934. Repr. New York, 1964.

256 GATES, Paul W. *The Farmer's Age: Agriculture, 1815–1860.* New York, 1960. †

257 GIPSON, Lawrence H. *The British Empire before the American Revolution.* 15 vols. Caldwell, Idaho, and New York, 1936–1970.

258 HALLER, William, Jr. *The Puritan Frontier: Town Planting in New England Colonial Development, 1630–1660.* New York, 1951. Repr. New York, 1969.

259 HAMILTON, William B. "The Southwestern Frontier, 1795–1817: An Essay in Social History." *J S Hist,* X (1944), 389–403.

260 HEIMERT, Alan. "Puritanism, the Wilderness, and the Frontier." *N Eng Q,* XXVI (1953), 361–382.

261 HIGGINS, Ruth L. *Expansion in New York, With Especial Reference to the Eighteenth Century.* Columbus, Ohio, 1931.

262 HOLMES, Jack D. L. "Interpretations and Trends of Study of the Spanish Borderlands: The Old Southwest." *S W Hist Q,* LXXIV (1971), 461–477.

263 HORSMAN, Reginald. *The Frontier in the Formative Years, 1783–1815.* New York, 1970. †

264 JAMES, Alfred P. "The First English-Speaking Trans-Appalachian Frontier." *Miss Val Hist Rev.* XVIII (1930), 55–71.

265 JAMES, James A. *The Life of George Rogers Clark.* Chicago, 1928, 1929. Repr. New York, 1969; St. Clair Shores, Mich., 1971.

266 JELLISON, Charles A. *Ethan Allen: Frontier Rebel.* Syracuse, N.Y., 1969. †

267 KELLOGG, Louise P. *The British Regime in Wisconsin and the Northwest.* Madison, Wis., 1935.

267A KLINGAMAN, David C., and Richard K. VEDDER, eds. *Essays in Nineteenth Century Economic History: The Old Northwest.* Athens, Ohio, 1975.

268 KOONTZ, Louis K. *The Virginia Frontier, 1754–1763.* Baltimore, Md., 1925.

269 LEACH, Douglas E. *Flintlock and Tomahawk: New England in King Philip's War.* New York, 1958. †

270 LEACH, Douglas E. *The Northern Colonial Frontier, 1607–1763.* New York, 1966. †

271 MCDERMOTT, John F., ed. *The French in the Mississippi Valley.* Urbana, Ill., 1965.

272 MCDERMOTT, John F., ed. *Travelers on the Western Frontier.* Urbana, Ill., 1970.

273 MATHEWS, Lois K. *The Expansion of New England: The Spread of New England Settlement and Institutions to the Mississippi River, 1620–1865.* Boston and New York, 1909.

274 MERRENS, H. Roy. "Historical Geography and Early American History." *Wm Mar Q,* 3d ser., XXII (1965), 529–548. A geographer's criticism of some well-established historical assumptions.

275 MILLER, Perry. *Errand into the Wilderness.* Cambridge, Mass., 1956 †

276 MOORE, Arthur K. *The Frontier Mind: A Cultural Analysis of the Kentucky Frontiersman.* Lexington, Ky., 1957. †

277 NASH, Gary B. *Red, White and Black: The Peoples of Early America.* Englewood Cliffs, N.J., 1974.

278 OWSLEY, Frank L. "The Pattern of Migration and Settlement on the Southern Frontier." *J S Hist,* XI (1945), 147–176.

279 PAGE, Evelyn. "The First Frontier—The Swedes and the Dutch." *Pa Hist,* XV (1948), 276–304.

280 PARKMAN, Francis. *The Discovery of the Great West.* Boston, 1869. Later eds. revised and retitled *La Salle and the Discovery of the Great West.*

281 PARKMAN, Francis. *A Half-Century of Conflict.* 2 vols. Boston, 1892. †

282 PARKMAN, Francis. *Montcalm and Wolfe.* 2 vols. Boston, 1884

283 PEASE, Theodore C. *The Frontier State, 1818–1848.* Springield, Ill., 1918; Chicago, 1922. Illinois as it emerged from its frontier era.

284 PECKHAM, Howard H. "Books and Reading on the Ohio Valley Frontier." *Miss Val Hist Rev,* XLIV (1958), 649–663.

285 PECKHAM, Howard H. *The Colonial Wars, 1689–1762.* Chicago, 1964. †

286 PHILBRICK, Francis S. *The Rise of the West, 1754–1830.* New York, 1965. †

287 PHILLIPS, Paul C. *The West in the Diplomacy of the American Revolution.* Urbana, Ill., 1913. Repr. New York, 1967.

288 POMFRET, John E. *Founding the American Colonies, 1583–1660.* New York, 1970.

289 RAMSEY, Robert W. *Carolina Cradle: Settlement of the Northwest Carolina Frontier, 1747–1762.* Chapel Hill, N.C., 1964.

290 RICE, Otis K. *The Allegheny Frontier: West Virginia Beginnings, 1730–1830.* Lexington, Ky., 1970.

290A RICE, Otis K. *Frontier Kentucky.* Lexington, Ky., 1975.

291 RUSSELL, Nelson V. *The British Regime in Michigan and the Old Northwest, 1760–1796.* Northfield, Minn., 1939.

292 SAUER, Carl O. *Sixteenth Century North America: The Land and the People as Seen by Europeans.* Berkeley, Calif., 1971.

293 SEVERIN, Timothy. *Explorers of the Mississippi.* New York, 1968.

294 SLOTKIN, Richard. *Regeneration Through Violence: The Mythology of the American Frontier, 1600–1860.* Middletown, Conn., 1973. †

295 SOSIN, Jack M. *The Revolutionary Frontier, 1763–1783.* New York, 1967. †

296 TURNER, Frederick J. *Rise of the New West, 1819–1829.* New York, 1906.

297 VAIL, R. W. G. *The Voice of the Old Frontier.* Philadelphia, 1949. Bibliography plus introductory essays.

298 VAN EVERY, Dale. *Ark of Empire, The American Frontier, 1784–1803.* New York, 1963.

299 VAN EVERY, Dale. *A Company of Heroes: The American Frontier, 1775–1783.* New York, 1962.

300 VAN EVERY, Dale. *The Final Challenge: The American Frontier, 1804–1845.* New York, 1964.

301 VAN EVERY, Dale. *Forth to the Wilderness: The First American Frontier, 1754–1774.* New York, 1961.

302 VAUGHAN, Alden T. *New England Frontier: Puritans and Indians, 1620–1675.* Boston, 1965.

303 WADE, Richard C. *The Urban Frontier: The Rise of Western Cities, 1790–1830.* Cambridge, Mass., 1959.

304 WASHBURN, Wilcomb E. *The Governor and the Rebel: A History of Bacon's Rebellion in Virginia.* Chapel Hill, N.C., 1957.

305 WEBB, Walter Prescott. *The Great Frontier.* See 22.

306 WEBB, Walter Prescott. "The Western World Frontier." *The Frontier in Perspective.* Eds. Walker D. Wyman and Clifton B. Kroeber. Madison, Wis., 1957, 1965.

307 WELTER, Rush."The Frontier West as Image of American Society, 1776–1860." *Pac N W Q,* LII (1961), 1–6.

308 WERTENBAKER, Thomas J. *Torchbearer of the Revolution: The Story of Bacon's Rebellion and Its Leader.* Princeton, N.J., 1940.

309 WHITAKER, Arthur P. *The Mississippi Question, 1795–1803; A Study in Trade, Politics, and Diplomacy.* New York, 1934. Repr. Gloucester, Mass., 1962.

310 WHITAKER, Arthur P. *The Spanish-American Frontier: 1783–1795; the Westward Movement and the Spanish Retreat in the Mississippi Valley.* Boston, 1927. Repr. Lincoln, Neb., 1969. †

311 WRIGHT, Louis B. *The Atlantic Frontier: Colonial American Civilization, 1607–1763.* New York, 1947. Repr. Ithaca, N.Y., 1963. †

312 WRIGHT, Louis B. *Culture on the Moving Frontier.* Bloomington, Ind., 1955. Repr. New York, 1961. †

IV. Indians

See also: Fur Trade; Frontiers East of the Missouri; The Army

1. Reference Materials and Documentary Collections

313 ABLER, Thomas S., Sally M. WEAVER, and Douglas E. SANDERS, comps. *A Canadian Indian Bibliography, 1960–1970.* Toronto, 1974. An elaborate bibliography that covers much more than the decade specified.

314 *The American Indian: Select Catalog of National Archives Microfilm Publications.* Washington, D.C., 1972.

315 CURTIS, Edward S. *The North American Indian, Being a Series of Volumes Picturing and Describing the Indians of the United States and Alaska.* Ed. Frederick W. Hodge. 20 vols. [Cambridge, Mass.], 1907–1930. Repr. New York, 1970.

316 DOCKSTADER, Frederick J., comp. *The American Indian in Graduate Studies: A Bibliography of Theses and Dissertations.* In 2 parts. New York, 1957, 1973. † Covers 1890–1970.

317 DRIVER, Harold E. *Indians of North America.* 2d ed. Chicago, 1969. The basic handbook of modern anthropological knowledge.

318   HEIZER, Robert F., Karen M. NISSEN, and Edward D. CASTILLO, comps. *California Indian History: A Classified and Annotated Guide to Source Materials.* Ramona, Calif., 1975.

319   HIRSCHFELDER, Arlene B., comp. *American Indian and Eskimo Authors: A Comprehensive Bibliography.* New York, 1973. †

320   HODGE, Frederick W., ed. *Handbook of American Indians North of Mexico.* 2 vols. Washington, D.C., 1907–10. Now being revised in many vols., William C. Sturtevant, ed.

321   HORR, David A., comp. and ed. *American Indian Ethnohistory.* Introductions by Robert A. Manners and Ralph A. Barney. 118 vols. New York, c. 1974. A massive collection of scholarly papers prepared for the Indian Claims Commission.

322   *Index to Literature on the American Indian, 1970–.* New York, 1972–. Annual volumes, edited since 1972 by Jeannette Henry. †

322A JOHNSON, Steven L., comp. *Guide to American Indian Documents in the Congressional Serial Set: 1817–1899.* New York, 1976.

323   KAPPLER, Charles J., comp. *Indian Affairs: Laws and Treaties.* 5 vols. Washington, D.C., 1903–1941.

324   KELSAY, Laura E., comp. *Cartographic Records in the National Archives of the United States Relating to American Indians.* Washington, D.C., 1974.

325   KLEIN, Barry T., and Dan ICOLARI, eds. *Reference Encyclopedia of the American Indian.* 2d ed. 2 vols. Rye, N.Y., 1973–1974. Includes elaborate bibliography and Who's Who in Indian Affairs.

326   KROEBER, Alfred L. *Cultural and Natural Areas of Native North America.* Berkeley, Calif., 1939.

327   KROEBER, Alfred L. *Handbook of the Indians of California.* Washington, D.C., 1925. Repr. Berkeley, Calif., 1953.

328   MARKEN Jack W., comp. *The Indians and Eskimos of North America: A Bibliography of Books in Print Through 1972.* Vermillion, S.D., 1973. †

329   MARQUIS, Arnold. *A Guide to America's Indians: Ceremonials, Reservations, and Museums.* Norman, Okla., 1974. †

330   MURDOCK, George Peter, comp. *Ethnographic Bibliography of North America.* 3d ed. New Haven, Conn., 1960.

331   *The New American State Papers: Indian Affairs.* Introduction by Loring B. Priest. 13 vols. Wilmington, Del., 1972.

332   PRICE, Monroe E., comp. and ed. *Law and the American Indian: Readings, Notes, and Cases.* Indianapolis, Kansas City, and New York, 1973. Careful "notes" supplement a very good collection of court decisions.

332A ROYCE, Charles C., comp. *Indian Land Cessions in the United States (18th Ann Rep Bur Am Eth, 1896–1897, part 2).* Washington, D.C., 1899.

333   SMITH, Dwight L., ed. *Indians of the United States and Canada: A Bibliography.* Santa Barbara, calif., 1974.

334   SNODGRASS, Marjorie P., comp. *Economic Development of American Indians and Eskimos, 1930 through 1967: A Bibliography* (U.S. Dept. of the Interior, Library Bibliography Series No. 10). Washington, D.C., 1968.

335 STENSLAND, Anna L. *Literature by and about the American Indian: An Annotated Bibliography.* Urbana, Ill., 1973.

336 STOUTENBURGH, John L., Jr. *Dictionary of the American Indian.* New York, 1960.

336A SUTTON, Imre. *Indian Land Tenure: Bibliographical Essays and a Guide to the Literature.* New York, 1975.

337 SWANTON, John R. *The Indian Tribes of North America* (Smithsonian Inst., Bur of Amer Ethn, Bull 145). Washington, D.C., 1952. Repr. Saint Clair Shores, Mich., 1968.

338 U.S. Bureau of the Census. *Indian Population of the United States and Alaska, 1910.* Washington, D.C., 1915.

339 U.S. Bureau of the Census. *Report on Indians Taxed and Indians not Taxed in the United States (Except Alaska) at the Eleventh Census: 1890.* Washington, D.C., 1894. A massive special report, much of it by Thomas Donaldson.

340 U.S. Bureau of Indian Affairs. *Biographical and Historical Index of American Indians and Persons Involved in Indian Affairs.* 8 vols. Boston, 1966. The old Bureau of Indian Affairs card catalog in book form.

341 U.S. Office of Indian Affairs. *Annual Reports of the Commissioner of Indian Affairs, 1824–1899.* Originally pub. Washington, D.C., 1825–1899. Repr. in 65 vols., New York, 1974.

342 U.S. Solicitor for the Department of the Interior. *Federal Indian Law.* Washington, D.C., 1958. Repr. New York, 1966. Replaces *Handbook of Federal Indian Law.* Ed. Felix S. Cohen. Washington, D.C., 1942.

343 VOEGELIN, C. F., and F. M. VOEGELIN, comps. *Map of North American Indian Languages.* Rev. ed. Seattle, Wash., 1966. Sponsored by the American Ethnological Society. A large wall-sized map.

344 WASHBURN, Wilcomb E. *The American Indian and the United States: A Documentary History.* 4 vols. New York, 1973. Includes selections from reports of the Commissioners of Indian Affairs, congressional debates, laws, ordinances, treaties, and judicial decisions.

345 WRIGHT, Muriel H. *A Guide to the Indian Tribes of Oklahoma.* Norman, Okla., 1951. Repr. Norman, 1971. Covering 67 tribes, this was intended to be in part a revision of Hodge's *Handbook;* see 320.

2. A Selection of Books and Articles

346 BEAL, Merrill D. *"I Will Fight No More Forever": Chief Joseph and the Nez Perce War.* Seattle, Wash., 1963. †

347 BERKHOFER, Robert F., Jr. "Native Americans and United States History." *The Reinterpretation of American History and Culture.* Ed. William H. Cartwright and Richard L. Watson, Jr. Washington, D.C., 1973.

348 BERKHOFER, Robert F., Jr. "The Political Context of a New Indian History." *Pac Hist Rev,* XL (1971), 357–382.

349 BERKHOFER, Robert F., Jr. *Salvation and the Savage: An Analysis of Protestant Missions and American Indian Response, 1787–1862.* Lexington, Ken., 1965. †

350 BERTHRONG, Donald J. *The Southern Cheyennes.* Norman, Okla., 1963.

INDIANS

351 BRANDON, William. *The Last Americans: The Indians in American Culture.* New York, 1974. Revises and adds bibliography to *The American Heritage Book of Indians.* New York, 1961. †

352 BRIGGS, Jean L. *Never in Anger: Portrait of an Eskimo Family.* Cambridge, Mass., 1970.†

353 BROPHY, William A., and Sophie D. ABERLE, comps. *The Indian: America's Unfinished Business. Report of the Commission on the Rights, Liberties, and Responsibilities of the American Indian.* Norman, Okla., 1966.

354 CATLIN, George. *Letters and Notes on the Manners, Customs, and Condition of the North American Indians.* 2 vols. New York, London, 1841. Repr. 2 vols. New York, 1973. †

355 CAUGHEY, John W. *McGillivray of the Creeks.* Norman, Okla., 1938.

356 COLLIER, John. *The Indians of the Americas.* New York, 1947. Abridged ed., 1952. †

357 COOK, Sherburne. *The Conflict Between the California Indian and White Civilization.* 4 vols. Berkeley, Calif., 1943, repr. 1976.

358 CORKRAN, David H. *The Cherokee Frontier: Conflict and Survival, 1740–1762.* Norman, Okla., 1962.

359 CORKRAN, David H. *The Creek Frontier, 1540–1783.* Norman, Okla., 1967.

360 COTTERILL, Robert S. *The Southern Indians: The Story of the Civilized Tribes before Removal.* Norman, Okla., 1954. †

361 CROSBY, Alfred W., Jr. *The Columbian Exchange: Biological and Cultural Consequences of 1492.* Westport, Conn., 1972. †

362 DALE, Edward Everett. *The Indians of the Southwest: A Century of Their Development under the United States.* Norman, Okla., 1949.

363 DANZIGER, Edmund J., Jr. *Indians and Bureaucrats: Administering the Reservation Policy During the Civil War.* Urbana, Ill., 1974.

364 DELORIA, Vine. *Custer Died For Your Sins: An Indian Manifesto.* New York, 1969, 1970. †

365 DE ROSIER, Arthur H., Jr. *The Removal of the Choctaw Indians.* Knoxville, Tenn., 1970.†

366 DIPPIE, Brian W. "The Vanishing American: Popular Attitudes and American Army Policy in the Nineteenth Century." Doctoral dissertation, University of Texas, Austin, 1970.

366A DOBYNS, Henry F. "Estimating Aboriginal American Population: An Appraisal of Techniques with a New Hemispheric Estimate." *Curr Anth,* VII (1966), 395–449.

367 DOCKSTADER, Frederick J. *Indian Art in America: The Arts and Crafts of the North American Indian.* 3d ed. Greenwich, Conn., 1966.

368 DOLLAR, Clyde D. "The Second Tragedy at Wounded Knee: a 1970s Confrontation and Its Historical Roots." *Am W,* X (September 1973), 4–11, 58–61.

369 DOWNES, Randolph C. "A Crusade for Indian Reform, 1922–1934." *Miss Val Hist Rev,* XXXII (1945), 331–354.

370 DOZIER, Edward P. *The Pueblo Indians of North America.* New York, 1970. †

371 DRUCKER, Philip. *Cultures of the North Pacific Coast.* San Francisco, 1965. †

372 DRUCKER, Philip. *Indians of the Northwest Coast.* New York, 1955; Garden City, N.Y., 1963. †

373 DUNN, Jacob P., Jr. *Massacres of the Mountains: a History of the Indian Wars of the Far West.* New York, 1886. †

374 ELLIS, Richard N., ed. *The Western American Indian: Case Studies in Tribal History.* Lincoln, Neb., 1972. †

375 EWERS, John C. *The Blackfeet: Raiders on the Northwestern Plains.* Norman, Okla., 1958.

376 EWERS, John C. *Indian Life on the Upper Missouri.* Norman, Okla., 1968.

377 EWERS, John C. "Intertribal Warfare as the Precursor of Indian-White Warfare on the Northern Great Plains." *W Hist Q,* VI (1975), 397–410.

378 EWERS, John C. "Mothers of the Mixed-Bloods: The Marginal Woman in the History of the Upper Missouri." *Probing the American West: Papers from the Santa Fe Conference.* Ed. K. Ross Toole, John A. Carroll, and others. Santa Fe, N.M., 1962.

379 EWERS, John C. "When Red and White Men Meet." *W Hist Q,* II (1971), 133–150.

380 FARB, Peter. *Man's Rise to Civilization as Shown by the Indians of North America From Primeval Times to the Coming of the Industrial State.* New York, 1968. †

381 FEHRENBACH, T. R. *Comanches: The Destruction of a People.* New York, 1974.

382 FENTON, William N., Lyman H. BUTTERFIELD, and Wilcomb E. WASH-BURN. *American Indian and White Relations to 1830: Needs and Opportunities for Study.* Chapel Hill, N.C., 1957.

383 FORBES, Jack D. *Apache, Navaho, and Spaniard.* Norman, Okla., 1960. † "From the first written records until 1698."

384 FOREMAN, Grant. *The Five Civilized Tribes.* Norman, Okla., 1934. †

385 FOREMAN, Grant. *Indian Removal: The Emigration of the Five Civilized Tribes of Indians.* Norman, Okla., 1932: rev. ed., 1953. †

386 FOREMAN, Grant. *The Last Trek of the Indians.* Chicago, 1946. Repr. New York, 1972.

387 FRITZ, Henry E. *The Movement for Indian Assimilation, 1860–1890.* Philadelphia, 1963.

388 GATES, Paul W. "Indian Allotments Preceding the Dawes Act." *The Frontier Challenge: Reponses to the Trans-Mississippi West.* Ed. John G. Clark. Lawrence, Kan., 1971.

389 GIBSON, Arrell M. *The Chickasaws.* Norman, Okla., 1971. †

390 GIBSON, Arrell M. *The Kickapoos: Lords of the Middle Border.* Norman, Okla., 1963.

391 GRINNELL, George Bird. *The Cheyenne Indians: Their History and Ways of Life.* 2 vols. New Haven, Conn., 1923. Repr. 2 vols. Lincoln, Neb., 1972. †

392 GUNTHER, Erna. *Indian Life on the Northwest Coast of North America as Seen by the Early Explorers and Fur Traders during the Last Decades of the Eighteenth Century.* Chicago, 1972.

393 HAGAN, William T. *American Indians.* Chicago, 1961. † A terse historical synthesis.

394 HAGAN, William T. *The Indian in American History.* New York, 1963; Washington, D.C., 1971. † Short bibliographical survey.

395 HAGAN, William T. *Indian Police and Judges: Experiments in Acculturation and Control.* New Haven, Conn., 1966.

396 HEIZER, Robert F., and Mary A. WHIPPLE, eds. *The California Indians: A Source Book.* 2d ed. Berkeley, Calif., 1971. †

397 HERTZBERG, Hazel W. *The Search for an American Indian Identity: Modern Pan-Indian Movements.* Syracuse, N.Y., 1971.

397A HILL, Edward E. *The Office of Indian Affairs, 1824–1880: Historical Sketches.* New York, 1974.

398 HOOPES, Alban W. *Indian Affairs and their Administration, with Special Reference to the Far West, 1849–1860.* Philidelphia, 1932.

399 HORSMAN, Reginald. *Expansion and American Indian Policy, 1783–1812.* East Lansing, Mich., 1967.

400 HUDSON, Charles M. *The Southeastern Indians.* Knoxville, Tenn., 1976.

400A HUNDLEY, Norris, Jr., ed. *The American Indian: Essays from the Pacific Historical Review.* Santa Barbara, Calif., 1975. Foreword by Vine Deloria, Jr. Includes essays by Wilcomb Washburn, Wilbur R. Jacobs, Nancy Oestreich Lurie, William T. Hagan, Robert F. Berkhofer, Jr., and Donald Parman.

401 HYDE, George E. *Indians of the High Plains: From the Prehistoric Period to the Coming of Europeans.* Norman, Okla., 1959.

402 HYDE, George E. *Indians of the Woodlands: From Prehistoric Times to 1725.* Norman, Okla., 1962. †

403 JACKSON, Helen Hunt. *A Century of Dishonor: A Sketch of the United States Government's Dealings with Some of the Indian Tribes.* New York, 1881. Repr., *Century of Dishonor: The Early Crusade for Indian Reform.* Intro. and ed. by Andrew F. Rolle, New York, 1965. †

404 JACOBS, Wilbur R. *Dispossessing the American Indian: Indians and Whites on the Colonial Frontier.* New York, 1972. †

405 JACOBS, Wilbur R. "The Indian and the Frontier in American History—A Need for Revision." *W Hist Q,* IV (1973), 43–56.

406 JACOBS, Wilbur R. "Native American History: How It Illuminates Our Past." *Am Hist Rev,* LXXX (1975), 595–609.

406A JOHN, Elizabeth A. H. *Storms Brewed in Other Men's Worlds: The Confrontation of Indians, Spanish, and French in the Southwest, 1540–1795.* College Station, Tex., 1975.

407 JORGENSEN, Joseph G. *The Sun Dance Religion: Power for the Powerless.* Chicago, 1972. †

408 JOSEPHY, Alvin M. *The Indian Heritage of America.* New York, 1968. †

409 JOSEPHY, Alvin M. *The Nez Perce Indians and the Opening of the Northwest.* New Haven, Conn., 1965. †

410 KELLY, Lawrence C. "The Indian Reorganization Act: The Dream and the Reality." *Pac Hist Rev,* XLIV (1975), 291–312. John Collier's experience with the Wheeler-Howard Act of 1934.

411 KELLY, Lawrence C. *The Navajo Indians and Federal Indian Policy, 1900–1935.* Tucson, Ariz., 1968.

412 KINNEY, Jay P. *A Continent Lost—A Civilization Won: Indian Land Tenure in America.* Baltimore, 1937. Detailed history of land tenure, by a veteran employee of the Indian Bureau.

413 KLUCKHOHN, Clyde, and Dorothea LEIGHTON. *The Navaho.* Rev. by Lucy H. Wales and Richard Kluckhohn. New York, 1962. †

414 KROEBER, Theodora. *Ishi in Two Worlds: A Biography of the Last Wild Indian in North America.* Berkeley, Calif., 1961. †

415 LEACH, Douglas E. *Flintlock and Tomahawk.* See 269.

416 LEACOCK, Eleanor B., and Nancy O. LURIE, eds. *North American Indians in Historical Perspective.* New York, 1971.

417 LEVINE, Stuart, and Nancy O. LURIE, eds. *The American Indian Today.* Deland, Florida, 1968; Baltimore, Md., 1970. †

418 LLEWELLYN, Karl N. and E. Adamson HOEBEL. *The Cheyenne Way: Conflict and Case Law in Primitive Jurisprudence.* Norman, 1941. A unique study important for all Indian jurisprudence.

419 LOWIE, Robert H. *Indians of the Plains.* New York, 1954; Garden City, N.Y., 1963. †

420 LURIE, Nancy Oestreich. "Indian Cultural Adjustment to European Civilization." *Seventeenth-Century America: Essays in Colonial History.* Ed. James Morton Smith. Chapel Hill, N.C., 1959. †

421 LURIE, Nancy Oestreich. "The World's Oldest On-Going Protest Demonstration: North American Indian Drinking Patterns." *Pac Hist Rev,* XL (1971), 311–332.

422 MCKENNEY, Thomas L. and James HALL. *History of the Indian Tribes of North America, with Biographical Sketches and Anecdotes of the Principal Chiefs.* 3 vols. Philadelphia, 1838–1844.

423 MCLOUGHLIN, William G. "Red Indians, Black Slavery and White Racism: America's Slaveholding Indians." *Am Q,* XXVI (1974), 367–385.

424 MCNICKLE, D'Arcy. *Native American Tribalism: Indian Survivals and Renewals.* New York, 1973.

425 MCNITT, Frank. *The Indian Traders.* Norman, Okla., 1962. Chiefly Southwest.

426 MARDOCK, Robert W. *The Reformers and the American Indian.* Columbia, Mo., 1971.

426A MARTIN, Calvin. "Wildlife Diseases as a Factor in the Depopulation of the North American Indian." *W Hist Q,* VII (1976), 47–62.

427 MARTIN, Douglas D. "Indian-White Relations on the Pacific Slope, 1850–1890." Doctoral dissertation, University of Washington, 1969.

428 MATHEWS, John J. *The Osages: Children of the Middle Waters.* Norman, Okla., 1961.

429 MERIAM, Lewis, and staff. *The Problem of Indian Administration* (Stud. in Admin. Inst. Govt. Res. Brook., no. 17). Baltimore, 1928. A highly influential report.

430 MEYER, Roy W. *History of the Santee Sioux: United States Indian Policy on Trial.* Lincoln, Neb., 1967, 1968.

INDIANS

431 MOHR, Walter H. *Federal Indian Relations, 1774–1788.* Philadelphia, Pa., 1933.

432 MORGAN, Lewis H. *League of the Ho-de-no-sau-nee, or Iroquois.* Rochester, N.Y., 1851. New ed. with notes by Herbert M. Lloyd. 2 vols. New York, 1901. New ed. with introduction by William N. Fenton, New York, 1962. †

433 NASH, Gary B. *Red, White, and Black: The Peoples of Early America.* See 277.

434 NEWCOMB, William W., Jr. *The Indians of Texas: From Prehistoric to Modern Times.* Austin, Tex., 1961. †

435 NICHOLS, Roger L. "The Army and the Indians, 1800–1830—A Reappraisal: The Missouri Valley Example." *Pac Hist Rev,* XLI (1972), 151–168.

436 OGLE, Ralph H. *Federal Control of the Western Apaches, 1848–1886.* Albuquerque, N.M., 1970.

437 OLSON, James C. *Red Cloud and the Sioux Problem.* Lincoln, Neb., 1965. †

438 ORTIZ, Alfonso, ed. *New Perspectives on the Pueblos.* Albuquerque, N.M., 1972.

439 OSWALT, Wendell H. *This Land Was Theirs: A Study of the North American Indian.* New York, 1966. Anthropological essays on selected Indian groups.

440 OTIS, D. S. *The Dawes Act and the Allotment of Indian Lands.* Ed. Francis Paul Prucha. Norman, Okla., 1973.

440A PARMAN, Donald L. *The Navajos and the New Deal.* New Haven, Conn., 1976.

441 PEAKE, Ora B. *A History of the United States Indian Factory System, 1795–1822.* Denver, Colo., 1954.

442 PEARCE, Roy Harvey. *The Savages of America: A Study of the Indian and the Idea of Civilization.* Rev. ed. Baltimore, Md., 1965. Reissued with new title: *Savagism and Civilization: A Study of the Indian and the American Mind.* Baltimore, 1967.

443 PECKHAM, Howard H. *Pontiac and the Indian Uprising.* Princeton, N.J., 1947.

444 PHILLIPS, George H. *Chiefs and Challengers: Indian Resistance and Cooperation in Southern California.* Berkeley, Calif., 1975.

445 PRIEST, Loring B. *Uncle Sam's Stepchildren: The Reformation of United States Indian Policy, 1865–1887.* New Brunswick, N.J., 1942. †

446 PRUCHA, Francis P. "American Indian Policy in the 1840's: Visions of Reform." *The Frontier Challenge.* Ed. John G. Clark. Lawrence, Kan., 1971.

447 PRUCHA Francis P. *American Indian Policy in the Formative Years: The Indian Trade and Intercourse Acts 1790–1834.* Cambridge, Mass., 1962. †

448 PRUCHA, Francis P. "Andrew Jackson's Indian Policy: A Reassessment." *J Am Hist,* LVI (1969), 527–539.

449 RAY, Arthur J. *Indians in the Fur Trade: Their Role as Trappers, Hunters, and Middlemen in the Lands Southwest of Hudson Bay, 1660–1870.* Toronto, 1974. † Deals chiefly with Canada.

450 RICHARDSON, Rupert N. *The Commanche Barrier to South Plains Settlement: A Century and a Half of Savage Resistance to the Advancing White Frontier.* Glendale, Calif., 1933.

451 RIDLEY, Jack. "Current Trends in Indian Education." *Ind Hist,* VI (1973), 8–13.

452 SATZ, Ronald N. *American Indian Policy in the Jacksonian Era.* Lincoln, Neb., 1974, 1975.

453 SAUM, Lewis O. *The Fur Trader and the Indian.* Seattle, Wash., 1965. †

454 SCHMECKEBIER, Laurence F. *The Office of Indian Affairs: Its History, Activities, and Organization (Serv. Mono. U.S. Govt.* Inst. Govt. Res. Brook., no. 48). Baltimore, 1927. Note important bibliography, 537–580, and digest of laws, 397–508.

455 SCHOOLCRAFT, Henry R. *Historical and Statistical Information, Respecting the History, Condition, and Prospects of the Indian Tribes of the United States.* 6 vols. Philadelphia, 1851–1857. (Titles of successive volumes vary considerably.) Index to Schoolcraft, comp. by Frances S. Nichols (*Bull. Bur. Am. Eth.,* no. 152). Washington, D.C., 1954.

456 SEYMOUR, Flora W. *Indian Agents of the Old Frontier.* New York, 1941.

457 SHAMES, Priscilla. "The Treatment of the American Indian in Western American Fiction." Doctoral dissertation, University of California, Los Angeles, 1970.

458 SHEEHAN, Bernard W. "Indian-White Relations in Early America: A Review Essay." *Wm Mar Q,* 3d ser., XXVI (1969), 267–286.

459 SHEEHAN, Bernard W. *Seeds of Extinction: Jeffersonian Philanthropy and the American Indian.* Chapel Hill, N.C., 1973 †

460 SONNICHSEN, C. L. *The Mescalero Apaches.* 2d ed. Norman, Okla., 1973.

461 SPICER, Edward H. *Cycles of Conquest: The Impact of Spain, Mexico, and the United States on the Indians of the Southwest, 1533–1960.* Tucson, Ariz., 1962. †

462 SPICER, Edward H., ed. *Perspectives in American Indian Culture Change.* Chicago, 1961. †

463 SPICER, Edward H. *A Short History of the Indians of the United States.* New York. 1969. †

464 STAUSS, Joseph H. "Modernization: The Urban Indian Experience." Doctoral dissertation, Washington State University, 1972.

464A STRICKLAND, Rennard. *Fire and the Spirits: Cherokee Law from Clan to Court.* Norman, Okla., 1975.

465 SZASZ, Margaret. *Education and the American Indian: The Road to Self-Determination, 1928–1973.* Albuquerque, N.M., 1974.

466 TAYLOR, Graham D. "Anthropologists, Reformers, and the Indian New Deal." *Prologue,* VII (1975), 151–162. Experience in the Bureau of Indian Affairs under John Collier and the Wheeler-Howard Act.

467 THOMPSON, Laura. *Culture in Crisis: A Study of the Hopi Indians.* New York, 1950.

468 TRENNERT, Robert A., Jr. *Alternative to Extinction: Federal Indian Policy and the Beginnings of the Reservation System, 1846–1851.* Philadelphia, 1975.

468A TYLER, S. Lyman. *A History of Indian Policy.* Washington, 1973. A factual summary prepared for the Bureau of Indian Affairs.

469 TYLER, S. Lyman. "The Recent Urbanization of the American Indian." *Essays on the American West, 1973–1974.* Ed. Thomas G. Alexander. Provo, Utah, 1975. †

470 UNDERHILL, Ruth M. *The Navajos.* Norman, Okla., 1956. Rev. ed. Norman, Okla., 1971.

471 UNDERHILL, Ruth M. *Red Man's America: A History of Indians in the United States.* Rev. ed. Chicago, 1971. †

472 UNDERHILL, Ruth M. *Red Man's Religion: Beliefs and Practices of the Indians North of Mexico.* Chicago, 1965. †

472A UNRAU, William E. "An International Perspective on American Indian Policy: The South Australian Protector and Aborigines Protection Society." *Pac Hist Rev,* XLV (1976), 519–538.

473 UTLEY, Robert M. *Frontier Regulars: The United States Army and the Indian, 1866–1891.* New York, 1973, 1974.

474 UTLEY, Robert M. *Frontiersmen in Blue: The United States Army and the Indian, 1848–1865.* New York, 1967.

475 UTLEY, Robert M. *The Last Days of the Sioux Nation.* New Haven, Conn., 1963. †

476 VAUGHAN, Alden T. *New England Frontier: Puritans and Indians.* See 302.

477 WALLACE, Anthony F. C. *The Death and Rebirth of the Seneca.* New York, 1969, 1970. †

478 WALLACE, Anthony F. C. *King of the Delawares: Teedyuscung, 1700–1763.* Philadelphia, 1949.

479 WASHBURN, Wilcomb E. *The Assault on Indian Tribalism: The General Allotment Law (Dawes Act) of 1887.* Philadelphia, Pa., 1975.

479A WASHBURN, Wilcomb E. *The Indian in America.* New York, 1975.

480 WASHBURN, Wilcomb E. *Red Man's Land/White Man's Law: A Study of the Past and Present Status of the American Indian.* New York, 1971. †

481 WASHBURN, Wilcomb E. "The Writing of American Indian History: A Status Report." *Pac Hist Rev,* XL (1971), 261–281.

482 WISSLER, Clark. *Indians of the United States: Four Centuries of Their History and Culture.* Garden City, N.Y., 1946. Rev. ed. Ed. Lucy W. Kluckhohn. New York, 1966. †

483 ZOLLA, Elémire. *The Writer and the Shaman: A Morphology of the American Indian.* Translated by Raymond Rosenthal. New York, 1973.

V. The Fur Trade and the Trappers

See also: Indians

484 ALTER, J. Cecil. *James Bridger, Trapper, Frontiersman, Scout, and Guide: A Historical Narrative.* Salt Lake City, 1925. Rev. ed. Norman, Okla., 1962.

485 ATKIN, W. T. "Snake River Fur Trade, 1816–24." *Ore Hist Q,* XXXV (1934), 295–312.

486 BABCOCK, Willoughby M. "The Fur Trade as Aid to Settlement." *N D Hist Q,* VII (1933), 82–93.

487 BECKWOURTH, James P. *The Life and Adventures of James P. Beckwourth, as Told to Thomas D. Bonner.* Ed. Delmont R. Oswald. Lincoln, Neb., 1972. (Original ed. 1856)

488 CARTER, Harvey L. *"Dear Old Kit," the Historical Christopher Carson, with a New Edition of the Carson Memoirs.* Norman, Okla., 1968.

489 CHITTENDEN, Hiram M. *The American Fur Trade of the Far West: A History of the Pioneer Trading Posts and Early Fur Companies. . . .* 3 vols. New York, 1902. Ed. Stallo Vinton. 2 vols. New York, 1935. 2 vols. Stanford, Calif., 1954.

490 CLELAND, Robert G. *This Reckless Breed of Men: The Trappers and Fur Traders of the Southwest.* New York, 1950.

491 CLINE, Gloria Griffen. *Exploring the Great Basin.* Norman, Okla., 1963.†

492 CLINE, Gloria Griffen. *Peter Skene Ogden and the Hudson's Bay Company.* Norman, Okla., 1973.

493 CLYMAN, James. *James Clyman, American Frontiersman, 1792–1881: The Adventures of a Trapper and Covered Wagon Emigrant. . . .* Ed. Charles L. Camp. San Francisco, 1928. Rev. ed. Portland, Ore., 1960.

494 COWAN, Ian McT. "The Fur Trade and the Fur Cycle: 1825–1857." *Brit Col Hist Q,* II (1938), 19–30.

495 COYNER, David H. *The Lost Trappers.* Ed. David J. Weber. Albuquerque, N.M., 1970. (Original ed. 1847)

496 CROUSE, Nellis M. *La Vérendrye, Fur Trader and Explorer.* Ithaca, N.Y., 1956.

497 CUTHBERTSON, Stuart, and John C. EWERS, comps. *A Preliminary Bibliography on the American Fur Trade.* Mimeograph, St. Louis, Mo., 1939.

498 DAVIDSON, Gordon C. *The North West Company.* Berkeley, Calif., 1918.

499 DE VOTO, Bernard. *Across the Wide Missouri.* Boston, 1947. †

500 DE VOTO, Bernard. *The Year of Decision, 1846.* Boston, 1943. †

501 DONNELLY, Joseph P., comp. *A Tentative Bibliography for the Colonial Fur Trade in the American Colonies: 1608–1800.* St. Louis, Mo., 1947.

502 ESTERGREEN, M. Morgan. *Kit Carson: A Portrait in Courage.* Norman, Okla., 1962.

503 FAVOUR, Alpheus H. *Old Bill Williams, Mountain Man.* Chapel Hill, N.C., 1936; Norman, Okla., 1962.

504 FISHER, Raymond H. *The Russian Fur Trade, 1550–1700.* Berkeley, Calif., 1943.

505 FUCHS, Victor R. *The Economics of the Fur Industry.* New York, 1957.

506 GALBRAITH, John S. "British-American Competition in the Border Fur Trade of the 1820's." *Minn Hist,* XXXVI (1959), 241–249.

507 GALBRAITH, John S. *The Hudson's Bay Company as an Imperial Factor, 1821–1869.* Berkeley, Calif., 1957.

508 GALBRAITH, John S. "A Note on the British Fur Trade in California, 1821–1846." *Pac Hist Rev,* XXIV (1955), 253–260.

509 GARRARD, Lewis H. *Wah-to-Yah and the Taos Trail.* Ed. Ralph P. Bieber. Glendale, Calif., 1938. Norman, Okla., 1955, 1966. † (Original ed. 1850)

510 GATES, Charles M., ed., *Five Fur Traders of the Northwest; Being the Narrative of Peter Pond and the Diaries of John Macdonell, Archibald N. McLeod, Hugh Faries, and Thomas Connor.* Minneapolis, Minn., 1933.

511 GLUEK, Alvin C., Jr. "Industrial Experiments in the Wilderness: A Sidelight in the Business History of the Hudson's Bay Company." *Bus Hist Rev,* XXXII (1958), 423–433.

512 GOETZMANN, William H. "The Mountain Man as Jacksonian Man." *Am Q,* XV (1963), 402–415.

513 GREGG, Josiah. *Commerce of the Prairies.* Ed. Max L. Moorhead. Norman, Okla., 1954. † (Original ed. 1844)

514 HAFEN, LeRoy R., ed. *The Mountain Men and the Fur Trade of the Far West; Biographical Sketches. . . .* 10 vols. Glendale, 1965–1972. Vol X contains extensive bibliography and statistical review, plus detailed index. First nine volumes consist of biographical essays by leading authorities.

515 HAFEN, LeRoy R., and W. J. GHENT. *Broken Hand: The Life Story of Thomas Fitzpatrick, Chief of the Mountain Men.* Denver, Colo., 1931. Rev. ed. by Hafen, Denver, 1973.

516 HAINES, Francis D., Jr. "The Relations of the Hudson's Bay Company with the American Fur Trade in the Pacific Northwest." *Pac N W Q,* XL (1949), 273–294.

517 HARRIS, Burton. *John Colter: His Years in the Rockies.* New York, 1952.

518 HOLDER, Preston. "The Fur Trader as Seen from the Indian Point of View." *The Frontier Re-Examined.* Ed. John F. McDermott. Urbana, Ill., 1967.

519 HOLMAN, Frederick V. *Dr. John McLoughlin, the Father of Oregon.* Cleveland, Ohio, 1907.

520 HOLMES, Kenneth L. *Ewing Young, Master Trapper.* Portland, Ore., 1967.

521 HUSSEY, John A. *The History of Fort Vancouver and its Physical Structure.* Tacoma, Wash., 1957.

522 INNIS, Harold A. *The Fur-Trade of Canada.* Toronto, 1927.

523 INNIS, Harold A. *The Fur Trade in Canada: An Introduction to Canadian Economic History.* New Haven, 1930. Rev. ed. Toronto, 1956. †

524 INNIS, Harold A. "Interrelations between the Fur Trade of Canada and the United States." *Miss Val Hist Rev,* XX (1933), 321–332.

525 INNIS, Harold A. "The North West Company." *Can Hist Rev,* VIII (1927), 308–321.

526 IRVING, Washington. *The Adventures of Captain Bonneville, U.S.A. in the Rocky Mountains and the Far West.* Ed. Edgeley W. Todd. Norman, Okla., 1961. (Original ed. 1837)

527 IRVING, Washington. *Astoria, or Anecdotes of an Enterprise beyond the Rocky Mountains.* Ed. Edgeley W. Todd. Norman, Okla., 1964 † (Original ed., 1836)

528 KANE, Lucile M. "New Light on the Northwestern Fur Company." *Minn Hist,* XXXIV (1955), 325–329.

529 LARPENTEUR, Charles. *Forty Years a Fur Trader on the Upper Missouri; the Personal Narrative of Charles Larpenteur, 1833–1872.* Ed. Elliott Coues. 2 vols. New York, 1898. Ed. Milo M. Quaife, Chicago, 1933. Repr. Minneapolis, Minn., 1962.

530 LAUT, Agnes C. *The Fur Trade of America.* New York, 1921.

531 LAVENDER, David. *Bent's Fort.* Garden City, N.Y., 1954. †

532 LAVENDER, David. *The Fist in the Wilderness.* New York, 1964. The history of the American Fur Company. ∂

533 LAWSON, Murray, G. *Fur, a Study in English Mercantilism, 1700–1775.* Toronto, 1943.

534 LENT, D. Geneva. *West of the Mountains: James Sinclair and the Hudson's Bay Company.* Seattle, Wash., 1963.

535 LEONARD, Zenas. *Narrative of the Adventures of Zenas Leonard.* Ed. Milo M. Quaife, Chicago, 1934. Ed. John C. Ewers, Norman, Okla., 1959. (Original ed., 1839)

536 LIPPINCOTT, Isaac. "A Century and a Half of Fur Trade at St. Louis." *Wash Univ Stud* (Humanistic Ser), III, Part 2 (1916), 205–242.

537 LUTTIG, John C. *Journal of a Fur-Trading Expedition on the Upper Missouri, 1812– 1813.* Ed. Stella M. Drum. St. Louis, Mo., 1920. New ed. New York, 1964.

538 MACKAY, Douglas. *The Honourable Company; a History of the Hudson's Bay Company.* Indianapolis, Ind., 1936. Rev. by Alice MacKay, Indianapolis, 1949.

539 MATTISON, Ray H. "Fort Union: its Role in the Upper Missouri Trade." *N D Hist Q,* XXIX (1962), 180–208.

540 MATTISON, Ray H. "The Upper Missouri Fur Trade: Its Methods of Operation." *Neb Hist,* XLII (1961), 1–28.

541 MERK, Frederick, ed. *Fur Trade and Empire: George Simpson's Journal.* Cambridge, Mass., 1931; with new introduction, 1968.

542 MERK, Frederick. "Snake Country Expedition, 1824–25: An Episode of Fur Trade and Empire." *Miss Val Hist Rev,* XXI (1934), 49–75.

543 MOLONEY, Francis X. *The Fur Trade of New England, 1620–1676.* Cambridge, Mass., 1931.

544 MONTGOMERY, Richard G. *The White-Headed Eagle, John McLoughlin, Builder of an Empire.* New York, 1934.

545 MORGAN, Dale L. *Jedediah Smith and the Opening of the West.* Indianapolis, Ind., 1953. Repr. Lincoln, Neb., 1964. †

546 MORGAN, Dale L. *The West of William Ashley; the International Struggle for the Fur Trade of the Missouri, the Rocky Mountains, and the Columbia, with Explorations beyond the Continental Divide, Recorded in the Diaries and Letters of William H. Ashley and his Contemporaries, 1822–1838.* Denver, Colo., 1964.

547 MORGAN, Dale L., and Eleanor T. HARRIS, eds. *The Rocky Mountain Journals of William Marshall Anderson: The West in 1834.* San Marino, Calif., 1967. Includes biographical sketches of mountain men, pp. 249–391.

548 MURRAY, Keith A. "The Role of the Hudson's Bay Company in Pacific Northwest History." *Pac N W Q,* LII (1961), 24–31.

549 NASATIR, Abraham P. *Before Lewis and Clark: Documents Illustrating the History of the Missouri, 1785–1804.* 2 vols. St. Louis, Mo., 1952.

550 NORTON, Thomas E. *The Fur Trade in Colonial New York, 1686–1776.* Madison, Wis., 1974.

551 NUNIS, Doyce B., Jr., *Andrew Sublette: Rocky Mountain Prince, 1808–1853.* Los Angeles, Calif., 1960.

552 NUNIS, Doyce B., Jr. "The Fur Men: Key to Westward Expansion, 1822–1830." *Hist,* XXIII (1961), 167–190.

553 OGLESBY, Richard E. "The Fur Trade as Business." *The Frontier Re-Examined.* Ed. John F. McDermott. Urbana, Ill., 1967.

554 OGLESBY, Richard E. *Manuel Lisa and the Opening of the Missouri Fur Trade.* Norman, Okla., 1963.

555 O'MEARA, Walter. *Daughters of the Country: The Women of the Fur Traders and Mountain Men.* New York, 1968.

556 "Papers on the North American Fur Trade." *Minn Hist,* XL (1966), 149–220. Symposium: nine papers by leading authorities.

557 PATTIE, James Ohio. *The Personal Narrative of James O. Pattie, of Kentucky during an Expedition from St. Louis through the Vast Regions between that Place and the Pacific.* . . . Ed. Reuben Gold Thwaites, Cleveland, Ohio, 1905. Ed. Milo M. Quaife, Chicago, 1930. (Original ed. 1831; 2d ed. 1833) Repr. 1833 ed., Ann Arbor, Mich., 1966, 1831 ed., New York, 1973.

558 PHILLIPS, Paul C. with concluding chapters by J. W. SMURR. *The Fur Trade.* 2 vols. Norman, Okla., 1961. Extensive bibliography, pp. 577–656.

559 PORTER, Kenneth W. *John Jacob Astor, Business Man.* 2 vols. Cambridge, Mass., 1931. Repr. New York, 1966.

560 PORTER, Kenneth W. "Negroes and the Fur Trade." *Minn Hist,* XV (1934), 421–433.

561 RICH, Edwin E. *The Fur Trade and the Northwest to 1857.* Toronto, 1967.

562 RICH, Edwin E. *The History of the Hudson's Bay Company, 1670–1870.* 2 vols. London, 1958–1959; 3 vols. New York, 1961.

563 RICH, Edwin E. *Montreal and the Fur Trade.* Montreal, 1966.

564 ROSS, Alexander. *The Fur Hunters of the Far West.* Ed. Kenneth A. Spaulding. Norman, Okla., 1956. (Original ed. 1855)

565 RUSSELL, Carl P. *Firearms, Traps, and Tools of the Mountain Men.* New York, 1967.

566 RUSSELL, Carl P. "Wilderness Rendezvous Period of the American Fur Trade." *Ore Hist Q,* XLII (1941), 1–47.

567 RUXTON, George F. *Life in the Far West.* Eds. LeRoy R. Hafen and Mae R. Porter. Norman, Okla., 1951. (Original ed., 1849)

568 SAUM, Lewis O. *The Fur Trader and the Indian.* Seattle, Wash., 1965. †

569 STEVENS, Wayne E. *The Northwest Fur Trade, 1763–1800.* Urbana, Ill., c. 1928.

570 SUNDER, John E. *Bill Sublette, Mountain Man.* Norman, Okla., 1959. †

571 SUNDER, John E. *The Fur Trade on the Upper Missouri, 1840–1865.* Norman, Okla., 1965.

572 SUNDER, John E. *Joshua Pilcher, Fur Trader and Indian Agent.* Norman, Okla., 1968.

573 THORP, Raymond W., and Robert BUNKER. *Crow Killer, the Saga of Liver-Eating Johnson.* Bloomington, Ind., 1958.

574 TOBIE, Harvey E. *No Man Like Joe: The Life and Times of Joseph L. Meek.* Portland, Ore., 1949.

575 TODD, Edgeley W. "Literary Interest in the Fur Trade and Fur Trapper of the Trans-Mississippi West." Doctoral dissertation, Northwestern University, 1952.

576 Toronto Public Library. *The Canadian North West: A Bibliography of the Sources of Information in the Public Reference Library of the City of Toronto, Canada, in Regard to the Hudson's Bay Company, the Fur Trade, and the Early History of the Canadian North West.* Toronto, 1931.

577 VICTOR, Frances Fuller. *The River of the West. Life and Adventures in the Rocky Mountains and Oregon; Embracing Events in the Life-Time of a Mountain Man. . . .* Hartford, San Francisco, etc. 1870. The "mountain man" was Joseph Meek, whose story is told at length.

578 VOEKLER, Frederick E. "The Mountain Men and their Part in the Opening of the West." *Mo Hist Soc Bull,* III (1947), 151–162.

579 WALKER, Don D. "The Mountain Man as Literary Hero." *W Am Lit,* I (1966), 15–25.

580 WEBER, David J. *The Taos Trappers: The Fur Trade in the Far Southwest, 1540–1846.* Norman, Okla., 1971.

581 WEISEL, George F., ed. *Men and Trade on the Northwest Frontier as Shown in the Fort Owen Ledger.* Missoula, Mont., 1955.

582 WESTBROOK, Harriette J. "The Chouteaus and their Commercial Enterprises." *Chron Okla,* XI (1933), 786–797, 942–966.

583 WILSON, Elinor. *Jim Beckwourth: Black Mountain Man and War Chief of the Crows.* Norman, Okla., 1972.

584 YOUNT, George C. *George C. Yount and his Chronicles of the West, Comprising Extracts from his "Memoirs" and from the Orange Clark "Narrative".* Ed. Charles L. Camp. Denver, Colo., 1966.

VI. Manifest Destiny: Diplomacy and Wars of Westward Expansion

See also: The Army; Indians; Spanish-Americans.

585 ACUÑA, Rodolfo. *Sonoran Strongman: Ignacio Pesqueira and His Times.* Tucson, Ariz., 1974. † Includes material on the American filibusters of the mid-nineteenth century.

586 ADAMS, Ephraim D. *British Interests and Activities in Texas, 1838–1846.* Baltimore, Md., 1910.

587 AMBLER, Charles H. "The Oregon Country, 1810–1830: A Chapter in Territorial Expansion." *Miss Val Hist Rev,* XXX (1943), 3–24.

588 ANDREWS, Thomas F. " The Ambitions of Lansford W. Hastings: A Study in Western Myth-Making." *Pac Hist Rev,* XXXIX (1970), 473–491.

589 ANDREWS, Thomas F. "The Controversial Hastings Overland Guide: A Reassessment." *Pac Hist Rev,* XXXVII (1968), 21–34.

590 BARKER, Eugene C. *The Life of Stephen F. Austin, Founder of Texas, 1793–1836: A Chapter in the Westward Movement of the Anglo-American People.* Nashville, Tenn., 1925. Repr. New York, 1968. †

591 BAUER, K. Jack. *The Mexican War: 1846–1848.* New York, 1974.

592 BEMIS, Samuel Flagg. *John Quincy Adams and the Foundations of American Foreign Policy.* New York, 1949. †

593 BENGE, Dennis E. "Mexican Response to United States' Expansionism, 1841–1848." Doctoral dissertation, University of California, Berkeley, 1965.

594 BILL, Alfred H. *Rehearsal For Conflict: The War with Mexico, 1846–1848.* New York, 1947.

595 BINKLEY, William C. *The Expansionist Movement in Texas, 1836–1850.* Berkeley, Calif., 1925.

596 BINKLEY, William C. *The Texas Revolution.* Baton Rouge, La., 1952.

597 BLOOM, John P. "New Mexico Viewed by Anglo-Americans, 1846–1849." *N M Hist Rev,* XXXIV (1959), 165–198.

598 BOURNE, Kenneth. *Britain and the Balance of Power in North America, 1815–1908.* Berkeley, Calif., 1967.

599 BRACK, Gene M. "Mexican Opinion, American Racism, and the War of 1846." *W Hist Q,* I (1970), 161–174.

600 BRACK, Gene M. *Mexico Views Manifest Destiny, 1821–1846: An Essay on the Origins of the Mexican War.* Albuquerque, N.M., 1975.

601 BRAUER, Kinley J. *Cotton versus Conscience: Massachusetts Whig Politics and Southwestern Expansion, 1843–1848.* Lexington, Ky., 1967.

602 BREBNER, John B. *North Atlantic Triangle: The Interplay of Canada, the United States and Great Britain.* New Haven, Conn., 1945.

603 BURT, Alfred L. *The United States, Great Britain and British North America, from the Revolution to the Establishment of Peace after the War of 1812.* New Haven, Conn., 1940.

604 CHAMBERS, William N. *Old Bullion Benton: Senator from the New West: Thomas Hart Benton, 1782–1858.* Boston, 1956.

605 COLLINS, John R. "The Mexican War: A Study in Fragmentation." *J W,* XI (1972), 225–234.

606 CONNOR, Seymour V. "Attitudes and Opinions about the Mexican War, 1846–1976." *J W,* XI (1972), 361–366.

607 CONNOR, Seymour V., and Odie B. FAULK. *North America Divided: The Mexican War, 1846–1848.* New York, 1971. Contains an extensive annotated bibliography.

608 DE VOTO, Bernard. *The Year of Decision, 1846.* Boston, 1943. †

609 FAULK, Odie B., and Joseph A. STOUT, Jr. *The Mexian War: Changing Interpretations.* Chicago, 1973. †

610 FEHRENBACHER, Don E., comp. *Manifest Destiny and the Coming of the Civil War, 1840–1861.* New York, 1970. †

611 FOWLER, Nolan. "Territorial Expansion—A Threat to the Republic?" *Pac N W Q,* (1962), 34–42.

612 FRIEND, Llerena. *Sam Houston: The Great Designer.* Austin, Tex., 1954. †

613 FULLER, John D. P. *The Movement for the Acquisition of All of Mexico, 1846–1848.* Baltimore, Md., 1936.

614 GARBER, Paul N. *The Gadsden Treaty.* Philadelphia, 1923.

615 GOETZMANN, William H. *When the Eagle Screamed: The Romantic Horizon in American Diplomacy, 1800–1860.* New York, 1966. †

616 GRAEBNER, Norman A. *Empire on the Pacific: A Study in American Continental Expansion.* New York, 1955.

617 GRAEBNER, Norman A., ed. *Manifest Destiny.* Indianapolis, Ind., 1968. †

618 GRAEBNER, Norman A. "Politics and the Oregon Compromise." *Pac N W Q,* LII (1961), 7–14.

619 HANSEN, William A. "Thomas Hart Benton and the Oregon Question." *Mo Hist Rev,* LXIII (1969), 489–497.

620 HARSTAD, Peter T., and Richard W. RESH. "The Causes of the Mexican War: A Note on Changing Interpretations." *Ariz W,* VI (1964), 289–302.

621 HAWGOOD, John A. "John C. Frémont and the Bear Flag Revolution: A Reappraisal. " *S Calif Q,* XLIV (1962), 67–96.

622 HENRY, Robert S. *The Story of the Mexican War.* Indianapolis, Ind., 1950. Repr. New York, 1960.

623 HINE, Robert V. *Edward Kern and American Expansion.* New Haven, Conn., 1962.

624 HORSMAN, Reginald. *The Causes of the War of 1812.* Philadelphia, Pa., 1962. †

625 JACOBS, Melvin C. *Winning Oregon: A Study of an Expansionist Movement.* Caldwell, Idaho, 1938.

625A JENSEN, Ronald J. *The Alaska Purchase and Russian-American Relations.* Seattle, Wash., 1975.

626 JOHANNSEN, Robert W. "Stephen A. Douglas and the American Mission." *The Frontier Challenge.* Ed. John G. Clark. Lawrence, Kan., 1971.

627 JOHANNSEN, Robert W. "Stephen A. Douglas, Popular Sovereignty and the Territories." *Hist,* XXII (1960), 378–395.

628 JOHANSEN, Dorothy O. "Oregon's Role in American History: An Old Theme Recast." *Pac N W Q,* XL (1949), 85–92.

629 JONES, Wilbur D. *The American Problem in British Diplomacy, 1841–1861.* Athens, Ga., 1974.

630 JONES, Wilbur D., and J. Chal VINSON. "British Preparedness and the Oregon Settlement." *Pac Hist Rev,* XXII (1953), 353–364.

631 KING, James C. "Daniel Webster and Westward Expansionism." Doctoral dissertation, University of Utah, 1949.

632 KNAPP, F. A., Jr. "Mexican Fear of Manifest Destiny in California." *Essays in Mexican History.* Ed. T. E. Cotner and C. E. Castañeda. Austin, Tex., 1958.

632A KUSHNER, Howard I. *Conflict on the Northwest Coast: American-Russian Rivalry in the Pacific Northwest, 1790–1867.* Westport, Conn., 1975.

633 LAVENDER, David S. *Climax at Buena Vista: The American Campaigns in Northeastern Mexico, 1846–47.* Philadelphia, 1966.

634 LYON, E. Wilson. *Louisiana in French Diplomacy, 1759–1804.* Norman, Okla. 1934. Repr. Norman, Okla., 1974.

635 MERK, Frederick. *Albert Gallatin and the Oregon Problem: A Study in Anglo-American Diplomacy.* Cambridge, Mass., 1950.

636 MERK, Frederick. *Manifest Destiny and Mission in American History: A Reinterpretation.* New York, 1963. †

637 MERK, Frederick. *The Monroe Doctrine and American Expansionism, 1843–1849.* New York, 1966. †

638 MERK, Frederick. *The Oregon Question: Essays in Anglo-American Diplomacy and Politics.* Cambridge, Mass., 1967.

639 MERK, Frederick, with the collaboration of Lois Bannister MERK. *Fruits of Propaganda in the Tyler Administration.* Cambridge, Mass., 1971. Includes "A Safety Valve Thesis and Texan Annexation."

640 MERK, Frederick, with the collaboration of Lois Bannister MERK. *Slavery and the Annexation of Texas.* New York, 1972.

641 MILES, Edwin A. " 'Fifty-four Forty or Fight'—An American Political Legend." *Miss Val Hist Rev,* XLIV (1957), 291–309.

642 NANCE, Joseph M. *After San Jacinto: Texas-Mexican Frontier, 1836–1841.* Austin, Tex., 1963.

643 PLETCHER, David M. *The Diplomacy of Annexation: Texas, Oregon, and the Mexican War.* Columbia, Mo., 1973.

644 PRATT, Julius W. *Expansionists of 1812.* New York, 1925.

645 PRATT, Julius W. "The Ideology of American Expansionism." *Essays in Honor of William E. Dodd.* Ed. Avery Craven. Chicago, 1935.

646 PRICE, Glenn W. *Origins of the War with Mexico: The Polk-Stockton Intrigue.* Austin, Tex., 1967.

647 RIVES, George L. *The United States and Mexico, 1821–1848.* 2 vols. New York, 1913.

648 SCHMIDT, Louis B. "Manifest Opportunity and the Gadsden Purchase." *Ariz W,* III (1961), 245–264.

649 SCHNELL, J. Christopher. "William Gilpin: Advocate of Expansionism." *Mont: Mag W Hist,* XIX (July 1969), 30–37.

650 SCHROEDER, John H. *Mr. Polk's War: American Opposition and Dissent, 1846–1848.* Madison, Wis., 1973.

651 SELLERS, Charles G. *James K. Polk, Continentalist: 1843–1846.* Princeton, N.J., 1966.

652 SHARP, Paul F. *Whoop-Up Country.* See 76.

653 SHARROW, Walter G. "William Henry Seward and the Basis for American Empire, 1850–1860." *Pac Hist Rev,* XXXVI (1967), 325–342.

654 SINGLETARY, Otis. *The Mexican War.* Chicago, 1960. †

655 SMITH, George W., and Charles JUDAH, eds. *Chronicles of the Gringos: The U.S. Army in the Mexican War, 1846–1848; Accounts of Eye-Witnesses and Combatants.* Albuquerque, N.M., 1968.

656 SMITH, Justin H. *The Annexation of Texas.* New York, 1911. "Corrected ed.," New York, 1941.

657 SMITH, Justin H. *The War with Mexico.* 2 vols. New York, 1919.

658 SNOKE, Elizabeth R., comp. *The Mexican War: A Bibliography of MHRC Holdings for the Period 1835–1850.* Carlisle, Pa., 1973. An extensive listing of the U.S. Military History Research Collection.

659 STENBERG, Richard R. "The Failure of Polk's Mexican War Intrigue of 1845." *Pac Hist Rev,* IV (1935), 39–68.

660 STENBERG, Richard R. "Polk and Frémont, 1845–1846." *Pac Hist Rev,* VII (1938), 211–227.

661 STOUT, Joseph A., Jr. *The Liberators: Filibustering Expeditions into Mexico, 1848–1862 and the Last Thrust of Manifest Destiny.* Los Angeles, 1973.

662 ULIBARRI, George S., and John P. HARRISON. *Guide to Materials on Latin America in the National Archives of the United States.* Washington, D.C., 1974. Includes much on relations with Mexico over the acquisition of the southwest and later disputes.

663 VAN ALSTYNE, Richard W. "International Rivalries in [the] Pacific Northwest." *Ore Hist Q,* XLVI (1945), 185–218.

664 VAN ALSTYNE, Richard W. *The Rising American Empire.* New York, 1960. †

665 VEVIER, Charles. "American Continentalism: An Idea of Expansionism, 1845–1910." *Am Hist Rev,* LXV (1960), 323–335.

666 VIGNESS, David M. *The Revolutionary Decades, 1810–1836.* Austin, Tex., 1965.

667 WARNER, Donald F. *The Idea of Continental Union: Agitation for the Annexation of Canada to the United States, 1849–1893.* Lexington, Ky., 1960.

668 WEEMS, John E. *To Conquer a Peace: The War between the United States and Mexico.* Garden City, N.Y., 1974.

669 WEINBERG, Albert K. *Manifest Destiny: A Study of Nationalist Expansionism in American History.* Baltimore, Md., 1935. Repr. Gloucester, Mass., 1958; New York, 1963. †

669A WINTHER, Oscar O. "British in Oregon Country: A Triptych View." *Pac N W Q,* LVIII (1967), 179–187.

670 WRIGHT, J. Leitch, Jr. *Britain and the American Frontier, 1783–1815.* Athens, Ga., 1975.

671 ZWELLING, Shomer S. *Expansionism and Imperialism.* Chicago, 1970.

VII. The Army in the Nineteenth-Century West

See also: Indians; Manifest Destiny; Explorers and Scientists; Irrigation, Reclamation, and Water Supply; and Conservation and Concern for the Environment.

672 ATHEARN, Robert G. *Forts of the Upper Missouri.* Englewood Cliffs, N.J., 1967. †

673 ATHEARN, Robert G. *William Tecumseh Sherman and the Settlement of the West.* Norman, Okla., 1956.

674 BEAL, Merrill D. *"I Will Fight No More Forever": Chief Joseph and the Nez Perce War.* See 346.

675 BEERS, Henry P. "The Army and the Oregon Trail to 1846." *Pac N W Q,* XXVIII (1937), 339–362.

676 BEERS, Henry P. "A History of the U.S. Topographical Engineers, 1813–1863." *Mil Engin,* XXXIV (1942), 287–291, 384–352.

677 BEERS, Henry P. "Military Protection of the Santa Fe Trail to 1843." *N M Hist Rev,* XII (1937), 113–133.

678 BEERS, Henry P. *The Western Military Frontier, 1815–1846.* Philadelphia, 1935.

679 BENDER, Averam B. *The March of Empire: Frontier Defense in the Southwest, 1848–1860.* Lawrence, Kan., 1952.

680 BROWN, Dee A. *The Galvanized Yankees.* Urbana, Ill., 1963. †

681 BROWN, Mark H. *The Flight of the Nez Perce.* New York, 1967. †

682 BURLINGAME, Merrill G. "The Influence of the Military in the Building of Montana." *Pac N W Q,* XXIX (1938), 135–150.

683 CALDWELL, Norman W. "Civilian Personnel at the Frontier Military Post (1790–1814)." *Mid-Am,* XXXVIII (1956), 101–119.

684 CALDWELL, Norman W. "The Enlisted Soldier at the Frontier Post, 1790–1814." *Mid-Am,* XXXVII (1955), 195–204.

685 CALDWELL, Norman W. "The Frontier Army Officer, 1790–1814." *Mid-Am,* XXXVII (1955), 101–128.

686 CARPENTER, John A. *Sword and Olive Branch: Oliver Otis Howard.* Pittsburgh, Pa., 1964.

687 CARROLL, John M., ed. *The Black Military Experience in the American West.* New York, 1971. †

688 "The Civil War in Indian Territory." *J W,* XII (July 1973).

689 "Civil War in the West." *Mont: Mag W Hist,* XII (Spring 1962).

690 CLARKE, Dwight L. *Stephen Watts Kearny: Soldier of the West.* Norman, Okla., 1961.

691 CLENDENEN, Clarence C. *Blood on the Border: The United States Army and the Mexican Irregulars.* New York, 1969.

692 CLENDENEN, Clarence C. *The United States and Pancho Villa: A Study in Unconventional Diplomacy.* Ithaca, N.Y., 1961; Port Washington, N.Y., 1972.

693 COFFMAN, Edward M. "Army Life on the Frontier, 1865–1898." *Mil Aff,* XX (1956), 193–201.

694 COLTON, Ray C. *The Civil War in the Western Territories: Arizona, Colorado, New Mexico, and Utah.* Norman, Okla., 1959.

695 CORNISH, Dudley T. *The Sable Arm: Negro Troops in the Union Army, 1861–1865.* New York, 1956. †

696 CROGHAN, George. *Army Life on the Western Frontier: Selections from the Official Reports Made between 1826 and 1845.* Ed. Francis Paul Prucha. Norman, Okla., 1958.

697 CUSTER, George Armstrong. *My Life on the Plains or, Personal Experiences with Indians.* Ed. Edgar I. Stewart. Norman, Okla., 1962. †

698 DIPPIE, Brian W. "The Vanishing American: Popular Attitudes and American Army Policy in the Nineteenth Century." Doctoral dissertation, University of Texas, Austin, 1970.

699 EDWARDS, Glenn Thomas. "The Department of the Pacific in the Civil War Years." Doctoral dissertation, University of Oregon, 1963.

700 EDWARDS, Glenn Thomas. "Holding the Far West for the Union: The Army in 1861." *Civil War Hist,* XIV (1968), 307–324.

701 ELLIS, Richard N. *General Pope and U. S. Indian Policy.* Albuquerque, N.M., 1970.

702 ELLIS, Richard N. "The Humanitarian Generals." *W Hist Q,* III (1972), 169–178.

703 EMMETT, Chris. *Fort Union and the Winning of the Southwest.* Norman, Okla., 1965.

704 EMMETT, Chris. "The Rough Riders." *N M Hist Rev,* XXX (1955), 177–189.

704A FLETCHER, Marvin E. *The Black Soldier and Officer in the United States Army, 1891–1917.* Columbia, Mo., 1974.

705 FLIPPER, Henry O. *Negro Frontiersman: The Western Memoirs of Henry O. Flipper, First Negro Graduate of West Point.* Ed. Theodore D. Harris. El Paso, Tex., 1963.

706 FOWLER, Arlen L. *The Black Infantry in the West, 1869–1891.* Westport, Conn., 1971.

707 FRAZER, Robert W. *Forts of the West: Military Forts and Presidios and Posts Commonly Called Forts West of the Mississippi River to 1898.* Norman, Okla., 1965.

708 GAMBLE, Richard D. "Garrison Life at Frontier Military Posts, 1830–1860." Doctoral dissertation, University of Oklahoma, 1956.

709 GILBERT, Benjamin F. "California and the Civil War: A Bibliographical Essay." *Calif Hist Soc Q,* XL (1961), 289–307.

710 GOETZMANN, William H. *Army Exploration in the American West 1803–1863.* New Haven, Conn., 1959.

711 GRAHAM, Stanley S. "Life of the Enlisted Soldier on the Western Frontier, 1815–1845." Doctoral dissertation, North Texas State University, 1972.

712 HILL, Forest G. *Roads, Rails & Waterways: The Army Engineers and Early Transportation.* Norman, Okla., 1957.

713 HILL, Gertrude. "The Civil War in the Southwest, 1861–1862: A List of Books, Old and New." *Ariz Q,* XVIII (1962), 166–170.

714 HINTON, Harwood P. "The Military Career of John Ellis Wool, 1812–1863." Doctoral dissertation, University of Wisconsin, 1960.

715 HUGHES, Willis B. "The First Dragoons on the Western Frontier, 1834–1846." *Ariz W,* XII (1970), 115–138.

716 HUNT, Aurora. *The Army of the Pacific: Its Operations in California, Texas, Arizona, New Mexico, Utah, Nevada, Oregon, Washington, Plains Region, Mexico, etc., 1860–1866.* Glendale, Calif., 1950, 1951.

717 HUTCHINS, James S. "Mounted Riflemen: The Real Role of Cavalry in the Indian Wars." *Probing the American West.* Ed. K. Ross Toole, *et al.* Santa Fe, N.M., 1962.

718 JOHNSON, Virginia W. *The Unregimented General: A Biography of Nelson A. Miles.* Boston, 1962.

719 JOSEPHY, Alvin M., Jr. *The Nez Perce Indians and the Opening of the Northwest.* New Haven, Conn., 1965. †

720 KIBBY, Leo P. "California, the Civil War, and the Indian Problem: An Account of California's Participation in the Great Conflict." *J W,* IV (1965), 183–209, 377–410.

721 KING, James T. "George Crook: Indian Fighter and Humanitarian." *Ariz W,* IX (1967), 333–348.

722 KING, James T. "Needed: A Re-evaluation of General George Crook." *Neb Hist,* XLV (1964), 223–235.

723 LECKIE, William H. *The Buffalo Soldiers: A Narrative of the Negro Cavalry in the West.* Norman, Okla., 1967.

724 LECKIE, William H. *The Military Conquest of the Southern Plains.* Norman, Okla., 1963.

725 LEONARD, Thomas C. "Red, White, and the Army Blue: Empathy and Anger in the American West." *Am Q,* XXVI (1974), 176–190.

726 MARSHALL, S. L. A. *Crimsoned Prairie: The Wars between the United States and the Plains Indians during the Winning of the West.* New York, 1972.

727 MATTISON, Ray H. "The Military Frontier on the Upper Missouri." *Neb Hist,* XXXVII (1956), 159–182.

728 MONAGHAN, Jay. *Civil War on the Western Border, 1854–1865.* Boston, 1955.

729 MONAGHAN, Jay. *Custer: The Life of General George Armstrong Custer.* Boston, 1959. †

730 MURRAY, Keith A. *The Modocs and Their War.* Norman, Okla., 1959.

731 MURRAY, Robert A. *Military Posts in the Powder River Country of Wyoming, 1865–1894.* Lincoln, Neb., 1968.

732 MYERS, Lee. "Military Establishments in Southwestern New Mexico: Stepping Stones to Settlement." *N M Hist Rev,* XLIII (1968), 5–48.

733 NELSON, Harold L. "Military Roads for War and Peace—1791–1836." *Mil Aff,* XIX (1955), 1–14.

734 NEVINS, Allan. *The War for the Union.* 4 vols. New York, 1959–1971.

735 *New Mexico Historical Review,* XLVII (January 1972), 1–60. Special issue on western military history.

736 NICHOLS, Roger L. "The Army and the Indians." See 435

737 NICHOLS, Roger L. *General Henry Atkinson: A Western Military Career.* Norman, Okla., 1965.

738 OEHLER, Charles M. *The Great Sioux Uprising.* New York, 1959.

739 OGLE, Ralph H. *Federal Control of the Western Apaches, 1848–1886.* Albuquerque, N.M., 1970.

740 OLIVA, Leo E. *Soldiers on the Santa Fe Trail.* Norman, Okla., 1967. †

741 PRUCHA, Francis Paul. *Broadax and Bayonet: The Role of the United States Army in the Development of the Northwest, 1815–1860.* Lincoln, Neb., 1953, 1967. †

742 PRUCHA, Francis Paul. *A Guide to the Military Posts of the United States, 1789–1895.* Madison, Wis., 1964.

743 PRUCHA, Francis Paul. *The Sword of the Republic: The United States Army on the Frontier, 1783–1846.* New York, 1968.

744 RICKEY, Don. *Forty Miles a Day on Beans and Hay: The Enlisted Soldier Fighting the Indian Wars.* Norman, Okla., 1963. †

745 RISCH, Erna. *Quartermaster Support of the Army: A History of the Corps, 1775–1939.* Washington, D.C., 1962.

746 RISTER, Carl C. *Border Command: General Phil Sheridan in the West.* Norman, Okla., 1944.

747 SACCONAGHI, Charles D. "A Bibliographical Note on the Civil War in the West." *Ariz W,* VIII (1966), 349–364.

748 SAVAGE, W. Sherman. "The Role of Negro Soldiers in Protecting the Indian Frontier from Intruders." *J Neg Hist,* XXXVI (1951), 25–34.

749 SHIRK, George A. "Military Duty on the Western Frontier." *Chron Okla,* XLVII (1969), 118–125.

750 SIEVERS, Michael. "Sands of Sand Creek Historiography." *Colo Mag,* XLIX (1972), 116–142.

751 "Special Custer Edition." *Mont: Mag W Hist,* XVI (Spring 1966).

752 STEWART, Edgar I. *Custer's Luck.* Norman, Okla., 1955.

753 SULLY, Langdon. *No Tears for the General: The Life of Alfred Sully, 1821–1879.* Palo Alto, Calif., 1974.

754 THRAPP, Dan L. *The Conquest of Apachería.* Norman, Okla., 1967.

755 *Utah Historical Quarterly,* XLII (Winter 1974). Special issue on the Mormons and western military history.

756 UTLEY, Robert M. *Custer and the Great Controversy: The Origin and Development of a Legend.* Los Angeles, 1962.

757 UTLEY, Robert M. *Frontier Regulars: The United States Army and the Indian, 1866–1891.* New York, 1973.

758 UTLEY, Robert M. *Frontiersmen in Blue: The United States Army and the Indian, 1848–1865.* New York, 1967.

759 WEIGLEY, Russell F. *History of the United States Army.* New York, 1967.

760 WELTY, Raymond L. "The Policing of the Frontier by the Army, 1860–1870." *Kan Hist Q,* VII (1938), 246–257.

761 WESLEY, Edgar B. *Guarding the Frontier: A Study of Frontier Defense from 1815 to 1825.* Minneapolis, Minn., 1935.

762 WHITE, Lonnie J., ed. *Hostiles and Horse Soldiers: Indian Battles and Campaigns in the West.* Boulder, Colo., 1972.

763 WOOD, Richard G. *Stephen Harriman Long, 1784–1864, Army Engineer, Explorer, Inventor.* Glendale, Calif., 1966.

764 YOUNG, Otis E., Jr. "Military Protection of the Santa Fe Trail and Trade." *Mo Hist Rev,* XLIX (1954), 19–32.

765 YOUNG, Otis E., Jr. *The West of Philip St. George Cooke, 1809–1895.* Glendale, Calif., 1955.

VIII. Explorers and Scientists in the Nineteenth-Century West

766 ALLEN, John L. *Passage Through the Garden: Lewis and Clark and the Image of the American Northwest.* Urbana, Ill., 1975.

767 ANDERSON, Bern. *Surveyor of the Sea: The Life and Voyages of Captain George Vancouver.* Seattle, Wash., 1960. †

768 BAKELESS, John. *Lewis and Clark: Partners in Discovery.* New York, 1947. †

769 BARTLETT, Richard A. *Great Surveys of the American West.* Norman, Okla., 1962.

770 BARTLETT, Richard A. "John Wesley Powell and the Great Surveys: A Problem in Historiography." *The American West: An Appraisal.* Ed. Robert G. Ferris. Santa Fe, N.M., 1963.

771 BEAGLEHOLE, J. C. *The Life of Captain James Cook.* Stanford, Calif., 1974.

772 BENSON, Maxine F. "Edwin James: Scientist, Linguist, Humanitarian." Doctoral dissertation, University of Colorado, 1968.

773 BLOMKVIST, E. E. "A Russian Scientific Expedition to California and Alaska, 1839–1849: The Drawings of I. G. Voznesenskii." *Ore Hist Q,* LXXIII (1972), 101–170.

774 BOLTON, Herbert E., ed. *Anza's California Expeditions.* 5 vols. Berkeley, Calif., 1930.

775 BOLTON, Herbert E., ed. *Spanish Exploration in the Southwest, 1542–1706.* New York, 1925.

776 CLINE, Gloria Griffen. *Exploring the Great Basin.* Norman, Okla., 1963. †

777 CUTRIGHT, Paul R. *Lewis and Clark: Pioneering Naturalists.* Urbana, Ill., 1969.

778 CUTTER, Donald C. "Spanish Scientific Exploration Along the Pacific Coast." *The American West: An Appraisal.* Ed. Robert G. Ferris. Santa Fe, N.M., 1963.

779 DALE, Harrison C. *The Ashley-Smith Explorations and the Discovery of a Central Route to the Pacific, 1822–1829.* Cleveland, 1918. Rev. ed. Glendale, Calif., 1941.

780 DARRAH, William C. *Powell of the Colorado.* Princeton, N.J., 1951. †

781 DE VOTO, Bernard. *The Course of Empire.* See 246.

782 DILLON, Richard. *Meriwether Lewis: A Biography.* New York, 1965.

783 DUPREE, A. Hunter. *Science in the Federal Government: A History of Policies and Activities to 1940.* Cambridge, Mass., 1957. Repr. New York, 1964.

784 EWAN, Joseph A. *Rocky Mountain Naturalists.* Denver, Colo., 1950.

785 FRIIS, Herman R. "The Image of the American West at Mid-Century (1840–60): A Product of the Scientific Geographical Exploration by the United States Government." *The Frontier Re-examined.* Ed. John Francis McDermott. Urbana, Ill., 1967.

786 FRIIS, Herman R., ed. *The Pacific Basin: A History of its Geographical Exploration.* New York, 1967.

787 GEISER, Samuel W. *Naturalists of the Frontier.* Dallas, Tex., 1937.

788 GILBERT, Edmund W. *The Exploration of Western America, 1800–1850: An Historical Geography.* Cambridge, Eng., 1933. Repr., New York, 1966.

789 GOETZMANN, William H. *Army Exploration in the American West 1803–1863.* New Haven, Conn., 1959.

790 GOETZMANN, William H. *Exploration and Empire: The Explorer and the Scientist in the Winning of the American West.* New York, 1966.

791 GOETZMANN, William H. "The West and the American Age of Exploration." *Ariz W,* II (1960), 265–278.

792 GRAUSTEIN, Jeannette E. *Thomas Nuttall, Naturalist: Explorations in America, 1808–1841.* Cambridge, Mass., 1967.

793 HOLLON, W. Eugene. *The Lost Pathfinder: Zebulon Montgomery Pike.* Norman, Okla., 1949.

794 IRVING, Washington. *The Adventures of Captain Bonneville, U.S.A., in the Rocky Mountains and the Far West. . . .* New York, 1850.

795 JACKSON, Donald, ed. *The Journals of Zebulon Montgomery Pike with Letters and Related Documents.* 2 vols. Norman, Okla., 1966.

796 JACKSON, Donald, ed. *Letters of the Lewis and Clark Expedition with Related Documents 1783–1854.* Urbana, Ill., 1962.

797 JACKSON, Donald. "The Public Image of Lewis and Clark." *Pac N W Q,* LVII (1966), 1–7.

798 JACKSON, Donald, and Mary Lee SPENCE, eds. *The Expeditions of John Charles Frémont.* 2 vols; vol. 2 Supplement; map portfolio volume. Urbana, Ill., 1970–

799 "John Wesley Powell and the Colorado River Centennial." *Utah Hist Q,* XXXVII (Spring 1969). Special issue.

800 MCDERMOTT, John Francis, ed. *Travelers on the Western Frontier.* Urbana, Ill., 1970.

801 MANNING, Thomas G. *Government in Science: The U.S. Geological Survey, 1867–1894.* Lexington, Ky., 1967.

802 MEISEL, Max, comp. *A Bibliography of American Natural History: The Pioneer Century, 1769–1865. . . .* 3 vols. Brooklyn, N.Y. 1924–1929.

803 MORGAN, Dale L. *Jedediah Smith and the Opening of the West.* See 545.

804 MORGAN, Dale L., and Eleanor Towles HARRIS, eds. *The Rocky Mountain Journals of William Marshall Anderson: The West in 1834.* San Marino, Calif., 1967.

805 NEVINS, Allan. *Frémont, Pathmarker of the West.* New York, 1939, 1955.

806 NICHOLS, Roger L. "Stephen Long and Scientific Exploration on the Plains." *Neb Hist,* LII (1971), 51–64.

807 RAMSEY, Bobby Gene. "Scientific Exploration and Discovery in the Great Basin from 1831–1891." Doctoral dissertation, Brigham Young University, 1972.

808 SHERWOOD, Morgan B. *Exploration of Alaska, 1865–1900.* New Haven, Conn., 1965.

809 SHERWOOD, Morgan B. "Science in Russian America, 1741 to 1865." *Pac N W Q,* LVIII (1967), 33–39.

810 SMITH, Henry Nash. "Clarence King, John Wesley Powell, and the Establishment of the United States Geological Survey." *Miss Val Hist Rev,* XXXIV (1947), 37–58.

811 STANTON, William. *The Great United States Exploring Expedition of 1838–1842.* Berkeley, Calif., 1975. The Wilkes Expedition.

812 STEGNER, Wallace E. *Beyond the Hundredth Meridian: John Wesley Powell and the Second Opening of the West.* Boston, 1954. †

813 STUART, Robert. *On the Oregon Trail: Robert Stuart's Journey of Discovery.* Ed. Kenneth A. Spaulding. Norman, Okla., 1953.

814 THAXTER, B. A. "Scientists in Early Oregon." *Ore Hist Q,* XXXIV (1933), 330–344.

815 THWAITES, Reuben Gold, ed. *Early Western Travels, 1748–1846. . . .* See 20.

816 THWAITES, Reuben Gold, ed. *Original Journals of the Lewis and Clark Expedition, 1804–1806, Printed from the Original Manuscripts. . . .* 7 vols and atlas. New York, 1904–05.

817 TYLER, David B. *The Wilkes Expedition: The First United States Exploration Expedition, 1838–1842.* Philadelphia, 1968.

818 WAGNER, Henry R. *The Cartography of the Northwest Coast of America to the Year 1800.* 2 vols. Berkeley, Calif., 1937.

819 WAGNER, Henry R., and Charles L. CAMP. *The Plains and the Rockies.* See 119.

820 WALLACE, Edward S. *The Great Reconnaissance: Soldiers, Artists, and Scientists on the Frontier, 1848–1861.* Boston, 1955.

821 WHEAT, Carl I. *Mapping the Trans-Mississippi West, 1540–1861.* 3 vols. San Francisco, 1957–58.

822 WILKINS, Thurman. *Clarence King: A Biography.* New York, 1958.

823 WILSON, Iris H. "Spanish Scientists in the Pacific Northwest, 1790–1792." *Reflections of Western Historians.* Ed. John A. Carroll. Tucson, Ariz., 1969.

824 WOOD, Richard G. *Stephen Harriman Long, 1784–1864: Army Engineer, Explorer, Inventor.* Glendale, Calif., 1966.

IX. The Spanish-Speaking Peoples in the West

1. Before 1900: the Pioneer and Transitional Eras—and Herbert Eugene Bolton

825 ALMARÁZ, Felix D. *Tragic Cavalier: Governor Manuel Salcado of Texas, 1803–1818.* Austin, Tex., 1971.

826 BANCROFT, Hubert H. *Works* (volumes on California, Arizona, New Mexico, Texas). See 1.

827 BANNON, John F. "Herbert Eugene Bolton—Western Historian." *W Hist Q,* II (1971), 261–282.

828 BANNON, John F. *The Spanish Borderlands Frontier, 1513–1821.* New York, 1970 †

829 BEILHARZ, Edwin A. *Felipe de Neve: First Governor of California.* San Francisco, 1971.

830 BOLTON, Herbert E. *Bolton and the Spanish Borderlands.* Ed. John F. Bannon. Norman, Okla., 1964. A collection of important essays by Bolton.

831 BOLTON, Herbert E. *Coronado: Knight of Pueblos and Plains.* New York, 1949. Published simultaneously in Albuquerque with slightly different title. †

832 BOLTON, Herbert E. *Rim of Christendom: A Biography of Eusebio Francisco Kino, Pacific Coast Pioneer.* New York, 1936. Repr. New York, 1960.

833 BOLTON, Herbert E. *The Spanish Borderlands: A Chronicle of Old Florida and the Southwest.* New Haven, Conn., 1921.

834 BOLTON, Herbert E. *Texas in the Middle Eighteenth Century: Studies in Spanish Colonial History and Administration.* Berkeley, Calif., 1915. Repr. New York, 1962.

835 BOLTON, Herbert E. *Wider Horizons of American History.* New York, 1939. Repr. Notre Dame, Ind., 1967. † Contains his best known essays, including "Defensive Spanish Expansion and the Significance of the Borderlands" and "The Mission as a Frontier Institution in the Spanish-American Colonies."

836 BRINCKERHOFF, Sidney R. "The Last Years of Spanish Arizona, 1786–1821." *Ariz W,* IX (1967), 5–20.

837 CASTAÑEDA, Carlos E. *Our Catholic Heritage in Texas, 1519–1936.* 7 vols. Austin, Tex., 1936–1958.

838 CHAPMAN, Charles E. *A History of California: The Spanish Period.* New York, 1921. Repr. Saint Clair Shores, Mich., 1971.

839 CLINE, Howard F. "Imperial Perspectives on the Borderlands." *Probing the American West.* Ed. K. Ross Toole, *et al.* Santa Fe, N.M., 1962.

840 COOK, Warren L. *Flood Tide of Empire: Spain and the Pacific Northwest, 1543–1819.* New Haven, Conn., 1973.

841 DANIEL, James M. "The Spanish Frontier in West Texas and Northern Mexico." *S W Hist Q*, LXXI (1968), 481–495.

841A DYSART, Jane. "Mexican Women in San Antonio, 1830–1860: The Assimilation Process." *W Hist Q*, VII (1976), 365–375.

842 FAULK, Odie B. *The Last Years of Spanish Texas, 1778–1821*. The Hague, Netherlands, 1964.

843 GARR, Daniel J. "A Rare and Desolate Land: Population and Race in Hispanic California." *W Hist Q*, VI (1975), 133–148.

844 GIBSON, Charles. *Spain in America*. New York, 1966. † A general survey of Spain's role throughout the Americas.

845 *Greater America: Essays in Honor of Herbert Eugene Bolton*. Ed. Adele Ogden and Engel Sluiter. Berkeley, Calif., 1945.

846 HAMMOND, George P. *Don Juan de Oñate, Colonizer of New Mexico, 1595–1628*. Albuquerque, N.M., 1953.

847 HARING, Clarence H. *The Spanish Empire in America*. New York, 1947. Repr. New York, 1963. †

848 HOLMES, Jack D. L. "Interpretations and Trends in the Study of the Spanish Borderlands: The Old Southwest." See 262.

849 HORGAN, Paul. *Conquistadors in North American History*. New York, 1963.

850 HORGAN, Paul. *Great River: The Rio Grande in North American History*. 2 vols. New York, 1954. †

851 HUTCHINSON, C. Alan. *Frontier Settlement in Mexican California: The Híjar-Padrés Colony and Its Origins, 1769–1835*. New Haven, Conn., 1969.

852 JONES, Oakah L., Jr., ed. "The Spanish Borderlands." *J W*, VIII (January 1969), 1–142. Special issue that contains nine essays.

853 JONES, Oakah L., Jr., comp. "The Spanish Borderlands: A Selected Reading List." *J W*, VIII (January 1969), 137–142.

854 *Latin American Research Review*, VII (Summer 1972). Special issue on Spanish Borderlands.

855 LEHMER, Donald J. "The Second Frontier: The Spanish." *The American West: An Appraisal*. Ed. Robert G. Ferris. Santa Fe, N.M., 1963.

856 MCDERMOTT, John F., ed. *The Spanish in the Mississippi Valley, 1762–1804*. Urbana, Ill., 1974. Sixteen papers.

857 NASATIR, Abraham P. *Before Lewis and Clark: Documents Illustrating the History of the Missouri, 1785–1804*. 2 vols. St. Louis, Mo., 1952.

858 NASATIR, Abraham P. "The Shifting Borderlands." *Pac Hist Rev*, XXXIV (1965), 1–20.

859 NOGGLE, Burl. "Anglo Observers of the Southwest Borderlands, 1825–1890: The Rise of a Concept." *Ariz W*, I (1959), 105–131.

860 NOSTRAND, Richard L. "The Hispanic-American Borderland: A Regional, Historical Geography." Doctoral dissertation, University of California, Los Angeles, 1968.

861 PAUL, Rodman W. "The Spanish-Americans in the Southwest, 1848–1900." *The Frontier Challenge: Responses to the Trans-Mississippi West*. Ed. John G. Clark. Lawrence, Kansas, 1971.

862 PITT, Leonard. *The Decline of the Californios: A Social History of Spanish-Speaking Californians, 1846–1890.* Berkeley, Calif., 1966. †

863 SAUER, Carl O. *Sixteenth Century North America: The Land and the People as Seen by the Europeans.* Berkeley, Calif., 1971. †

864 SCHOLES, Frances V. "Civil Government and Society in New Mexico in the Seventeenth Century." *N M Hist Rev,* X (1935), 71–111.

865 SCHOLES, Frances V. "Historiography of the Spanish Southwest: Retrospect and Prospect." *Probing the American West.* Ed. K. Ross Toole, *et al.* Santa Fe, N.M., 1962.

866 SIMMONS, Marc. *Spanish Government in New Mexico.* Albuquerque, N.M., 1968.

867 STECK, Francis B. *A Tentative Guide to Historical Materials on the Spanish Borderlands.* Philadelphia, Pa., 1943.

868 SWADESH, Frances L. *Los Primeros Pobladores: Hispanic Americans of the Ute Frontier.* Notre Dame, Ind., 1974. †

869 ULIBARRI, Richard O. "American Interest in the Spanish-Mexican Southwest, 1803–1848," Doctoral dissertation, University of Utah, 1963.

870 VIGIL, Ralph H. "The New Borderlands History: A Critique." *N M Hist Rev,* XLVIII (1973), 189–208.

871 WAGNER, Henry R., comp. *The Spanish Southwest, 1542–1794: An Annotated Bibliography.* Berkeley, Calif., 1924. Rev. ed., 2 vols. Albuquerque, N.M., 1937. Repr., 2 vols. New York, 1967.

872 WEBER, David J., ed. *Foreigners in Their Native Land: Historical Roots of the Mexican American.* Albuquerque, N.M., 1973.

872A WEBER, David J. "Mexico's Far Northern Frontier, 1821–1854: Historiography Askew." *W Hist Q,* VII (1976), 279–293.

873 WHITAKER, Arthur P. *The Spanish-American Frontier, 1783–1795: The Westward Movement and the Spanish Retreat in the Mississippi Valley.* Boston, 1927. †

873A WORCESTER, Donald E. "The Significance of the Spanish Borderlands to the United States." *W Hist Q,* VII (1976), 5–18.

874 WRIGHT, J. Leitch, Jr. *Anglo-Spanish Rivalry in North America.* Athens, Ga., 1971.

2. Since 1900: the Era of Large-Scale Immigration

See also: Labor; Agriculture

875 ACUÑA, Rodolfo. "Freedom in a Cage: the Subjugation of the Chicano in the United States." *The Reinterpretation of American History and Culture.* Ed. William H. Cartwright and Richard L. Watson. Washington, D.C., 1973. Includes brief bibliography.

876 BRUNTON, Anne M. "The Decision to Settle: A Study of Mexican-American Migrants." Doctoral dissertation, Washington State University, 1971.

877 CAMARILLO, Albert M. "Chicano Urban History: A Study of Compton's Barrio, 1936–1970." *Aztlán,* II (1971), 79–106.

878 CAMPBELL, Howard L. "Bracero Migration and the Mexican Economy, 1951–1964." Doctoral dissertation, American University, 1972.

879 "The Chicano Experience in the United States." *Soc Sci Q,* LIII (March 1973). Special issue containing 22 essays.

880 COPP, Nelson G. " 'Wetbacks' and *Braceros:* Mexican Migrant Laborers and American Immigration Policy." Doctoral dissertation, Boston University, 1963.

881 CORWIN, Arthur F. "Mexican-American History: An Assessment." *Pac Hist Rev,* XLII (1973), 269–308. A comprehensive and discriminating annotated bibliographical essay.

882 CORWIN, Arthur F. "Mexican Migration History, 1900–1970: Literature and Research." *Latin Am Res Rev,* VIII (1973), 3–24.

883 CRAIG, Richard B. *The Bracero Program: Interest Groups and Foreign Policy.* Austin, Tex., 1971.

884 FINCHER, Ernest B. "The Spanish-Americans as a Political Factor in New Mexico, 1912–1950." Doctoral dissertation, New York University, 1950.

885 FODELL, Beverly, comp. *Cesar Chavez and the United Farm Workers: A Selective Bibliography.* Detroit, Mich., 1974. †

886 GALARZA, Ernesto. *Merchants of Labor: The Mexican Bracero Story: An Account of the Managed Migration of Mexican Farm Workers in California, 1942–1960.* Santa Barbara, Calif., 1964. †

887 GAMIO, Manuel, comp. *The Mexican Immigrant, his Life-Story: Autobiographical Documents.* Chicago, 1931. Repr. with slightly varying titles. New York, 1969, 1972.

888 GAMIO, Manuel. *Mexican Immigration to the United States: A Study of Human Migration and Adjustment.* Chicago, 1930. Repr. New York, 1969. †

889 GARDNER, Richard M. *Grito! Reies Tijerina and the New Mexico Land Grant War of 1967.* Indianapolis, Ind., 1970. †

890 GILMORE, N. Ray, and Gladys W. GILMORE. "The Bracero in California." *Pac Hist Rev,* XXXII (1963), 265–282.

891 GÓMEZ-QUIÑONES, Juan. "The First Steps: Chicano Labor Conflict and Organizing, 1900–1920." *Aztlán,* III (1972), 13–49.

892 GÓMEZ-QUIÑONES, Juan. "Toward a Perspective on Chicano History." *Aztlán,* II (1971), 1–49.

892A GÓMEZ-QUIÑONES, Juan, and Luis LEOBARDO ARROYO. "On the State of Chicano History: Observations on Its Development, Interpretations, and Theory, 1970–1974." *W Hist Q,* VII (1976), 155–185.

893 GONZALEZ, Nancie L. *The Spanish-Americans of New Mexico: A Heritage of Pride.* Rev. and enlarged ed. Albuquerque, N. M., 1969. † (Originally pub. in preliminary form Los Angeles, 1967.)

894 GREBLER, Leo. *Mexican Immigration to the United States: The Record and Its Implications.* Los Angeles, Calif., 1966.

895 GREBLER, Leo, Joan W. MOORE, Ralph C. GUZMAN. *The Mexican-American People: The Nation's Second Largest Minority.* New York, 1970.

896 GUZMAN, Ralph. "The Function of Anglo-American Racism in the Political Development of Chicanos." *Calif Hist Q,* L (1971), 321–337.

897 HOFFMAN, Abraham. "Chicano History: Problems and Potentialities." *J Eth Stud,* I (1973), 6–12.

898 HOFFMAN, Abraham. *Unwanted Mexican Americans in the Great Depression: Repatriation Pressures, 1929–1939.* Tucson, Ariz., 1974. †

899 HUNDLEY, Norris, Jr., ed. *The Chicano: Essays from the Pacific Historical Review.* Santa Barbara, Calif., 1975. [Originally published as vol. XLII (August 1973) of the *Pac Hist Rev.*]

900 JORDAN, Lois B., comp. *Mexican Americans: Resources to Build Cultural Understanding.* Littleton, Colo., 1973. An annotated bibliography.

901 KIBBE, Pauline R. *Latin Americans in Texas* (Inter-Americana Stud., III). Albuquerque, N.M., 1946.

902 LARSON, Robert W. "The White Caps of New Mexico: A Study of Ethnic Militancy in the Southwest." *Pac Hist Rev,* XLIV (1975), 171–185.

903 MCWILLIAMS, Carey. *North from Mexico: The Spanish-Speaking People of the United States.* Philadelphia, 1949. Repr. New York, 1968.

904 MARTÍNEZ, John R. *Mexican Emigration to the United States, 1910–1930.* San Francisco, 1971. Offset copy of doctoral dissertation, University of California, Berkeley, 1957.

905 MEIER, Matt S., and Feliciano RIVERA. *A Bibliography for Chicano History.* San Francisco, 1972. †

906 MEIER, Matt S., and Feliciano RIVERA. *The Chicanos: A History of Mexican Americans.* New York, 1972. †

907 METZGAR, Joseph V. "The Ethnic Sensibility of Spanish New Mexicans: A Survey and Analysis." *N M Hist Rev,* XLIX (1974), 49–73.

908 MOORE, Joan W. *The Mexican American.* Englewood Cliffs, N.J., 1970.

909 NAVARRO, Joseph P. "The Condition of Mexican-American History." *J Mex-Am Hist,* I (1970), 25–52.

910 NAVARRO, Joseph P. "The Contributions of Carey McWilliams to American Ethnic History." *J Mex-Am Hist,* II (1971), 1–21.

911 NOGALES, Luis, G., ed. *The Mexican American: A Selected and Annotated Bibliography.* 2d ed., rev. and enl. Stanford, Calif., 1971.

912 NORQUEST, Carrol. *Rio Grande Wetbacks: Migrant Mexican Workers.* Albuquerque, N.M., 1972.

913 PINO, Frank, comp. *Mexican Americans: A Research Bibliography.* 2 vols., index. East Lansing, Mich., 1974.

914 REISLER, Mark. "Always the Laborer, Never the Citizen: Anglo Perceptions of the Mexican Immigrant during the 1920s." *Pac Hist Rev,* XLV (1976), 231–254.

914A REISLER, Mark. "Mexican Unionization in California Agriculture, 1927–1936." *Labor Hist,* XIV (1973), 562–579.

915 ROBINSON, Cecil. *With the Ears of Strangers: The Mexican in American Literature.* Tucson, Ariz., 1963. †

916 SAMORA, Julian. *Los Mojados: The Wetback Story.* Notre Dame, Ind., 1971.

917 SAMORA, Julian, ed. *La Raza: Forgotten Americans.* Notre Dame, Ind., 1966.

918 SANCHEZ, George I. *Forgotten People: A Study of New Mexicans.* Albuquerque, N.M., 1940.

919 SCRUGGS, Otey M. "Evolution of the Mexican Farm Labor Agreement of 1942." *Ag Hist,* XXXIV (1960), 140–149.

920 SCRUGGS, Otey M. "The First Mexican Farm Labor Program." *Ariz W,* II (1960), 319–326.

921 SCRUGGS, Otey M. "Texas and the Bracero Program, 1942–1947." *Pac Hist Rev,* XXXII (1963), 251–264.

922 SCRUGGS, Otey M. "The United States, Mexico, and the Wetbacks." *Pac Hist Rev,* XXX (1961), 149–164.

923 SERVÍN, Manuel, comp. *The Mexican-Americans: An Awakening Minority.* Beverly Hills, Calif., 1970.

924 SERVÍN, Manuel. "The Pre-World War II Mexican American: An Interpretation." *Calif Hist Soc Q,* XLV (1966), 325–338.

925 SIMMONS, Ozzie G. *Anglo-Americans and Mexican Americans in South Texas.* New York, 1974. A reprint of a doctoral dissertation at Harvard, 1952.

926 TAYLOR, Paul S. *An American-Mexican Frontier: Nueces County, Texas.* Chapel Hill, N.C., 1934.

927 TAYLOR, Paul S. *Mexican Labor in the United States.* 2 vols. in 3. Berkeley, Calif., 1928–1934.

928 WOLLENBERG, Charles. "*Huelga,* 1928 Style: The Imperial Valley Cantaloupe Workers' Strike." *Pac Hist Rev,* XXXVIII (1969), 45–58.

X. The Mormons

929 ALEXANDER, Thomas G., and James B. ALLEN. "The Mormons in the Mountain West: A Selective Bibliography." *Ariz W,* IX (1967), 365–384.

930 ALLEN, James B., and Richard O. COWAN. *Mormonism in the Twentieth Century.* 2d ed. Provo, Utah, 1967.

930A ALLEN, James B., and Glen M. LEONARD. *The Story of the Latter-day Saints.* Salt Lake City, Utah, 1976. A comprehensive modern history written from a Mormon point of view. Extensive bibliography.

931 ANDERSON, Nels. *Desert Saints: The Mormon Frontier in Utah.* Chicago, 1942. New ed. Chicago, 1966. † Especially strong on southwestern Utah.

932 ARRINGTON, Leonard J. "Blessed Damozels: Women in Mormon History." *Dialogue,* VI (Summer 1971), 22–31.

933 ARRINGTON, Leonard J. *Charles C. Rich: Mormon General and Western Frontiersman.* Provo, Utah, 1974.

934 ARRINGTON, Leonard J. *Great Basin Kingdom: An Economic History of the Latter-day Saints, 1830–1900.* Cambridge, Mass., 1958. Repr. Lincoln, Neb., 1966. † A major study that examines the Mormon achievement as a whole in addition to presenting excellent economic history.

935 ARRINGTON, Leonard J. "The Intellectual Tradition of the Latter-day Saints." *Dialogue,* IV (Spring 1969), 13–26.

936 ARRINGTON, Leonard J. "Scholarly Studies of Mormonism in the Twentieth Century." *Dialogue,* I (Spring 1966), 15–32.

937 ARRINGTON, Leonard J. "The Search for Truth and Meaning in Mormon History." *Dialogue,* III (Summer 1968), 56–65.

937A ARRINGTON, Leonard J., Feramorz Y. FOX, and Dean L. MAY. *Building the City of God: Community and Cooperation among the Mormons.* Salt Lake City, Utah, 1976. Essentially case studies in cooperative communities and businesses.

938 ARRINGTON, Leonard J., and Wayne K. HINTON. "Origin of the Welfare Plan of the Church of Jesus Christ of Latter-day Saints." *Brig You Univ Stud,* V (1964), 67–85.

939 BANCROFT, Hubert H. *Works.* Volume on Utah. See 1.

940 BITTON, Davis. "Anti-Intellectualism in Mormon History." *Dialogue,* I (Autumn 1966), 111–134. With rejoinder by James B. Allen, pp. 134–140.

941 *The Book of Mormon: An Account Written by the Hand of Mormon upon Plates Taken from the Plates of Nephi.* Salt Lake City, Utah, 1920 and subsequent printings. † (Original ed. 1830).

942 *Brigham Young University Studies,* IX (Spring 1969). Special issue on Joseph Smith, the beginning of Mormonism, and the influence of New England and New York on the Mormon mind. XI (Summer 1971) and XII (Summer 1972). Special issues on the Mormons at Kirtland, Ohio. XIII (Autumn 1972 and Summer 1973). Special issues on the Mormons in Missouri.

943 BRODIE, Fawn M. *No Man Knows My History: The Life of Joseph Smith.* New York, 1945. Rev. ed. New York, 1971.

944 BROOKS, Juanita. *John Doyle Lee: Zealot—Pioneer Builder—Scapegoat.* Glendale, Calif., 1962. New ed. Glendale, 1972.

945 BROOKS, Juanita. *The Mountain Meadows Massacre.* Stanford, Calif., 1950. New ed. Norman, Okla., 1962.

946 BROOKS, Juanita, ed. *On the Mormon Frontier: The Diary of Hosea Stout, 1844–1861.* 2 vols. Salt Lake City, Utah, 1964.

947 CANNON, Charles A. "The Awesome Power of Sex: The Polemical Campaign Against Mormon Polygamy." *Pac Hist Rev,* XLIII (1974), 61–82.

948 CHRISTENSEN, Harold T. "Stress Points in Mormon Family Culture." *Dialogue,* VII (Winter 1972), 20–34.

949 COWAN, Richard O. "Mormonism in National Periodicals." Doctoral dissertation, Stanford University, 1961.

950 CRACROFT, Richard H., and Neal E. LAMBERT, eds. *A Believing People: Literature of the Latter-day Saints.* Provo, Utah, 1974. †

951 CRAWLEY, Peter. "A Bibliography of the Church of Jesus Christ of Latter-day Saints in New York, Ohio, and Missouri." *Brig You Univ Stud,* XII (1972), 465–537.

952 DAVIES, J. Kenneth. "The Accommodation of Mormonism and Politico-Economic Reality." *Dialogue,* III (Spring 1968), 42–54.

953 DE PILLIS, Mario S. "The Social Sources of Mormonism." *Church Hist,* XXXVII (1968), 50–79.

954 DE VOTO, Bernard. "The Centennial of Mormonism: A Study in Utopia and Dictatorship." *Forays and Rebuttals.* Boston, 1936.

955 *Dialogue,* IV (Spring 1969). Special issue on religion, the Mormon Church, Joseph Smith's first vision, and the contemporaneous revival at Palmyra, VII (Spring 1972). Special issue on "the Mormon Experience" in the twentieth century.

956 DURHAM, G. Homer. "A Political Interpretation of Mormon History." *Pac Hist Rev,* XIII (1944), 136–150.

957 FIFE, Austin, and Alta FIFE. *Saints of Sage and Saddle: Folklore Among the Mormons.* Bloomington, Ind., 1956.

958 FLANDERS, Robert B. *Nauvoo: Kingdom on the Mississippi.* Urbana, Ill., 1965.

959 FLANDERS, Robert B. "To Transform History: Early Mormon Culture and the Concept of Time and Space." *Church Hist,* XL (1971), 108–117.

960 FLANDERS, Robert B. "Writing on the Mormon Past." *Dialogue,* I (Autumn 1966), 47–61.

961 FOX, Feramorz Y. "Experiment in Utopia: The United Order of Richfield, 1874–1877." *Utah Hist Q,* XXXII (1964), 355–380.

962 FURNISS, Norman F. *The Mormon Conflict, 1850–1859.* New Haven, Conn., 1960. A study of Federal military intervention under President Buchanan.

963 GODFREY, Kenneth W. "The Coming of the Manifesto." *Dialogue,* V (Autumn 1970), 11–25. The decision to perform no more marriage ceremonies involving polygamy.

964 HANSEN, Klaus J. "The Metamorphosis of the Kingdom of God: Toward a Reinterpretation of Mormon History." *Dialogue,* I (Autumn 1966), 63–83.

965 HANSEN, Klaus J. *Quest for Empire: The Political Kingdom of God and Council of Fifty in Mormon History.* East Lansing, Mich., 1967. †

966 HILL, Marvin S. "The Historiography of Mormonism." *Church Hist,* XXVIII (1959), 418–426.

967 HILL, Marvin S. "The Role of Christian Primitivism in the Origin and Development of the Early Mormon Kingdom, 1830–1844." Doctoral dissertation, University of Chicago, 1968.

968 HILL, Marvin S., and James B. ALLEN, eds. *Mormonism and American Culture.* New York, 1972. † Reprints important essays by David B. Davis, Mario De Pillis, Leonard J. Arrington, William Mulder, Stanley S. Ivins, Klaus Hansen, and Howard R. Lamar, plus two new essays: Thomas F. O'Dea, "Sources of Strain in Mormon History Reconsidered", and Arrington, "Crisis in Identity: Mormon Responses in the Nineteenth and Twentieth Centuries."

969 HIRSHSON, Stanley P. *The Lion of the Lord: A Biography of Brigham Young.* New York, 1969. A strangely one-sided biography.

970 HOWARD, Richard P. "The Reorganized Church in Illinois, 1852–82: Search for Identity." *Dialogue,* V (Spring 1970), 63–75.

971 HUNSAKER, Kenneth B. "The Twentieth Century Mormon Novel." Doctoral dissertation, Pennsylvania State University, 1968.

972 HUNTER, Milton R. *Brigham Young, the Colonizer.* Salt Lake City, Utah, 1940. Rev. ed. Santa Barbara, Calif., and Salt Lake City, 1973. While giving chief attention to the founding of new settlements, this book also discusses Mormon economic and political policy.

973 IVINS, Stanley S. "Notes on Mormon Polygamy." *W Hum Rev,* X (1956), 229–239. Repr. *Utah Hist Q,* XXXV (1967), 309–321. The best available estimates as to the number of polygamous families.

974 JACKSON, Richard H. "Righteousness and Environmental Change: The Mormons and the Environment." *Essays on the American West, 1973–1974.* Ed. Thomas G. Alexander. Provo, Utah, 1975. † Especially good on the beginning of irrigation.

975 *Journal of Discourses.* 26 vols. Liverpool and London, 1854–1886. Repr. Los Angeles, 1956. Index Provo, Utah, 1959. Discourses by Brigham Young, his associates, and successors.

976 KANE, Elizabeth Wood. *Twelve Mormon Homes Visited in Succession on a Journey through Utah to Arizona.* Ed. Everett L. Cooley. Salt Lake City, Utah, 1974. A reprint of a description written in 1872 by Mrs. Thomas L. Kane.

977 LARSON, Gustive O. *The 'Americanization' of Utah for Statehood.* San Marino, Calif., 1971. The final drive against polygamy and the politics of admission to statehood.

978 LEE, Lawrence B. "Homesteading in Zion." *Utah Hist Q,* XXVIII (1960), 29–38.

979 LINFORD, Orma. "The Mormons and the Law: The Polygamy Cases." Doctoral dissertation, University of Wisconsin, 1964.

980 LYON, T. Edgar. "Religious Activities and Development in Utah, 1847–1910." *Utah Hist Q,* XXXV (1967), 292–306.

981 LYTHGOE, Dennis L. "The Changing Image of Mormonism in Periodical Literature, 1830–1969." Doctoral dissertation, University of Utah, 1969.

982 MCCLINTOCK, James H. *Mormon Settlement in Arizona: A Record of Peaceful Conquest of the Desert.* Phoenix, Ariz., 1921.

982A MCKIERNAN, F. Mark, Alma R. BLAIR, and Paul M. EDWARDS, eds. *The Restoration Movement: Essays in Mormon History.* Lawrence, Kan., 1973. Includes both the "Brighamite" and "Josephite" branches of the divided church.

983 MCMURRIN, Sterling M. *The Theological Foundations of the Mormon Religion.* Salt Lake City, Utah, 1965. †

984 MCNIFF, William J. *Heaven on Earth: A Planned Mormon Society.* Oxford, Ohio, 1940.

985 MAUSS, Armand L. "Saints, Cities, and Secularism: Religious Attitudes and Behavior of Modern Urban Mormons." *Dialogue,* VII (Summer 1972), 8–27.

986 MEINIG, Donald W. "The Mormon Culture Region: Strategies and Patterns in the Geography of the American West, 1847–1964." *Ann Ass Am Geog,* LV (1965), 191–220. An important interpretation.

987 MELVILLE, J. Keith. "Brigham Young's Ideal Society: The Kingdom of God." *Brig You Univ Stud,* V (1962), 3–18.

988 MORGAN, Dale L. "The State of Deseret." *Utah Hist Q,* VIII (1940), 65–251. Three full issues were devoted exclusively to Morgan's ninety-page history and to the texts of the constitution, statutes, and papers of this Mormon attempt at statehood.

989 MULDER, William. *Homeward to Zion: The Mormon Migration from Scandinavia.* Minneapolis, Minn., 1957.

990 MULDER, William. "The Mormons in American History." *Utah Hist Q,* XXVII (1959), 59–77.

991 MULDER, William, and A. Russell MORTENSEN, eds. *Among the Mormons: Historic Accounts by Contemporary Observers.* New York, 1958. †

992 NELSON, Lowry. *The Mormon Village: A Pattern and Technique of Land Settlement.* Salt Lake City, Utah, 1952. A classic sociological study.

993 NIBLEY, Preston. *Brigham Young: The Man and His Work.* Salt Lake City, Utah, 1936. "This book is written primarily for Latter-day Saints"—Foreword.

994 O'DEA, Thomas F. "Mormonism and the American Experience of Time." *W Hum Rev,* VIII (1954), 181–190.

995 O'DEA, Thomas F. *The Mormons.* Chicago, 1957. † A major study of Mormon religious and social organization and belief.

996 PAUL, Rodman W. "The Mormons as a Theme in Western Historical Writing." *J Am Hist,* LIV (1967), 511–523.

997 PETERSON, Charles S. " 'A Mighty Man Was Brother Lot': A Portrait of Lot Smith—Mormon Frontiersman." *W Hist Q,* I (1970), 393–414.

998 PETERSON, Charles S. *Take Up Your Mission: Mormon Colonizing Along the Little Colorado River, 1870–1900.* Tucson, Ariz., 1973. †

999 POLL, Richard D. "The Mormon Question Enters National Politics, 1850–1856." *Utah Hist Q,* XXV (1957), 117–131.

1000 POLL, Richard D. "The Political Reconstruction of Utah Territory, 1866–1890." *Pac Hist Rev,* XXVII (1958), 111–126.

1001 RICH, Russell R. *Ensign to the Nations: A History of the Church from 1846 to the Present.* Provo, Utah, 1972. The L. D. S. Church.

1002 RICKS, Joel E. *Forms and Methods of Early Mormon Settlement in Utah and the Surrounding Region, 1847 to 1877.* Logan, Utah, 1964.

1003 ROBERTS, Brigham H. *A Comprehensive History of the Church of Jesus Christ of Latter-day Saints.* 6 vols. Salt Lake City, Utah, 1930. Index, Provo, Utah, 1959.

1004 ROBERTS, Brigham H., ed. *History of the Church of Jesus Christ of Latter-day Saints.* 2d ed. 7 vols. Salt Lake City, Utah, 1948–1956. Index, Provo, Utah, 1962. The first 6 volumes are Joseph Smith's account, from his journals and papers. The seventh volume is from several sources.

1005 SMITH, Joseph. *The Doctrines and Convenants of the Church of Jesus Christ of Latter-day Saints.* Salt Lake City, Utah, 1921 and subsequent printings.

1006 SMITH, Joseph. *The Pearl of Great Price: A Selection from the Revelations, Translations, and Narrations of Joseph Smith.* Salt Lake City, Utah, 1921 and subsequent printings.

1007 STEGNER, Wallace. *The Gathering of Zion: The Story of the Mormon Trail.* New York, 1964. †

1008 STEGNER, Wallace. *Mormon Country.* New York, 1942.

1009 STENHOUSE, T. B. H. *The Rocky Mountain Saints: A Full and Complete History of the Mormons. . . .* New York, 1873. A detailed history by a prominent apostate.

1010 TAGGART, Stephen G. *Mormonism's Negro Policy: Social and Historical Origins.* Salt Lake City, Utah, 1970. †

1011 TANNER, Annie C. *A Mormon Mother: An Autobiography.* n.p., 1941. 2d ed. Salt Lake City, Utah, 1969.

1012 TARCAY, Eileen. "Among the Lamanites: The Indians and the Mormons." *W Folk,* XVIII (1959), 131–134.

1013 TAYLOR, Philip A. M. "Early Mormon Loyalty and the Leadership of Brigham Young." *Utah Hist Q,* XXX (1962), 103–132.

1014 TAYLOR, Philip A. M. *Expectations Westward: The Mormons and the Emigration of Their British Converts in the Nineteenth Century.* Edinburgh and London, 1965. Ithaca, N.Y., 1966.

1015 TAYLOR, Philip A. M. "The Life of Brigham Young: A Biography Which Will Not Be Written." *Dialogue,* I (Autumn 1966), 101–110.

1016 TAYLOR, Philip A. M. "The Mormon Crossing of the United States, 1840–1870." *Utah Hist Q,* XXV (1957), 319–337.

1017 TAYLOR, Philip A. M. "Recent Writing on Utah and the Mormons." *Ariz W,* IV (1962), 249–260.

1018 TAYLOR, Philip A. M., and Leonard ARRINGTON. "Religion and Planning in the Far West: The First Generation of Mormons in Utah." *Econ Hist Rev,* XI (1958), 71–86.

1019 THOMAS, George. *The Development of Institutions under Irrigation, with Special Reference to Early Utah Conditions.* New York, 1920.

1020 TURNER, Wallace. *The Mormon Establishment.* Boston, 1966. Contemporary survey by a *New York Times* reporter.

1021 WERNER, M. R. *Brigham Young.* New York, 1925.

1022 WEST, Ray B., Jr. *Kingdom of the Saints: The Story of Brigham Young and the Mormons.* New York, 1957.

1023 WHALEN, William J. *The Latter-day Saints in the Modern Day World: An Account of Contemporary Mormonism.* New York, 1964. †

1024 YOUNG, Karl. "Brief Sanctuary: The Mormon Colonies of Northern Mexico." *Am W,* IV (1967), 4–11, 66–67.

1025 YOUNG, Kimball. *Isn't One Wife Enough?* New York, 1954. This is a serious sociological-psychological study of polygamy.

XI. Mining and Miners

See also: Labor.

1026 ABUDU, Assibi O. "Establishing Gold Mining Rights in California, 1848–1853." Doctoral dissertation, University of California, Los Angeles, 1969.

1027 ALENIUS, E. M. J. *A Brief History of the United Verde Open Pit, Jerome, Arizona.* Tucson, Ariz., 1968.

1028 ARRINGTON, Leonard J. *Great Basin Kingdom.* See 934.

1029 ARRINGTON, Leonard J. "Planning an Iron Industry for Utah, 1851–1858." *Hunt Lib Q,* XXI (1958), 237–260.

1030 ARRINGTON, Leonard J., and Gary B. HANSEN. *"The Richest Hole on Earth": A History of the Bingham Copper Mine.* Logan, Utah, 1963. †

1031 ATHERTON, Lewis. "The Mining Promoter in the Trans-Mississippi West." *W Hist Q,* I (1970), 35–50.

1032 ATHERTON, Lewis. "Structure and Balance in Western Mining History." *Hunt Lib Q,* XXX (1966), 55–84.

1033 BAUR, John E. "The Health Factor in the Gold Rush Era." *Pac Hist Rev,* XVIII (1949), 97–108.

1034 BERTON, Pierre. *The Klondike Fever: The Life and Death of the Last Great Gold Rush.* New York, 1958.

1035 BIEBER, Ralph P. "California Gold Mania." *Miss Val Hist Rev,* XXXV (1948), 3–28.

1036 BOLINO, August C. "The Role of Mining in the Economic Development of Idaho Territory." *Ore Hist Q,* LIX (1958), 116–151.

1037 BURCH, Albert. "Development of Metal Mining in Oregon." *Ore Hist Q,* XLIII (1941), 105–128.

1038 CARLSON, Leland H. *An Alaskan Gold Mine: The Story of No. 9 Above.* Evanston, Ill., 1951.

1039 CASH, Joseph H. *Working the Homestake.* Ames, Iowa, 1973.

1040 CAUGHEY, John W. *Gold is the Cornerstone.* Berkeley, Calif., 1948. Repr. as *The California Gold Rush.* Berkeley, Calif., 1975. †

1041 CHADWICK, Robert A. "Coal: Montana's Prosaic Treasure." *Mont: Mag W Hist,* XXIII (October 1973), 18–31.

1042 CLELAND, Robert G. *A History of Phelps Dodge, 1834–1950.* New York, 1952.

1043 CLEMENS, Samuel L. (Mark Twain, pseud.). *Roughing It.* Hartford, Conn., 1872. Repr. with intro. by Rodman W. Paul, New York, 1953. Rev. ed., New York, 1964. †

1044 DAY, David T. *Report on Mineral Industries in the United States at the Eleventh Census: 1890.* Washington, D.C., 1892.

1045 DE ARMOND, R. N. *The Founding of Juneau.* Juneau, Alaska, 1967. Includes local mining laws, early mining, and mining rushes.

1046 ELLIOTT, Russell R. *Nevada's Twentieth Century Mining Boom: Tonopah—Goldfield—Ely.* Reno, Nev., 1966.

1047 ELLIOTT, Russell R. *Radical Labor in the Nevada Mining Booms, 1900–1920.* Reno, Nev., 1963.

1048 EMMONS, Samuel F., and George F. BECKER. *Statistics and Technology of the Precious Metals* (Bureau of the Census, *Tenth Census,* 1880, XIII). Washington, D.C., 1885.

1049 EVANS, William B., and Robert L. PETERSON. "Decision at Colstrip: The Northern Pacific Railway's Open-Pit Mining Operation." *Pac N W Q,* LXI (1970), 129–136.

1050 FAHEY, John. *The Ballyhoo Bonanza: Charles Sweeny and the Idaho Mines.* Seattle, Wash., 1971.

1051 GIBSON, Arrell M. *Wilderness Bonanza: The Tri-State District of Missouri, Kansas, and Oklahoma.* Norman, Okla., 1972.

1052 GREEVER, William S. *The Bonanza West: The Story of the Western Mining Rushes 1848–1900.* Norman, Okla., 1963.

1053 GRISWOLD, Don L., and Jean H. GRISWOLD. *The Carbonate Camp Called Leadville.* Denver, Colo., 1951.

1054 GURIAN, Jay. "Literary Convention and the Mining Romance." *J W,* V (1966), 106–114.

1055 HAMMOND, John Hayes. *Autobiography.* 2 vols., New York, 1935.

1056 HIGH, James. "William Andrews Clark, Westerner: An Interpretative Vignette." *Ariz W,* II (1960), 245–264.

1057 HINTON, Harwood P. "Frontier Speculation: A Study of the Walker Mining District." *Pac Hist Rev,* XXIX (1960), 245–255.

1058 HOLLIDAY, Jaquelin S. "The California Gold Rush in Myth and Reality." Doctoral dissertation, University of California, 1959.

1059 HUNT, William R. *North of 53°: The Wild Days of the Alaska-Yukon Mining Frontier, 1870–1914.* New York, 1974.

1060 HUNTTING, Marshall T. *Gold in Washington.* Olympia, Wash., 1955.

1061 JACKSON, W. Turrentine. "British Capital in Northwest Mines." *Pac N W Q,* XLVII (1956), 75–85.

1062 JACKSON, W. Turrentine. *The Enterprising Scot: Investors in the American West after 1873.* Edinburgh, 1968.

1063 JACKSON, W. Turrentine. "The Infamous Emma Mine: A British Interest in the Little Cottonwood District, Utah Territory." *Utah Hist Q,* XXIII (1955), 339–362.

1064 JACKSON, W. Turrentine. *Treasure Hill: Portrait of a Silver Mining Camp.* Tucson, Ariz., 1963. †

1065 JENSEN, Vernon H. *Heritage of Conflict: Labor Relations in the Nonferrous Metals Industry up to 1930.* Ithaca, N.Y., 1950. Repr. Westport, Conn., 1968. †

1066 KELLEY, Robert L. *Gold vs. Grain: The Hydraulic Mining Controversy in California's Sacramento Valley: A Chapter in the Decline of the Concept of Laissez Faire.* Glendale, Calif., 1959.

1067 KENNY, William R. "History of the Sonora Mining Region of California, 1848–1860." Doctoral dissertation, University of California, 1955.

1068 KENSEL, W. Hudson. "Inland Empire Mining and the Growth of Spokane, 1883–1905." *Pac N W Q,* LX (1969), 77–97.

1069 LAPP, Rudolph M. "The Negro in Gold Rush California." *J Neg Hist,* XLIX (1964), 81–98.

1070 LAPP, Rudolph M. "Negro Rights Activities in Gold Rush California." *Calif Hist Soc Q,* XLV (1966), 3–20.

1071 LAVENDER, David. *Nothing Seemed Impossible: William C. Ralston and Early San Francisco.* Palo Alto, Calif., 1975.

1072 LEWIS, Marvin, ed. *The Mining Frontier: Contemporary Accounts from the American West in the 19th Century.* Norman, Okla., 1967.

1073 LEWIS, Oscar. *Silver Kings: The Lives and Times of Mackay, Fair, Flood, and O'Brien, Lords of the Nevada Comstock Lode.* New York, 1947.

1074 LILLARD, Richard G. *Desert Challenge: An Interpretation of Nevada.* New York, 1942. †

1075 LINGENFELTER, Richard E. *The Hardrock Miners: A History of the Mining Labor Movement in the American West, 1863–1893.* Berkeley, Calif., 1974.

1076 LORD, Eliot. *Comstock Mining and Miners* (U.S. Geological Survey, Monographs, IV). Washington, 1883. Repr. with intro. by David F. Myrick, Berkeley, Calif., 1959.

1077 LYMAN, George D. *Ralston's Ring: California Plunders the Comstock Lode.* New York, 1937.

1078 MCNELIS, Sarah. *Copper King at War: The Biography of F. Augustus Heinze.* Missoula, Mont., 1968.

1079 MANN, Ralph E., II. "The Decade After the Gold Rush: Social Structure in Grass Valley and Nevada City, California, 1850–1860." *Pac Hist Rev,* XLI (1972), 484–504.

1080 MORRELL, W. P. *The Gold Rushes.* New York, 1941. Comparative study of rushes throughout the world.

1081 MURRAY, Robert A. "Miner's Delight, Investor's Despair: The Ups and Downs of a Sub-Marginal Mining Camp in Wyoming." *Ann Wyo,* XLIV (1972), 25–55.

1082 NORTHROP, Stuart A. *Minerals of New Mexico.* Rev. ed. Albuquerque, N.M., 1959.

1083 NUNIS, Doyce B., Jr., ed. *The Golden Frontier: The Recollections of Herman Francis Reinhart, 1851–1869.* Austin, Tex., 1962.

1083A PAHER, Stanley W. *Nevada Ghost Towns and Mining Camps.* Berkeley, Calif., 1970. An album of excellent contemporary photographs, plus brief comments.

1084 PARKER, Watson. *Gold in the Black Hills.* Norman, Okla., 1966.

1085 PARSONS, A. B., ed. *Seventy-Five Years of Progress in the Mineral Industry, 1871–1946.* New York, 1947. Essays on many aspects of mining and metallurgy.

1086 PAUL, Rodman W. *California Gold: The Beginning of Mining in the Far West.* Cambridge, Mass., 1947. Repr. Lincoln, Neb., 1965. †

1087 PAUL, Rodman W. *The California Gold Discovery: Sources, Documents, Accounts and Memoirs Relating to the Discovery of Gold at Sutter's Mill.* Georgetown, Calif., 1966.

1088 PAUL, Rodman W. "Colorado as a Pioneer of Science in the Mining West." *Miss Val Hist Rev,* XLVII (1960), 34–50.

1089 PAUL, Rodman W. "Mining Frontiers as a Measure of Western Historical Writing." *Pac Hist Rev,* XXXII (1964), 25–34.

1090 PAUL, Rodman W. *Mining Frontiers of the Far West, 1848–1880.* New York, 1963; Albuquerque, N.M., 1974. †

1091 PERRIGO, Lynn I. "Law and Order in Early Colorado Mining Camps." *Miss Val Hist Rev,* XXVIII (1941), 41–62.

1092 PETERSON, Richard H. "The Bonanza Kings: Mining Entrepreneurs of the Trans-Mississippi Frontier." Doctoral dissertation, University of California, Davis, 1971.

1093 PETERSON, Richard H. "Frontier Thesis and Social Mobility on the Mining Frontier." See 193.

1094 RICKARD, Thomas A. *A History of American Mining.* New York, 1932. Repr. New York, n.d.

1095 ROMIG, Robert L. "Stamp Mills in Trouble." *Pac N W Q,* XLIV (1953), 166–176.

1096 ROSKE, Ralph J. "The World Impact of the California Gold Rush, 1849–1857." *Ariz W,* V (1963), 187–232.

1097 ROWE, John. *The Hard-Rock Men: Cornish Immigrants and the North American Mining Frontier.* New York, 1974.

1098 SAVAGE, W. Sherman. "The Negro on the Mining Frontier." *J Neg Hist,* XXX (1945), 30–46.

1099 SHINN, Charles H. *Mining Camps: A Study in American Frontier Government.* New York, 1885. Repr. with intro. by Joseph H. Jackson, New York, 1948. Repr. with intro. by Rodman W. Paul, New York, 1965.

1100 SHINN, Charles H. *The Story of the Mine, as Illustrated by the Great Comstock Lode of Nevada.* New York, 1896.

1101 SMITH, Duane A. "Colorado's Urban-Mining Safety Valve." *Colo Mag,* XLVIII (1971), 299–318.

1102 SMITH, Duane A. *Horace Tabor: His Life and the Legend.* Boulder, Colo., 1973.

1103 SMITH, Duane A. "Mining Camps: Myth vs. Reality." *Colo Mag,* XLIV (1967), 93–110.

1104 SMITH, Duane A. *Rocky Mountain Mining Camps: The Urban Frontier.* Bloomington, Ind., 1967. †

1105 SMITH, Grant H. *The History of the Comstock Lode, 1850–1920.* Reno, Nev., 1943.

1106 SMITH, Robert W. *The Coeur d'Alene Mining War of 1892: A Case Study of an Industrial Dispute.* Corvallis, Ore., 1961.

1107 SONNICHSEN, C. L. *Colonel Greene and the Copper Skyrocket; The Spectacular Rise and Fall of William Cornell Greene: Copper King, Cattle Baron, and Promoter Extraordinary in Mexico, the American Southwest, and the New York Financial District.* Tucson, Ariz., 1974. †

1108 SPENCE, Clark C. *British Investments and the American Mining Frontier, 1860–1901.* Ithaca, N.Y., 1958.

1109 SPENCE, Clark C. *Mining Engineers and the American West: The Lace-Boot Brigade, 1849–1933.* New Haven, Conn., 1970.

1109A SPRAGUE, Marshall. *Money Mountain: The Story of Cripple Creek Gold.* Boston, 1953.

1110 SUGGS, George G. *Colorado's War on Militant Unionism: James H. Peabody and the Western Federation of Miners.* Detroit, Mich., 1972.

1111 THOMPSON, Thomas G. "The Cultural History of Colorado Mining Towns, 1859–1920." Doctoral dissertation, University of Missouri, 1966.

1112 THOMPSON, Thomas G. "The Far Western Mining Frontier: Trends and Unsolved Problems." *Colo Mag,* XLI (1964), 105–110.

1113 TODD, Arthur C. *The Cornish Miner in America: The Contribution to the Mining History of the United States by Emigrant Cornish Miners. . . .* Truro, Cornwall, and Glendale, Calif., 1967.

1114 TOOLE, K. Ross. "The Anaconda Copper Mining Company: A Price War and a Copper Corner." *Pac N W Q,* XLI (1950), 312–329.

1115 TOOLE, K. Ross. "A History of the Anaconda Mining Company: A Study in the Relationships between a State and Its People and a Corporation, 1880–1950." Doctoral dissertation, University of California at Los Angeles, 1954.

1116 TOOLE, K. Ross. "When Big Money Came to Butte: The Migration of Eastern Capital to Montana." *Pac N W Q*, XLIV (1953), 23–29.

1117 TOWNLEY, John M. "The Delamar Boom: Development of a Small, One-Company Mining District in the Great Basin." *Nev Hist Soc Q*, XV (1972), 3–19.

1118 TOWNLEY, John M. "The New Mexico Mining Company." *N M Hist Rev*, XLVI (1971), 57–73.

1119 TRIMBLE, William J. *The Mining Advance into the Inland Empire: A Comparative Study of . . . Idaho and Montana, Eastern Washington and Oregon, and the Southern Interior of British Columbia. . . .* Madison, Wis., 1914. Repr. with intro. by Rodman W. Paul, New York, 1972.

1120 *Utah Hist Q*, XXXI (Summer 1963). Special issue on mining in Utah, 1863–1963.

1120A WAGNER, Jack R. *Gold Mines of California: An Illustrated History of the Most Productive Mines with Descriptions of the Interesting People Who Owned Them.* Berkeley, Calif., 1970.

1121 WALKER, Arthur L. "Recollections of Early Day Mining in Arizona." *Ariz Hist Rev*, VI (1935), 14–43.

1122 WATERS, Frank, *Midas of the Rockies: The Story of Stratton and Cripple Creek.* New York, 1937. Repr., Denver, Colo., 1949.

1123 WATKINS, T. H. *Gold and Silver in the West: The Illustrated History of an American Dream.* Palo Alto, Calif., 1971.

1124 WELLS, Merle W. *Gold Camps and Silver Cities.* Moscow, Idaho, 1963. Repr., "with slight revisions," Boise, Idaho, 1974.

1125 WHARTON, David. *The Alaska Gold Rush.* Bloomington, Ind., 1972.

1126 WHEAT, Carl I. *Books of the California Gold Rush: A Centennial Selection.* San Francisco, 1949.

1127 WRIGHT, William (Dan De Quille, pseud.). *History of the Big Bonanza: An Authentic Account of the Discovery, History, and Working of the World Renowned Comstock Silver Lode. . . .* Hartford, Conn., 1876. Repr. with intro. by Oscar Lewis, New York, 1947.

1128 WYMAN, Mark. "Industrial Revolution in the West: Hard-Rock Miners and the New Technology." *W Hist Q*, V (1974), 39–57.

1129 WYMAN, Mark. "The Underground Miner, 1860–1910: Labor and Industrial Change in the Northern Rockies." Doctoral dissertation, University of Washington, 1971.

1130 YOUNG, Otis, E., Jr., with assistance of Robert LENON. *Black Powder and Hand Steel: Miners and Machines on the Old Western Frontier.* Norman, Okla., 1976.

1130A YOUNG, Otis E., Jr., with assistance of Robert LENON. *Western Mining: An Informal Account of Precious-Metals Prospecting, Placering, Lode Mining, and Milling on the American Frontier from Spanish Times to 1893.* Norman, Okla., 1970.

XII. Cattle and Sheep

1. Cattlemen and Cowboys

1131 ADAMS, Andy. *The Log of a Cowboy; a Narrative of the Old Trail Days.* Boston, 1903. †

1132 ADAMS, Ramon F., comp. *The Rampaging Herd: A Bibliography of Books and Pamphlets on Men and Events in the Cattle Industry.* Norman, Okla., 1959.

1133 *Agricultural History,* XXXV (July 1961). Entire issue devoted to early cattle industry of North America.

1134 ATHERTON, Lewis. *The Cattle Kings.* Bloomington, Ind., 1961. †

1135 AYDELOTTE, Frank. "The Literature of the Range Cattle Industry: A Critical Survey." *Trail Guide,* XV (1970), 3–19.

1136 BOX, Thadis W. "Range Deterioration in West Texas." *S W Hist Q,* LXXI (1967), 37–45.

1137 BRANCH, E. Douglas. *The Cowboy and His Interpreters.* New York, 1926. Repr. New York, 1961.

1138 BRAYER, Herbert O. "The L7 Ranches: An Incident in the Economic Development of the Western Cattle Industry." *Ann Wyo,* XV (1943), 5–37. Ranch economics in microcosm.

1139 BURCHAM, L. T. "Cattle and Range Forage in California, 1770–1880." *Ag Hist,* XXXV (1961), 140–149.

1140 BURMEISTER, Charles A. "Six Decades of Rugged Individualism: The American National Cattlemen's Association, 1898–1955." *Ag Hist,* XXX (1956), 143–150.

1141 BURROUGHS, John R. *Guardian of the Grasslands: The First Hundred Years of the Wyoming Stock Growers Association.* Cheyenne, Wyo., 1971.

1142 CALEF, Wesley C. *Private Grazing and Public Lands: Studies of the Local Management of the Taylor Grazing Act.* Chicago, 1960. Primarily Wyoming.

1143 CARPENTER, Clifford D. "The Early Cattle Industry in Missouri." *Mo Hist Rev,* XLVII (1953), 201–215.

1144 CARTER, George E. "The Cattle Industry of Eastern Oregon, 1880–1890." *Ore Hist Q,* LXVII (1966), 139–159.

1145 CAULEY, T. J. "Early Business Methods in the Texas Cattle Industry." *J Econ Bus Hist,* IV (1932), 461–486.

1146 CLAWSON, Marion. *The Western Range Livestock Industry.* New York, 1950.

1147 CLAY, John. *My Life on the Range.* Chicago, 1924. Repr. New York, 1961.

1148 CLELAND, Robert G. *The Cattle on a Thousand Hills; Southern California, 1850–1870.* San Marino, Calif., 1941. 2d ed., with chronological scope extended to 1880. San Marino, Calif., 1951.

1149 DALE, Edward E. *Cow Country.* Norman, Okla., 1942. † Essays on the history of the Great Plains.

1150 DALE, Edward E. *The Range Cattle Industry*. Norman, Okla., 1930. New ed. with new subtitle *Ranching on the Great Plains from 1865 to 1925*. Norman, Okla., 1960.

1151 DRAGO, Harry S. *Great American Cattle Trails: The Story of the Old Cow Paths of the East and the Longhorn Highways of the Plains*. New York, 1965.

1152 DURHAM, Philip, and Everett L. JONES. *The Negro Cowboys*. New York, 1965.

1153 DUSENBERRY, William. "Constitutions of Early and Modern American Stock Growers' Associations." *S W Hist Q*, LIII (1950), 255–275. Compares colonial Spanish practice with American.

1154 DYKSTRA, Robert R. *The Cattle Towns*. New York, 1968. † Five Kansas cattle towns, 1867–1885.

1155 EDWARDS, Everett E., comp. *A Bibliography of the History of Agriculture in the United States*. Washington, D.C., 1930.

1156 EMMETT, Chris. *Shanghai Pierce: A Fair Likeness*. Norman, Okla., 1953.

1157 FAULK, Odie B. "Ranching in Spanish Texas." *His-Am Hist Rev*, XLV (1965), 257–266.

1158 FEDEWA, Philip C. "Abel Stearns in Transitional California, 1848–1871." Doctoral dissertation, University of Missouri, 1970.

1159 FLETCHER, Robert H. *Free Grass to Fences: The Montana Cattle Range Story*. New York, 1960.

1160 FOSS, Philip O. *Politics and Grass: The Administration of Grazing on the Public Domain*. Seattle, Wash., 1960.

1161 FRANTZ, Joe B. "Cowboy Philosophy: A Cold Spoor." *The Frontier Re-examined*. Ed. John Francis McDermott. Urbana, Ill., 1967.

1162 FRANTZ, Joe B., and Julian E. CHOATE, Jr. *The American Cowboy: The Myth and the Reality*. Norman, Okla., 1955.

1163 FRINK, Maurice, *et al. When Grass Was King: Contributions to the Western Range Cattle Industry Study*. Boulder, Colo., 1956.

1164 FRITZ, Henry E., ed. "The Cattleman's Frontier in the Trans-Mississippi West: An Annotated Bibliography." *Ariz W*, XIV (1972), 45–70, 169–190.

1165 FUGATE, Francis L. "Origins of the Range Cattle Era in South Texas." *Ag Hist*, XXXV (1961), 155–158.

1166 GARD, Wayne. *The Chisholm Trail*. Norman, Okla., 1954.

1167 GARD, Wayne. "The Fence-Cutters." *S W Hist Q*, LI (1947), 1–15. Local illustration of a universal problem.

1168 GATES, Paul W. "Cattle Kings in the Prairies." *Miss Val Hist Rev*, XXXV (1948), 379–412.

1169 GATES, Paul W. *The Farmer's Age: Agriculture 1815–1860*. New York, 1960. †

1170 GIBSON, Arrell M., ed. "Ranching in the West." *J W*, XIV (July 1975). Special issue.

1171 GORDON, Clarence W. "Report on Cattle, Sheep, and Swine, Supplementary to Enumeration of Live Stock on Farms in 1880." Tenth Census (1880, *Report on the Productions of Agriculture*. Washington, D.C., 1883. Special report.

1172 GRESSLEY, Gene M. "The American Cattle Trust: A Study in Protest." *Pac Hist Rev*, XXX (1961), 61–77.

1173 GRESSLEY, Gene M. *Bankers and Cattlemen.* New York, 1966. †

1174 HALEY, J. Evetts. *Charles Goodnight: Cowman and Plainsman.* Boston, 1936.

1175 HALEY, J. Evetts. *The XIT Ranch of Texas, and the Early Days of the Llano Estacado.* Chicago, 1929. New ed. Norman, Okla., 1953.

1176 HATCHER, Averlyne M. "The Water Problem of the Matador Ranch." *W Tex Hist Assn Yrbk,* XX (1944), 51–76. Local illustration of a universal problem.

1177 HAVINS, T. R. "Livestock and Texas Law." *W Tex Hist Assn Yrbk,* XXXVI (1960), 18–32.

1178 "History of Western Range Research." *Ag Hist,* XVIII (1944), 127–143.

1179 HOLDEN, William C. *The Spur Ranch: A Study of the Inclosed Ranch Phase of the Cattle Industry in Texas.* Boston, 1934. Enlarged ed. with new title: *The Espuela Land and Cattle Company: A Study of a Foreign-Owned Ranch in Texas.* Austin, Tex., 1970.

1180 HOUGH, John. "Abel Stearns, 1848–1871." Doctoral dissertation, University of California at Los Angeles, 1961.

1181 JACKSON, W. Turrentine. "Railroad Relations of the Wyoming Stock Growers' Association." *Ann Wyo,* XIX (1947), 3–23.

1182 JACKSON, W. Turrentine. "The Wyoming Stock Growers' Association: Political Power in Wyoming Territory, 1873–1890." *Miss Val Hist Rev,* XXXIII (1947), 571–594.

1183 LAMBERT, C. Roger. "The Drought Cattle Purchase, 1934–35: Problems and Complaints." *Ag Hist,* XLV (1971), 85–93.

1184 LAMBERT, C. Roger. "New Deal Experiments in Production Control: The Livestock Program, 1933–1935." Doctoral dissertation, University of Oklahoma, 1962.

1185 LAMBERT, C. Roger. "Texas Cattlemen and the AAA, 1933–1935." *Ariz W,* XIV (1972), 137–154.

1186 LEA, Tom. *The King Ranch.* 2 vols. Boston, 1957.

1187 MCCALLUM, Henry D., and Frances T. MCCALLUM. *The Wire that Fenced the West.* Norman, Okla., 1965.

1188 MCCOY, Joseph G. *Historic Sketches of the Cattle Trade of the West and Southwest.* Kansas City, 1874. Ed. Ralph P. Bieber. Glendale, Calif., 1940.

1189 MAHNKEN, Norbert R. "Ogallala—Nebraska's Cowboy Capital." *Neb Hist,* XXVIII (1947), 85–110.

1190 MATTISON, Ray H. "The Hard Winter and the Range Cattle Business." *Mont: Mag W Hist,* I (1951), 5–21.

1191 MORRISEY, Richard J. "The Northward Expansion of Cattle Ranching in New Spain, 1550–1600." *Ag Hist,* XXV (1951), 115–121.

1192 MOSK, Sanford A. "Land Policy and Stock Raising in the Western United States." *Ag Hist,* XVII (1943), 14–30. The influence of stock raisers in the selection and use of state lands, with emphasis on Arizona and New Mexico.

1193 MOTHERSHEAD, Harmon R. *The Swan Land and Cattle Company, Ltd.* Norman, Okla., 1971.

1194 MYRES, Sandra L. "The Ranching Frontier: Spanish Institutional Backgrounds of the Plains Cattle Industry." *Essays on the American West.* Ed. Harold M. Hollingsworth and Sandra L. Myres. Austin, Tex., 1969.

1195 MYRES, Sandra L. *The Ranch in Spanish Texas, 1691–1800.* El Paso, Tex., 1969.

1196 NIMMO, Joseph, Jr. "The Range and Ranch Cattle Business of the United States." *Report on the Internal Commerce of the United States,* Part 3. Washington, D.C., 1885.

1197 OLIPHANT, J. Orin. "History of Livestock Industry in the Pacific Northwest." *Ore Hist Q,* XLIV (1948), 3–29. Historiographical.

1198 OLIPHANT, J. Orin. *On the Cattle Ranges of the Oregon Country.* Seattle, Wash., 1968.

1199 OSGOOD, Ernest S. *The Day of the Cattleman.* Minneapolis, Minn., 1929. Repr. Chicago, n.d. †

1200 PEAKE, Ora Brooks. *The Colorado Range Cattle Industry.* Glendale, Calif., 1937.

1201 PEARCE, William M. *The Matador Land and Cattle Company.* Norman, Okla., 1964.

1202 PELZER, Louis. *The Cattleman's Frontier: A Record of the Trans-Mississippi Cattle Industry from Oxen Trains to Pooling Companies, 1850–1890.* Glendale, Calif., 1936.

1203 PETERSON, Levi S. "The Development of Utah Livestock Law, 1848–1896." *Utah Hist Q,* XXXII (1964), 198–216

1204 PULLING, Hazel A. "California's Fence Laws and the Range-Cattle Industry." *Hist,* VIII (1946), 140–155.

1205 RENNER, G. K. "The Kansas City Meat Packing Industry before 1900." *Mo Hist Rev,* LV (1960), 18–29.

1206 ROLLINS, Philip Ashton. *The Cowboy: His Characteristics, his Equipment, and his Part in the Development of the West.* New York, 1922. Rev. ed. with new subtitle *An Unconventional History of Civilization on the Old-Time Cattle Range.* New York, 1936. †

1207 SALOUTOS, Theodore. "The New Deal and Farm Policy in the Great Plains." *Ag Hist,* XLVIII (1969), 345–355.

1208 SAVAGE, William W. *The Cherokee Strip Live Stock Association: Federal Regulation and the Cattleman's Last Frontier.* Columbia, Mo., 1973.

1209 SCHLEBECKER, John T., comp. *Bibliography of Books and Pamphlets on the History of Agriculture in the United States, 1607–1967.* Santa Barbara, Calif., 1969. †

1210 SCHLEBECKER, John T. *Cattle Raising on the Plains, 1900–1961.* Lincoln, Neb., 1963.

1211 SHANNON, Fred A. *The Farmer's Last Frontier: Agriculture 1860–1897.* New York, 1945.

1212 SHEFFY, Lester F. *The Francklyn Land and Cattle Company: A Panhandle Enterprise, 1882–1957.* Austin, Tex., 1963.

1213 SHIDELER, James H. *Farm Crisis, 1919–1923.* Berkeley, Calif., 1957.

1214 SKAGGS, Jimmy M. *The Cattle-Trailing Industry: Between Supply and Demand, 1866–1890.* Lawrence, Kan., 1973.

1215 SONNICHSEN, C. L. *Cowboys and Cattle Kings: Life on the Range Today.* Norman, Okla., 1950.

1216 STOUT, Joe A. "Cattlemen, Conservationists, and the Taylor Grazing Act." *N M Hist Rev,* XLV (1970), 311–332.

1217 TOWNE, Charles W., and Edward N. WENTWORTH. *Cattle and Men.* Norman, Okla., 1955.

1218 TRESSMAN, Ruth. "Home on the Range." *N M Hist Rev,* XXVI (1951), 1–17. Woman's place on cow ranches.

1219 *Utah Historical Quarterly,* XXXII (Summer 1964). Special issue on cattle industry in Utah.

1220 WAGONER, J. J. *The History of the Cattle Industry in Southern Arizona, 1540–1940.* Tucson, Ariz., 1952.

1221 WALKER, Don D. "The Cattle Industry of Utah: 1850–1900: An Historical Profile." *Utah Hist Q,* XXXII (1964), 182–197.

1222 WALKER, Don D. "From Self-Reliance to Cooperation: The Early Development of the Cattlemen's Associations in Utah." *Utah Hist Q,* XXXV (1967), 187–201.

1223 WEBB, Walter Prescott. *The Great Plains.* See 82.

1224 WESTERMEIER, Clifford P. "The Modern Cowboy—An Image." *The American West.* Ed. R. G. Ferris. Santa Fe, N.M., 1963.

1225 WESTERMEIER, Clifford P. *Trailing the Cowboy: His Life and Lore as told by Frontier Journalists.* Caldwell, Idaho, 1955.

1226 WILSON, James A. "Cattle and Politics in Arizona, 1886–1941." Doctoral dissertation, University of Arizona, 1967.

1227 WILSON, James A. "Cattlemen, Packers, and Government: Retreating Individualism on the Texas Range." *S W Hist Q,* LXXIV (1971), 525–534.

1228 WILSON, James A. "West Texas Influence on the Early Cattle Industry of Arizona." *S W Hist Q,* LXXI (1967), 26–36.

2. Sheep and Wool

1229 AUSTIN, Mary. *The Flock.* Boston, 1906. Vivid "local color" narrative.

1230 BRIGGS, Harold E. "The Early Development of Sheep Ranching in the Northwest." *Ag Hist,* XI (1937), 161–180.

1231 BRIGGS, Harold E. "Ranching and Stock-Raising in the Territory of Dakota." *S D Hist Coll,* XIV (1928), 417–465.

1232 BROWN, Harry James, ed. *Letters From a Texas Sheep Ranch.* Urbana, Ill., 1959.

1233 BROWN, Harry James. "The National Association of Wool Manufacturers, 1864–1897." Doctoral dissertation, Cornell University, 1949.

1234 Bureau of Statistics, United States Treasury Dept. *Wool and Manufactures of Wool. Special Report.* Treasury Dept. Document No. 1025. Washington, D.C., 1887.

1235 CARLSON, Alvar Ward. "New Mexico's Sheep Industry, 1850–1900: Its Role in the History of the Territory." *N M Hist Rev,* XLIV (1969), 25–49.

1236 CARMAN, Ezra A., H. A. HEATH, and John MINTO. *Special Report on the History and Present Condition of the Sheep Industry of the United States.* Washington, D.C., 1892.

1237 COLE, Arthur H. *The American Wool Manufacture.* 2 vols. Cambridge, Mass., 1926.

1238 CONNOR, L. G. "A Brief History of the Sheep Industry in the United States." *Ann Rep Am Hist Assoc,* 1918. Washington, D.C., 1921.

1239 FORD, Worthington C. *Wool and Manufactures of Wool.* Washington, D.C., 1894.

1240 GEORGETTA, Clel. *Golden Fleece in Nevada.* Reno, Nev., 1972.

1241 GILFILLAN, A. B. *Sheep: Life on a South Dakota Range.* Minneapolis, Minn., 1957.

1242 HASKETT, Bert. "History of the Sheep Industry in Arizona." *Ariz Hist Rev,* VII (1936), 3–49.

1243 HOLLIDAY, J. S. "The Lonely Sheepherder." *Am W,* I (1964), 37–42.

1244 HULTZ, Fred, and John A. HILL. *Range Sheep and Wool in the Seventeen Western States.* New York, 1931.

1245 KENNY, Judith Keyes. "Early Sheep Ranching in Eastern Oregon." *Ore Hist Q,* LXIV (1963), 101–122. Part history and part reminiscence, by the daughter and granddaughter of pioneer sheep raisers.

1246 KUPPER, Winifred. *The Golden Hoof: The Story of the Sheep of the Southwest.* New York, 1945.

1247 LEHMANN, Valgene W. *Forgotten Legions: Sheep in the Rio Grande Plain of Texas.* El Paso, Tex., 1969.

1248 MAUDSLAY, Robert. *Texas Sheepman; the Reminiscences of Robert Maudslay.* Ed. Winifred Kupper. Austin, Tex., 1951.

1249 MINTO, John. "Sheep Husbandry in Oregon." *Ore Hist Q,* III (1902), 219–247.

1250 RAKESTRAW, Lawrence. "Sheep Grazing in the Cascade Range: John Minto vs. John Muir." *Pac Hist Rev,* XXVII (1958), 371–382.

1251 ROSTAD, Lee. "Charley Bair: King of the Western Sheepmen." *Mont: Mag W Hist,* XX (October 1970), 50–61.

1252 SAWYER, Byrd W. *Nevada Nomads: A Story of the Sheep Industry.* San Jose, Calif., 1971.

1253 SHAW, R. M. "Range Sheep Industry in Kittitas County, Washington." *Pac N W Q,* XXXIII (1942), 153–170.

1254 SHEPHERD, William R. E. *Prairie Experiences in Handling Cattle and Sheep.* New York, 1885.

1255 SYPOLT, Charles M. "Keepers of the Rocky Mountain Flocks: A History of the Sheep Industry in Colorado, New Mexico, Utah and Wyoming to 1900." Doctoral dissertation, University of Wyoming, 1974.

1256 TOWNE, Charles W., and Edward N. WENTWORTH. *Shepherd's Empire.* Norman, Okla., 1945.

1257 U.S. Tariff Commission. *The Wool-Growing Industry.* Washington, D.C., 1921.

1258 WENTWORTH, Edward N. *America's Sheep Trails: History, Personalities.* Ames, Iowa, 1948.

1259 WENTWORTH, Edward N. "Trailing Sheep from California to Idaho in 1865: The Journal of Gorham Gates Kimball." *Ag Hist,* XXVIII (1954), 49–83.

1260 WHITE, Charles L. "Transhumance in the Sheep Industry of the Salt Lake Region." *Econ Geog,* II (1926), 414–425.

1261 WRIGHT, Chester W. *Wool-Growing and the Tariff; A Study in the Economic History of the United States.* Boston, 1910.

XIII. Agriculture

See also: Irrigation and Reclamation; Land and Land Policy; Cattle and Sheep; Western Politics; Labor; Spanish-Speaking Peoples; Chinese and Japanese.

1262 *Agricultural History,* XLI (January 1967), 1–35. Four articles on the sugar beet industry.

1263 AMERINE, Maynard A. "An Introduction to the Pre-Repeal History of Grapes and Wines in America." *Ag Hist,* XLIII (1969), 259–262. Contains a good bibliography.

1264 ARRINGTON, Leonard J. *Beet Sugar in the West: A History of the Utah-Idaho Sugar Company, 1891–1966.* Seattle, Wash., 1966.

1265 ARRINGTON, Leonard J. *Great Basin Kingdom.* See 934.

1266 ARRINGTON, Leonard J. "Western Agriculture and the New Deal." *Ag Hist,* XLIV (1970), 337–353.

1267 BALL, Carleton. "The History of American Wheat Improvement." *Ag Hist,* IV (1930), 48–71.

1268 BENNETT, M. K. "Climate and Agriculture in California." *Econ Geog,* XV (1939), 153–164.

1269 BENTLEY, Arthur F. *The Condition of the Western Farmer as Illustrated by the Economic History of a Nebraska Township* (Johns Hopkins Univ Stud in Hist and Polit Sci, XI). Baltimore, Md., 1893.

1270 BOGUE, Allan G. *From Prairie to Corn Belt: Farming on the Illinois and Iowa Prairies in the Nineteenth Century.* Chicago, 1963. This "modern classic" study of midwestern agriculture suggests important parallels for any student of agriculture in the farther west.

1271 BOWERS, William L. "Country Life Reform, 1900–1920: A Neglected Aspect of Progressive Era History." *Ag Hist,* XLV (1971), 211–221.

1272 BRIGGS, Harold E. *Frontiers of the Northwest.* See 44.

1273 BUCK, Solon J. *The Agrarian Crusade: A Chronicle of the Farmer in Politics.* New Haven, Conn., 1920.

1274 BUCK, Solon J. *The Granger Movement: A Study of Agricultural Organization and Its Political, Economic and Social Manifestations, 1870–1880.* Cambridge, Mass., 1913. Repr. Lincoln, Neb., 1963. †

AGRICULTURE

1275 CAROSSO, Vincent P. *The California Wine Industry, 1830–1895: A Study of the Formative Years.* Berkeley, Calif., 1951, 1976.

1276 CHAMBERS, Clarke A. *California Farm Organizations: A Historical Study of the Grange, the Farm Bureau, and the Associated Farmers, 1929–1941.* Berkeley, Calif., 1952.

1277 COULTER, C. Brewster. "The Big Y Country: Marketing problems and Organization, 1900–1920." *Ag Hist,* XLVI (1972), 471–488. Yakima Valley, Washington, apple marketing.

1278 CREEL, Cecil W. *A History of Nevada Agriculture.* Reno, Nev., 1964.

1279 DANHOF, Clarence H. *Change in Agriculture: The Northern United States, 1820–1870.* Cambridge, Mass., 1969. While dealing with eastern and midwestern agriculture, this book suggests sources and patterns of inquiry important for any area, and offers a detailed bibliography that includes the new economic history's materials.

1280 DETHLOFF, Henry C., comp. *A List of References for the History of the Farmers' Alliance and the Populist Party.* Davis, Calif., 1973.

1281 DICK, Everett. *The Sod-House Frontier, 1854–1890: A Social History of the Northern Plains. . . .* New York, 1937. Repr. Lincoln, Neb., 1954.

1282 DRACHE, Hiram M. *The Day of the Bonanza: A History of Bonanza Farming in the Red River Valley of the North.* Fargo, N. D., 1964. A classic example of large-scale, mechanized farming just east of the line of semiaridity.

1283 DUNBAR, Robert G. "Agricultural Adjustments in Eastern Colorado in the Eighteen-Nineties." *Ag Hist,* XVIII (1944), 41–52.

1284 DUNBAR, Robert G. "The Significance of the Colorado Agricultural Frontier." *Ag Hist,* XXXIV (1960), 119–125.

1285 DYKSTRA, Robert R. "The Last Days of 'Texan' Abilene: A Study in Community Conflict on the Farmer's Frontier." *Ag Hist,* XXXIV (1960), 107–119.

1286 EDWARDS, Edward E., comp. *A Bibliography of the History of Agriculture in the United States* (U.S. Department of Agriculture, Miscellaneous Publication No. 84). Washington, D.C., 1930. Over 4200 items, listed by major topics, periods, states, and crops.

1287 ERDMAN, H. E. "The Development and Significance of California Cooperatives, 1900–1915." *Ag Hist,* XXXII (1958), 179–184. Commentary by Reynold Wik, 185–186.

1288 EVANS, Samuel L. "Texas Agriculture, 1880–1930." Doctoral dissertation, University of Texas, 1960.

1289 FISHER, Lloyd H. "The Harvest Labor Market in California." *Q J Econ,* LXV (1951), 392–415. Discusses the past 100 years.

1290 FISHER, Mary Frances K., and Max YAVNO. *The Story of Wine in California.* Berkeley, Calif., 1962.

1291 FITE, Gilbert C. *American Agriculture and Farm Policy Since 1900.* New York, 1964. An introduction to the nature of the subject and to the bibliography of it.

1292 FITE, Gilbert C., "Farmer Opinion and the Agricultural Adjustment Act, 1933." *Miss Val Hist Rev,* XLVIII (1962), 656–673.

1293 FITE, Gilbert C. "The Farmers' Dilemma, 1919–1929." *Change and Continuity in Twentieth-Century America.* Ed. John Braeman, *et al.* New York, c. 1964.

1294 FITE, Gilbert C. *The Farmers' Frontier, 1865–1900.* New York, 1966. †

1295 FITE, Gilbert C. "Untapped Sources of Western Agricultural History." *Probing the American West."* Ed. K. Ross Toole, *et al.* Santa Fe, N.M., 1962.

1296 FITE, Gilbert C. "Western Farmers and the Decline of Laissez Faire, 1870–1900." *N D Hist Q,* XLI (1973), 40–53.

1297 FODELL, Beverly, comp. *Cesar Chavez and the United Farm Workers.* See 885.

1298 GATES, Paul W. *Agriculture and the Civil War.* New York, 1965. Detailed analysis and description of agriculture during that era.

1299 GATES, Paul W., ed. *California Ranchos and Farms, 1846–1862, Including the Letters of John Quincy Adams Warren. . . .* Madison, Wisc., 1967. Includes an 80-page introduction that is a good summary of California agricultural history for the period indicated.

1300 GEISER, Samuel W. *Horticulture and Horticulturists in Early Texas.* Dallas, Tex., 1945. †

1301 HARGREAVES, Mary W. M. *Dry Farming in the Northern Great Plains, 1900–1925.* Cambridge, Mass., 1957.

1302 HARGREAVES, Mary W. M. "Homesteading and Homemaking on the Plains: A Review." *Ag Hist,* XLVII (1973), 156–163. Discusses three books by women.

1303 HEINTZELMAN, Oliver H. "The Evolution of an Industry: The Dairy Economy of Tillamook County, Oregon." *Pac N W Q,* XLIX (1958), 77–81.

1303A HEWES, Leslie. *The Suitcase Farming Frontier: A Study in the Historical Geography of the Central Great Plains.* Lincoln, Neb., 1973. Twentieth century experience in western Kansas and eastern Colorado.

1304 HOLDEN, William C. "The Development of Agriculture in West Texas." *Readings in Texas History.* Ed. Eugene C. Barker. Dallas, Tex., 1929.

1305 HUTCHISON, Claude B., ed. *California Agriculture. By Members of the Faculty of the College of Agriculture.* Berkeley, Calif., 1946. One historical chapter plus much scattered historical information.

1306 ISE, John. *Sod and Stubble: The Story of a Kansas Homestead.* New York, 1936. Repr. Lincoln, Neb., 1967. †

1307 IWATA, Masakazu. "The Japanese Immigrants in California Agriculture." *Ag Hist,* XXXVI (1962), 25–37.

1308 JONES, Lamar B. "Labor and Management in California Agriculture, 1864–1964." *Labor Hist,* XI (1970), 23–40.

1309 KLOSE, Nelson. *America's Crop Heritage: The History of Foreign Plant Introduction by the Federal Government.* Ames, Iowa, 1950.

1310 KNAPP, Joseph G. "The Experience of Kansas with Wheat Pools." *J Farm Econ,* IX (1927), 318–332.

1311 KRAEMER, Erich, and H. E. ERDMAN. *History of Cooperation in the Marketing of California Fresh Deciduous Fruits* (California Agricultural Experiment Station Bulletin 557.) Berkeley, Calif., 1933.

1312 LANGE, Dorothea, and Paul S. TAYLOR. *An American Exodus: A Record of Human Erosion.* New York, 1939. Photographic history of the Dust Bowl migration.

1313 LEONARD, William E. "The Wheat Farmer of Southeastern Washington." *J Land and Public Utility Econ,* II (1926), 23–39.

1314 LEWIS, Howard T. "The Elevator Movement in the Pacific Northwest." *J Pol Econ,* XXIV (1916), 794–804.

1315 LLOYD, John W. *Cooperative and Other Organized Methods of Marketing California Horticultural Products* (Univ of Ill Stud Soc Sci, VIII). Urbana, Ill., c. 1919.

1316 MCCALLUM, Henry D., and Frances T. MCCALLUM. *Wire that Fenced the West.* See 1187.

1317 MCCLINTOCK, Thomas C. "Henderson Luelling, Seth Lewelling and the Birth of Pacific Coast Fruit Industry." *Ore Hist Q,* LXVIII (1967), 153–174.

1318 MCWILLIAMS, Carey. *Factories in the Field: The Story of Migratory Farm Labor in California.* Boston, 1939. Repr. Hamden, Conn., 1969. Repr. Salt Lake City, Utah, 1971. †

1319 MCWILLIAMS, Carey. *Ill Fares the Land: Migrants and Migratory Labor in the United States.* Boston, 1942. Repr. New York, 1967.

1320 MALIN, James C. *The Grassland of North America: Prolegomena to its History.* Lawrence, Kan., 1947. Repr. with addenda, Gloucester, Mass., 1967.

1321 MALIN, James C. "The Turnover of Farm Population in Kansas." *Kan Hist Q,* IV (1935), 339–359. Based on a study of rainfall belts and sample townships, 1860–1935.

1322 MALIN, James C. *Winter Wheat in the Golden Belt of Kansas: A Study in Adaption to Subhumid Geographical Environment.* Lawrence, Kan., 1944.

1323 MEERS, John R. "The California Wine and Grape Industry and Prohibition." *Calif Hist Soc Q,* XLVI (1967), 19–32.

1324 MEINIG, Donald W. *The Great Columbia Plain: A Historical Geography, 1805–1910.* See 64.

1325 MEINIG, Donald W. "The Growth of Agricultural Regions in the Far West, 1850–1910." *J Geog,* LIV (1955), 221–232.

1326 MEINIG, Donald W. "Wheat Sacks out to Sea." *Pac N W Q,* XLV (1954), 13–18. The export wheat trade of the Pacific Northwest.

1327 MEYER, Albert J. "History of the California Fruit Growers Exchange, 1893–1920." Doctoral dissertation, Johns Hopkins University, 1951.

1328 MILLER, Orlando W. *The Frontier in Alaska and the Matanuska Colony.* New Haven, Conn., 1975.

1329 MILLER, William H. "Agriculture in the High Plains: The History of a Struggle against Environment." Doctoral dissertation, University of California, Berkeley, 1951.

1330 MINTZ, Warren. "A Search for a Successful Agricultural Migrant: A Study of Five Fruit Harvests on the West Coast of the United States." Doctoral dissertation, New York University, 1971.

1331 NELSON, Lowry. *Mormon Village.* See 992.

1332 NESBIT, Robert C., and Charles M. GATES. "Agriculture in Eastern Washington, 1890–1910." *Pac N W Q,* XXXVII (1946), 279–302.

1333 NORDIN, Dennis Sven, comp. *A Preliminary List of References for the History of the Granger Movement.* Davis, Calif., 1967.

1334 NORDIN, Dennis Sven. *Rich Harvest: A History of the Grange, 1867–1900.* Jackson, Miss., 1974.

1335 OLSEN, Michael L. "The Beginnings of Agriculture in Western Oregon and Western Washington." Doctoral dissertation, University of Washington, 1970.

1336 OLSEN, Michael L., comp. *A Preliminary List of References for the History of Agriculture in the Pacific Northwest and Alaska.* Davis, Calif., 1968.

1337 ORSI, Richard J., comp. *A List of References for the History of Agriculture in California.* Davis, Calif., 1974. Comprehensive and thorough.

1338 PADFIELD, Harland, and William E. MARTIN. *Farmers, Workers and Machines: Technological and Social Change in Farm Industries of Arizona.* Tucson, Ariz., 1965.

1339 PAUL, Rodman W. "The Beginnings of Agriculture in California: Innovation vs. Continuity." *Calif Hist Q,* LII (1973), 16–27. Repr. in *Essays and Assays: California History Reappraised.* Ed. George H. Knoles. San Francisco, Calif., 1973. †

1340 PAUL, Rodman W. "The Great California Grain War: The Grangers Challenge the Wheat King." *Pac Hist Rev,* XXVII (1958), 331–349.

1341 PAUL, Rodman W. "The Wheat Trade between California and the United Kingdom." *Miss Val Hist Rev,* XLV (1958), 391–412.

1342 PAYLORE, Patricia, comp. *Seventy-Five Years of Arid-Lands Research at the University of Arizona: A Selective Bibliography, 1891–1965.* Tucson, Ariz., c. 1966. A comprehensive listing, including historical materials, that gives a surprisingly good insight into the problems of arid regions.

1343 PRESSLY, Thomas J., and William H. SCOFIELD, eds. *Farm Real Estate Values in the United States by Counties, 1850–1959.* Seattle, Wash., 1965.

1344 RASMUSSEN, Wayne D., ed. *Agriculture in the United States: A Documentary History.* 4 vols. New York, 1975.

1345 RASMUSSEN, Wayne D. "Forty Years of Agricultural History." *Ag Hist,* XXXIII (1959), 177–184.

1346 RASMUSSEN, Wayne D. "The Impact of Technological Change on American Agriculture, 1862–1962." *J Econ Hist,* XXII (1962), 578–591.

1347 RASMUSSEN, Wayne D., and Gladys L. BAKER. *The Department of Agriculture.* New York, 1972.

1348 ROGERS, Earl M., comp. *A List of References for the History of Agriculture in the Mountain States.* Davis, Calif., 1972.

1349 ROGIN, Leo. *The Introduction of Farm Machinery in its Relation to the Productivity of Labor in the Agriculture of the United States during the Nineteenth Century* (Univ of Calif Pubs in Econs, IX). Berkeley, Calif., 1931. Repr. New York, n.d. An excellent study of the evolution of farm machinery, with emphasis on the Pacific Coast.

1350 SALOUTOS, Theodore. "The New Deal and Farm Policy in the Great Plains." *Ag Hist,* XLIII (1969), 345–355.

1351 SALOUTOS, Theodore. "The Spring-Wheat Farmer in a Maturing Economy." *J Econ Hist,* VI (1946), 173–190.

1351A SCHAPSMEIER, Edward L., and Frederick H. SCHAPSMEIER. *Encyclopedia of American Agricultural History.* Westport, Conn., 1975.

1352 SCHLEBECKER, John T., comp. *Bibliography of Books and Pamphlets on the History of Agriculture in the United States, 1607–1967.* Santa Barbara, Calif., 1969. †

1353 SCHLEBECKER, John T. "Grasshoppers in American Agricultural History." *Ag Hist,* XXVII (1953), 85–93.

1354 SCHLEBECKER, John T. *Whereby We Thrive: A History of American Farming, 1607–1972.* Ames, Iowa, 1975.

1355 SCHMIDT, Louis B. "Agriculture in the West as a Field of Historical Study." *Ariz W,* I (1959), 331–342.

1356 SCHWARTZ, Harry. *Seasonal Farm Labor in the United States: With Special Reference to Hired Workers in Fruit and Vegetable and Sugar-Beet Production.* New York, 1945.

1357 SHANNON, Fred A. *The Farmers' Last Frontier, Agriculture, 1860–1897.* New York, 1945.

1358 SHIDELER, James H., ed. "Agriculture in the Development of the Far West: A Symposium." *Ag Hist,* XLIX (January 1975). Special issue, with 310 pages on Far Western farming and cattle raising and the technology, labor, law, and society connected with it.

1358A SHIDELER, James H. *Farm Crisis, 1919–1923.* Berkeley, Calif., 1957.

1359 SIMMS, D. Harper. *The Soil Conservation Service.* New York, 1970.

1360 STEIN, Walter J. *California and the Dust Bowl Migration.* Westport, Conn., 1973. †

1361 STEINEL, Alvin T., in collab. with D. W. WORKING. *History of Agriculture in Colorado.* Fort Collins, Colo., 1926.

1362 SUDWEEKS, Leslie L. "Early Agricultural Settlements in Southern Idaho." *Pac N W Q,* XXVIII (1937), 137–150.

1363 SUNDBORG, George, comp. *Bibliography and Abstracts on the Subject of Agriculture in Alaska, 1867–1942.* Juneau, Alaska, 1942.

1364 SWEEDLUN, Verne S. "A History of the Evolution of Agriculture in Nebraska, 1870–1930." Doctoral dissertation, University of Nebraska, 1940.

1365 TAYLOR, Paul S. "California Farm Labor: A Review." *Ag Hist,* XLII (1968), 49–54.

1366 TAYLOR, Paul S., and Edward J. ROWELL. "Patterns of Agricultural Labor Migration within California." *Monthly Labor Rev,* XLVII (1938), 980–990.

1367 TAYLOR, Paul S., and Tom VASEY. "Historical Background of California Farm Labor." *Rural Soc,* I (1936), 401–419.

1368 WEBB, Walter Prescott. *The Great Plains.* See 82.

1369 WHITAKER, James W., ed. "Farming in the Midwest, 1840–1900: A Symposium." *Ag Hist,* XLVIII (1974), 1–220. While concerned primarily with the region east of the line of semiaridity, much of the discussion has insights valuable for the farther west.

1370 WICKSON, Edward J. *California Nurserymen and the Plant Industry, 1850–1910.* . . . Los Angeles, 1921.

1371 WICKSON, Edward J. *Rural California.* New York, 1923. Contains many important historical insights and historical facts, as narrated by a pioneer teacher of agriculture.

1372 WIK, Reynold M. *Steam Power on the American Farm.* Philadelphia, 1953.

XIV. Irrigation, Reclamation, and Water Supply

1373 ADAMS, Frank. *Irrigation Districts in California, 1887–1915* (Calif. State Dept. of Engineering, Bull 2). Sacramento, Calif., 1916. The first of two reports in which Adams appraised the effects of the important Wright Act (irrigation district statute).

1374 ADAMS, Frank. *Irrigation Districts in California* (Calif. State Div. of Engineering and Irrigation, Bull 21). Sacramento, Calif., 1929. Important because of its discussion of the Wright Act and irrigation district laws in general.

1375 BAIN, Joe S., Richard E. CAVES, and Julius MARGOLIS. *Northern California's Water Industry: The Comparative Efficiency of Public Enterprise in Developing a Scarce Natural Resource.* Baltimore, Md., 1967.

1376 BOENING, Rose M. "History of Irrigation in the State of Washington." *Wash Hist Q,* IX (1918), 259–276; X (1919), 21–45.

1377 BRANDHORST, L. Carl. "The Panacea of Irrigation: Fact or Fancy." *J W,* VII (1968), 491–509. Western Nebraska, 1887–1956.

1378 BROUGH, Charles H. *Irrigation in Utah* (Johns Hopkins University Stud in Hist and Polit Sci, Extra vol. XIX). Baltimore, Md., 1898.

1378A CLARK, Ira G. "The Elephant Butte Controversy: A Chapter in the Emergence of Federal Water Law." *J Am Hist,* LXI (1975), 1006–1033.

1379 CONKIN, Paul K. "The Vision of Elwood Mead." *Ag Hist,* XXXIV (1960), 88–97.

1380 COOPER, Erwin. *Aqueduct Empire: A Guide to Water in California.* Glendale, Calif., 1968. Discusses every aspect of water, including irrigation.

1381 COULTER, Calvin Brewster. "Building the Tieton Irrigation Canal." *Pac N W Q,* XLIX (1958), 11–18. A part of the Yakima Project.

1382 COULTER, Calvin Brewster. "The New Settlers on the Yakima Project, 1880–1910." *Pac N W Q,* LXI (1970), 10–21.

1383 COULTER, Calvin Brewster. "The Victory of National Irrigation in the Yakima Valley, 1902–1906." *Pac N W Q,* XLII (1951), 99–122.

1384 DAVISON, Stanley R. "The Leadership of the Reclamation Movement, 1875–1902." Doctoral dissertation, University of California, Berkeley, 1951.

1385 DE ROOS, Robert. *The Thirsty Land: The Story of the Central Valley Project.* Stanford, Calif., 1948.

1386 DUNBAR, Robert G. "The Origins of the Colorado System of Water-Right Control." *Colo Mag.* XXVII (1950), 241–262.

1387 DURRENBERGER, Robert W., comp. "A Selected California Bibliography: Water Resources." *Calif Geog,* VIII (1967), 47–61, IX (1968), 65–77.

1388 FERRELL, John R. "Water in the Missouri Valley: The Inter-Agency River Committee Concept at Mid-Century." *J W,* VII (1968), 96–105.

1389 GANOE, John T. "The Beginnings of Irrigation in the United States." *Miss Val Hist Rev,* XXV (1938), 59–78.

1390 GANOE, John T. "The Origin of a National Reclamation Policy." *Miss Val Hist Rev*, XVIII (1931), 34–52. The Newlands Act of 1902.

1391 GLASS, Mary Ellen. *Water For Nevada: The Reclamation Controversy, 1885–1902*. Reno, Nev., 1964. †

1392 GREEN, Donald E. *Land of the Underground Rain: Irrigation on the Texas High Plains, 1910–1970*. Austin, Tex., 1973.

1393 GRESSLEY, Gene M. "Arthur Powell Davis, Reclamation, and the West." *Ag Hist*, XLII (1968), 241–257.

1394 HOLMES, Beatrice H. *A History of Federal Water Resources Programs, 1800–1960* (U.S. Dept. of Ag. Misc Pub 1233). Washington, D.C., 1972.

1395 HOSMER, Helen. "Imperial Valley." *Am W*, III (Winter 1966), 34–49, 79. Irrigation in what had been a desert.

1396 HUNDLEY, Norris, Jr. "Clio Nods: Arizona v. California and the Boulder Canyon Act—A Reassessment." *W Hist Q*, III (1972), 17–51.

1397 HUNDLEY, Norris, Jr. *Dividing the Waters: A Century of Controversy between the United States and Mexico*. Berkeley, Calif., 1966.

1398 HUNDLEY, Norris, Jr. "The Politics of Reclamation: California, the Federal Government, and the Origins of the Boulder Canyon Act—A Second Look." *Calif Hist Q*, LII (1973), 292–325.

1399 HUNDLEY, Norris, Jr. *Water and the West: The Colorado River Compact and the Politics of Water in the American West*. Berkeley, Calif., 1975.

1400 JACKSON, Richard H. "Righteousness and Environmental Change." See 974.

1401 JACOBSTEIN, J. Myron, and Roy M. MERSKY, comps. *Water Law Bibliography, 1847–1965; Source Book on U.S. Water and Irrigation Studies: Legal, Economic and Political*. Silver Spring, Md., 1966. Supplement for 1966–1967. Bibliographies and legislative histories for individual projects and states.

1402 JAMES, George Wharton, *Reclaiming the Arid West: The Story of the United States Reclamation Service*. New York, 1917.

1403 *Journal of the West*, VII (January 1968). Special issue on irrigation, reclamation, and conservation, with articles that include Martin E. Carlson, "William E. Smythe: Irrigation Crusader," 41–47; Thomas G. Alexander, "The Powell Irrigation Survey and the People of the Mountain West," 48–54; Mary Ellen Glass, "The Newlands Reclamation Project: Years of Innocence, 1903–1907," 55–63; H. L. Meredith, "Reclamation in the Salt River Valley, 1902–1917," 76–83.

1404 KLEINSORGE, Paul L. *The Boulder Canyon Project: Historical and Legal Aspects*. Stanford, Calif., 1941.

1405 LEE, Lawrence B. "William Ellsworth Smythe and the Irrigation Movement: A Reconsideration." *Pac Hist Rev*, XLI (1972), 289–311.

1406 LILLEY, William, III. "The Early Career of Frances G. Newlands, 1848–1897." Doctoral dissertation, Yale University, 1965.

1407 LILLEY, William, III, and Lewis L. GOULD. "The Western Irrigation Movement, 1878–1902: A Reappraisal." *The American West: A Reorientation*. Ed. Gene M. Gressley. Laramie, Wyo., 1966.

1408 MAAS, Arthur. *Muddy Waters: The Army Engineers and the Nation's Rivers*. Cambridge, Mass., 1951. Repr. New York, 1974.

1409 MEAD, Elwood, dir. *Report of Irrigation Investigations in California* (U.S. Dept. of Ag., Office of Expt. Stations, Bull 100). Washington, D.C., 1901. Especially important because of its discussion of riparian rights vs. prior appropriation, and the Wright Act.

1410 MEAD, Elwood, dir. *Report of Irrigation Ivestigations in Utah* (U.S. Dept. of Ag., Office of Expt. Stations, Bull 124). Washington, D.C. 1903. A highly realistic appraisal of how Mormon-dominated arrangements actually worked.

1411 MOELLER, Beverly B. *Phil Swing and Boulder Dam.* Berkeley, Calif., 1971.

1412 MORGAN, Arthur E. *Dams and Other Disasters: A Century of the Army Corps of Engineers in Civil Works.* Boston, 1971.

1413 MURPHY, Paul L. "Early Irrigation in the Boise Valley." *Pac N W Q,* XLIV (1953), 177–184.

1414 *New Mexico Historical Review,* XLVII (April 1972), 85–201. Special issue on land and water in New Mexico.

1415 NEWELL, F. H. *Report on Agriculture by Irrigation in the Western Part of the United States, Eleventh Census, 1890,* vol. V. Washington, D.C., 1894.

1416 "Personalities in the Development of the Columbia Basin." *Pac N W Q,* LII (1961), 139–154. Special section on this topic, includes articles: Bruce Mitchell, "Rufus Woods and Columbia River Development," 139–144; Click Relander, "The Battleground of National Irrigation," 144–150.

1417 SAGESER, A. Bower. "Windmill and Pump Irrigation on the Great Plains, 1890–1910." *Neb Hist,* XLVIII (1967), 107–118.

1418 SCHMALZ, Bruce L. "Headgates and Headaches: The Powell Tract." *Idaho Yes,* IX (1965–66), 22–25.

1419 SCHONFELD, Robert G. "The Early Development of California's Imperial Valley." *S Calif Q,* L (1968), 279–307, 395–426. Irrigation and community development.

1420 SMYTHE, William E. *The Conquest of Arid America.* New York, 1900. Rev. ed., New York, 1905. Repr. Ed. Lawrence B. Lee. Seattle, Wash., 1969. † A classic contemporary account that surveys the whole west.

1421 Special Committee of the U.S. Senate (William M. Stewart and J. H. Reagan). "Report on the Irrigation and Reclamation of Arid Lands." 51 Cong., 1 sess., *Senate Report* 928, in 6 parts, May 8, 1890 (Ser. nos. 2707 and 2708). Contains a vast amount of information.

1422 SPENCE, Clark C. "A Brief History of Pluviculture." *Pac N W Q,* LII (1961), 129–138. Attempts to "make rain."

1423 STEPHENSON, W. A. "Appropriation of Water in Arid Regions." *S W Soc Sci Q,* XVIII (1937), 215–226.

1424 SUNDBORG, George. *Hail Columbia: The Thirty Year Struggle for Grand Coulee Dam.* New York, 1954.

1425 SUTTON, Imre. "Geographical Aspects of Construction Planning: Hoover Dam Revisited.' *J W,* VII (1968), 301–344. Despite the title, this is an historical essay on the problems encountered in building the dam.

1426 SWAIN, Donald C. "The Bureau of Reclamation and the New Deal, 1933–1940." *Pac N W Q,* LXI (1970), 137–146.

1427 THOMAS, George. *Development of Institutions under Irrigation.* See 1019.

1428 THOMAS, George. *Early Irrigation in the Western States.* Salt Lake City, Utah, 1948.

1429 THOMPSON, John T. "Governmental Responses to the Challenge of Water Resources in Texas." *S W Hist Q,* LXX (1966), 44–64.

1430 U.S. Bureau of the Census. "Irrigation." *Twelfth Census, 1900,* VI (Washington, D.C., 1902), 797–880.

1431 VANDE VERE, Emmett K. "History of Irrigation in Washington." Doctoral dissertation, University of Washington, 1948.

1432 VOELTZ, Herman C. "Genesis and Development of a Regional Power Agency in the Pacific Northwest, 1933–43." *Pac N W Q,* LIII (1962), 65–76.

1433 WEBB, Walter Prescott. *More Water for Texas: The Problem and the Plan.* Austin, Tex., 1954.

XV. Land and Land Policy in the West

See also: Cattle and Sheep; Lumber and Forestry; Conservation; Mormons; Mining; Transportation (Railroads)

1434 ALEXANDER, Thomas G. "Senator Reed Smoot and Western Land Policy, 1905–1920." *Ariz W,* XIII (1971), 245–264.

1435 ANDERSON, George L. "The Administration of Federal Land Laws in Western Kansas, 1880–1890: A Factor in Adjustment to a New Environment." *Kan Hist Q,* XX (1952), 233–251.

1436 BERGQUIST, James M. "The Oregon Donation Act and the National Land Policy." *Ore Hist Q,* LVIII (1957), 17–35.

1437 BILLINGTON, Ray A. "The Origin of the Land Speculator as a Frontier Type." *Ag Hist.* XIX (1945), 204–212.

1438 BOGUE, Allan G., and Margaret B. BOGUE. "'Profits' and the Frontier Land Speculator." *J Econ Hist,* XVII (1957), 1–24.

1439 BRADFUTE, Richard W. *The Court of Private Land Claims: The Adjudication of Spanish and Mexican Land Grant Titles, 1891–1904.* Albuquerque, N.M., 1975. †

1440 BRAYER, Herbert O. *William Blackmore: The Spanish-Mexican Land Grants of New Mexico and Colorado, 1863-1878. A Case Study in the Economic Development of the West.* 2 vols. Denver, Colo., 1949.

1441 BROWN, Richard D. "The Agricultural College Land Grant in Kansas—Selection and Disposal." *Ag Hist,* XXXVII (1963), 94–102.

1442 CARR, Ralph. "Private Land Claims in Colorado." *Colo Mag,* XXV (1948), 11–30.

1443 CARSTENSEN, Vernon, ed. *The Public Lands: Studies in the History of the Public Domain.* Madison, Wis., 1963. † Important essays that in total come close to constituting a history of the disposal of the public domain.

1444 CHAPMAN, Berlin B. "The Legal Sooners of 1889 in Oklahoma." *Chron Okla*, XXXV (1957–58), 382–415.

1445 CLAWSON, Marion. *The Bureau of Land Management*. New York, 1971.

1446 CLAWSON, Marion. *The Federal Lands Since 1956: Recent Trends in Use and Management*. Washington, D.C., 1967. †

1447 CLAWSON, Marion. *Land for Americans: Trends, Prospects, and Problems*. Chicago, 1963.

1448 CLAWSON, Marion. *The Land System of the United States: An Introduction to the History and Practice of Land Use and Land Tenure*. Lincoln, Neb., 1968.

1449 CLAWSON, Marion. *Man and Land in the United States*. Lincoln, Neb., 1964.

1450 CLAWSON, Marion, and R. Burnell HELD. *The Federal Lands, Their Use and Management*. Baltimore, Md., 1957. Repr. Lincoln, Neb., 1965. †

1451 CONNOR, Seymour A. "Early Land Speculations in West Texas." *S W Soc Sci Q*, XLII (1962), 354–362.

1452 DECKER, Leslie E. "The Railroads and the Land Office: Administrative Policy and the Land Patent Controversy, 1864–1896." *Miss Val Hist Rev*, XLVI (1960), 679–699.

1453 DECKER, Leslie E. *Railroads, Lands, and Politics: The Taxation of the Railroad Land Grants, 1864–1897*. Providence, R.I., 1964.

1454 DICK, Everett. *The Lure of the Land: A Social History of the Public Lands from the Articles of Confederation to the New Deal*. Lincoln, Neb., 1970.

1455 DOZIER, Jack. "The Coeur d'Alene Land Rush, 1909–10." *Pac N W Q*, LIII (1962), 145–150.

1456 DUNHAM, Harold H. *Government Handout: A Study in the Administration of the Public Lands, 1875–1891*. Ann Arbor, Mich., 1941. Repr. New York, 1970.

1457 ELLIS, David M. "The Forfeiture of Railroad Land Grants, 1867–1894." *Miss Val Hist Rev*, XXXIII (1946), 27–60.

1458 EMMONS, David M. *Garden in the Grasslands: Boomer Literature of the Great Plains*. Lincoln, Neb., 1971.

1459 GANOE, John T. "The Desert Land Act in Operation, 1877–1891." *Ag Hist*, XI (1937), 142–157.

1460 GANOE, John T. "The Desert Land Act since 1891." *Ag Hist*, XI (1937), 266–277.

1461 GARDNER, Richard M. *Grito! Reies Tijerina and the New Mexico Land Grant War*. See 889.

1462 GATES, Paul W. "Adjudication of Spanish-Mexican Land Claims in California." *Hunt Lib Q*, XXI (1958), 213–236.

1463 GATES, Paul W. "California's Agricultural College Lands." *Pac Hist Rev*, XXX (1961), 103–122.

1464 GATES, Paul W. "California's Embattled Settlers." *Calif Hist Soc Q*, XLI (1962), 99–130.

1465 GATES, Paul W. "The California Land Act of 1851." *Calif Hist Q*, L (1971), 395–430.

1466 GATES, Paul W. *Fifty Million Acres: Conflicts over Kansas Land Policy, 1854–1890*. Ithaca, N.Y., 1954. †

1467 GATES, Paul W. *History of Public Land Law Development.* Washington, D.C., 1968. A massive study by the leading specialist in this field.

1468 GATES, Paul W. "The Homestead Law in an Incongruous Land System." *Am Hist Rev,* XLI (1936), 652–681.

1469 GATES, Paul W. "Land and Credit Problems in Underdeveloped Kansas." *Kan Hist Q,* XXXI (1965), 41–61.

1470 GATES, Paul W. "Pre-Henry George Land Warfare in California." *Calif Hist Soc Q,* XLVI (1967), 121–148.

1471 GATES, Paul W. "Public Land Issues in the United States." *W Hist Q,* II (1971), 363–376.

1472 GATES, Paul W. "Research in the History of the Public Lands." *Ag Hist,* XLVIII (1974), 31–50.

1473 GATES, Paul W. "The Role of the Land Speculator in Western Development." *Pa Mag Hist Biog,* LXVI (1942), 314–333.

1474 GATES, Paul W. "The Suscol Principle, Preemption, and California Latifundia." *Pac Hist Rev,* XXXIX (1970), 453–471.

1475 GEORGE, Henry. *Our Land and Land Policy, National and State.* San Francisco, 1871.

1476 GRAEBNER, Norman A. "The Public Land Policy of the Five Civilized Tribes." *Chron Okla,* XXIII (1945), 107–118.

1477 GREENLEAF, Richard E. "Land and Water in Mexico and New Mexico, 1700–1821." *N M Hist Rev,* XLVII (1972), 85–112.

1478 GREEVER, William S. *Arid Domain: The Santa Fe Railway and its Western Land Grant.* Stanford, Calif., 1954.

1479 HAFEN, LeRoy R. "Mexican Land Grants in Colorado." *Colo Mag,* IV (1927), 81–93.

1480 HEATHCOTE, Lesley M. "The Montana Arid Land Grant Commission, 1895–1903." *Ag Hist,* XXXVIII (1964), 108–117.

1481 HENRY, Robert S. "The Railroad Land Grant Legend in American History Texts." *Miss Val Hist Rev,* XXXII (1945), 171–194.

1482 HIBBARD, Benjamin. *A History of the Public Land Policies.* New York, 1924. Repr. Madison, Wis., 1965. †

1483 HOLLON, W. Eugene. "Rushing for Land: Oklahoma, 1889." *Am W,* III (Fall 1966), 4–15, 69–71.

1484 JENKINS, Myra E. "Spanish Land Grants in the Tewa Area." *N M Hist Rev,* XLVII (1972), 113–134.

1485 KNOWLTON, Clark S. "Cause of Land Loss among the Spanish Americans in Northern New Mexico." *Roc Mt Soc Sci J,* I (1964), 201–211.

1486 LAMAR, Howard R. "Land Policy in the Spanish Southwest, 1846–1891: A Study in Contrasts." *J Econ Hist,* XXII (1962), 498–515.

1487 LE DUC, Thomas. "The Disposal of the Public Domain on the Trans-Mississippi Plains: Some Opportunities for Investigation." *Ag Hist,* XXIV (1950), 199–204.

1488 LE DUC, Thomas. "Public Policy, Private Investment, and Land Use in American Agriculture, 1825–1875." *Ag Hist,* XXXVII (1963), 3–9.

1489 LEE, Lawrence B. "The Homestead Act: Vision and Reality." *Utah Hist Q*, XXX (1962), 215–234.

1490 LEE, Lawrence B. "Homesteading in Zion." See 978.

1491 LEE, Lawrence B. "Kansas and the Homestead Act, 1862–1905." Doctoral dissertation, University of Chicago, 1957.

1492 MCCLELLAND, Peter D. "New Perspectives on the Disposal of Western Lands in Nineteenth Century America." *Bus Hist Rev*, LXIII (1969), 77–83.

1493 MERCER, Lloyd, J. "Land Grants to American Railroads: Social Cost or Social Benefit?" *Bus Hist Rev*, XLIII (1969), 134–151.

1494 MESSING, John. "Public Lands, Politics, and Progressives: The Oregon Land Fraud Trials, 1903–1910." *Pac Hist Rev*, XXXV (1966), 35–66.

1495 MILLER, Thomas L. *Bounty and Donation Land Grants of Texas, 1835–1888.* Austin, Tex., 1967.

1496 MILLER, Thomas L. *The Public Lands of Texas, 1519–1970.* Norman, Okla., 1972.

1497 MOSK, Sanford A. *Land Tenure Problems in the Santa Fe Railroad Grant Area.* Berkeley, Calif., 1944.

1498 NASH, Gerald D. "The California State Land Office, 1858–1898." *Hunt Lib Q*, XXVII (1964), 347–356.

1499 NASH, Gerald D. "Henry George Reexamined: William S. Chapman's Views on Land Speculation in Nineteenth Century California." *Ag Hist*, XXXIII (1959), 133–137.

1500 NASH, Gerald D. "Problems and Projects in the History of Nineteenth-Century California Land Policy." *Ariz W*, II (1960), 327–340.

1501 NASH, Gerald D. *State Government and Economic Development: A History of Administrative Policies in California, 1849–1933.* Berkeley, Calif., 1964.

1502 *New Mexico Historical Review*, XLVII (April 1972). On land and water in New Mexico. See 1414.

1503 O'CALLAGHAN, Jerry A. *The Disposition of the Public Domain in Oregon. . . .* Washington, D.C., 1960.

1504 O'CALLAGHAN, Jerry A. "Senator Mitchell and the Oregon Land Frauds, 1905." *Pac Hist Rev*, XXI (1952), 255–261.

1505 OTTOSON, Howard W., *et al.,* eds. *Land and People in the Northern Plains Transition Area.* Lincoln, Neb., 1966.

1506 OTTOSON, Howard W., ed. *The Land Use Policy and Problems in the United States.* Lincoln, Neb., 1963.

1507 PEARSON, Jim B. *The Maxwell Land Grant.* Norman, Okla., 1961.

1508 PEFFER, E. Louise. *The Closing of the Public Domain: Disposal and Reservation Policies, 1900–1950.* Stanford, Calif., 1951. Repr. New York, 1972.

1509 PENNY, J. Russell, and Marion CLAWSON. "Administration of Grazing Districts." *Land Econ*, XXIX (1953), 23–34.

1510 RAKESTRAW, Lawrence. "The West, States' Rights, and Conservation: A Study of Six Public Lands Conferences." *Pac N W Q*, XLVIII (1957), 89–99.

1511 RISTER, Carl C. *Land Hunger: David L. Payne and the Oklahoma Boomers.* Norman, Okla., 1942.

1512 ROBBINS, Roy M. *Our Landed Heritage: The Public Domain, 1776–1936.* Princeton, N.J., 1942. Repr. Lincoln, Neb., 1962, rev. ed., 1976. †

1513 ROBINSON, William W. *Land in California: The Story of Mission Lands, Ranchos, Squatters, Mining Claims, Railroad Grants, Land Scrip [and] Homesteads.* Berkeley, Calif., 1948.

1514 ROHRBOUGH, Malcolm J. *The Land Office Business: The Settlement and Administration of American Public Lands, 1789–1837.* New York, 1968. †

1515 SALOUTOS, Theodore "Land Policy and Its Relation to Agricultural Production and Distribution, 1862–1933." *J Econ Hist,* XXII (1962), 445–460.

1516 SHANNON, Fred A. "The Homestead Act and Labor Surplus." *Am Hist Rev,* XLI (1936), 637–651.

1517 SHELDON, Addison E. *Land Systems and Land Policies in Nebraska. . . .* Lincoln, Neb., 1936.

1518 SOCOLOFSKY, Homer. "Land Disposal in Nebraska, 1854-1906: The Homestead Story." *Neb Hist,* XLVIII (1967), 225–248.

1519 STEWART, William J. "Speculation and Nebraska's Public Domain, 1863–1872." *Neb Hist,* XLV (1964), 265–272.

1520 STOWE, Noel J., ed. "Pioneering Land Development in the Californias: An Interview with David Otto Brant." *Calif Hist Soc Q,* XLVII (1968), 15–39, 141–155, 237–250.

1521 SWIERENGA, Robert P. *Pioneers and Profits: Land Speculation on the Iowa Frontier.* Ames, Iowa, 1968.

1522 WATKINS, T. H., and Charles S. WATSON, Jr. *The Lands No One Knows.* San Francisco, 1975. "America and the Public Domain."

1523 WESTPHALL, Victor. "Fraud and Implications of Fraud in the Land Grants of New Mexico." *N M Hist Rev,* XLIX (1974), 189–218.

1524 WESTPHALL, Victor. *The Public Domain in New Mexico, 1854–1891.* Albuquerque, N.M., 1965.

1525 WILLIAMS, R. Hal "George W. Julian and Land Reform in New Mexico, 1885–1889." *Ag Hist,* XLI (1967), 71–84.

1526 YONCE, Frederick J. "Public Land Disposal in Washington." Doctoral dissertation, University of Washington, 1969.

1527 YONCE, Frederick J. "The Public Land Surveys in Washington." *Pac N W Q,* LXIII (1972), 129–141.

XVI. Lumbering and Forestry in the West

See also: Conservation; Land and Land Policy; Labor

1528 ADAMS, Kramer A. *Logging Railroads of the West.* Seattle, Wash., 1961.

1529 ANDREWS, Ralph W. *"This Was Logging!" Selected Photographs of Darius Kinsey.* Seattle, Wash., 1954.

1530 ANDREWS, Ralph W. *Timber! Toil and Trouble in the Big Woods.* Seattle, Wash., 1968. A photographic history of lumbering.

1531 AYRES, Robert W. *History of Timber Management in the California National Forests, 1850 to 1937.* Washington, D.C., 1958.

1532 BECKHAM, Stephen Dow. "Asa Mead Simpson, Lumberman and Shipbuilder." *Ore Hist Q,* LXVIII (1967), 259–273.

1533 BERNER, Richard C. "The Port Blakely Mill Company, 1876–89." *Pac N W Q,* LVII (1966), 158–171.

1534 Bureau of Corporations. *The Lumber Industry.* Parts I–IV. Washington, D.C., 1913–1914.

1535 BURGESS, Sherwood D. "Lumbering in Hispanic California." *Calif Hist Soc Q,* XLI (1962), 237–248.

1536 CAMERON, Jenks. *The Development of Governmental Forest Control in the United States.* Baltimore, Md., 1928. Repr. New York, 1972.

1537 [CLAPP, Earle H., and others.] *Timber Depletion, Lumber Prices, Lumber Exports, and Concentration of Timber Ownership.* Washington, D.C., 1920. Commonly known as the Capper Report.

1538 CLAR, C. Raymond. *California Government and Forestry, from Spanish Days until the Creation of the Department of Natural Resources in 1927.* Sacramento, Calif., 1959.

1539 CLARK, Norman H. *Mill Town: A Social History of Everett, Washington. . . .* Seattle, Wash., 1970. †

1540 CLEPPER, Henry E., and Arthur B. MEYER, eds. *American Forestry: Six Decades of Growth.* Washington, D.C., 1960.

1541 COMAN, Edwin T., Jr., and Helen M. GIBBS. *Time, Tide, and Timber: A Century of Pope & Talbot.* Stanford, Calif., 1949.

1542 COMPTON, Wilson M. *The Organization of the Lumber Industry, with Special Reference to the Influences Determining the Prices of Lumber in the United States.* Princeton, N.J., 1916; Chicago, 1916.

1543 COWAN, Charles S. *The Enemy is Fire: The History of Forest Protection in the Big Timber Country.* Seattle, Wash., 1961.

1544 COX, John H. "Organizations of the Lumber Industry in the Pacific Northwest, 1889–1914." Doctoral dissertation, University of California, Berkeley, 1937.

1545 COX, John H. "Trade Associations in the Lumber Industry of the Pacific Northwest, 1899–1914." *Pac N W Q,* XLI (1950), 285–311.

1546 COX, Thomas R. *Mills and Markets: A History of the Pacific Coast Lumber Industry to 1900.* Seattle, Wash., 1974.

1547 DANA, Samuel T. *Forest and Range Policy: Its Development in the United States.* New York, 1956.

1548 DAVIS, Richard C., comp. *North American Forest History: A Guide to Archives and Manuscripts in the United States and Canada.* Santa Barbara, Calif., 1976.

1549 EASTON, Hamilton P. "The History of the Texas Lumbering Industry." Doctoral dissertation, University of Texas, 1947.

1550 ELCHIBEGOFF, Ivan M. *United States International Timber Trade in the Pacific Area.* Stanford, Calif., 1949.

1551 FAHL, Ronald J., comp. *North American Forest and Conservation History: A Bibliography.* Santa Barbara, Calif., 1976.

1552 FISCHER, Duane D. "The Short, Unhappy Story of the Del Norte Company." *For Hist,* XI (1967), 12–25.

1553 FRITZ, Emanuel, comp. *California Coast Redwood: An Annotated Bibliography to and Including 1955.* San Francisco, 1957

1554 FROME, Michael. *The Forest Service.* New York, 1971.

1555 FROME, Michael. *Whose Woods These Are: The Story of the National Forests.* Garden City, N.Y., 1962.

1556 GANNETT, Henry. "The Lumber Industry." *Twelfth Census* (1900), vol IX (Manufactures, Part III, Washington, D.C., 1902), 803–897.

1557 GILLIGAN, James P. "The Development of Policy and Administration of Forest Service Primitive and Wilderness Areas in the Western United States." Doctoral dissertation, University of Michigan, 1953.

1558 GREELEY, William B. *Forests and Men.* New York, 1951.

1559 GREELEY, William B. *Some Public and Economic Aspects of the Lumber Industry* (USDA, Off of Secy, *Rep* 114). Washington, D.C., 1917.

1560 HIDY, Ralph W. "Lumbermen in Idaho: A Study in Adaptation to Change in Environment." *Idaho Yes,* VI (1962), 2–17.

1561 HIDY, Ralph W., Frank E. HILL, and Allan NEVINS. *Timber and Men: The Weyerhaeuser Story.* New York, 1963.

1562 HOFFMAN, Daniel G. *Paul Bunyan, Last of the Frontier Demigods.* Philadelphia, Pa., 1952.

1563 HOLBROOK, Stewart H. *Burning an Empire: The Story of American Forest Fires.* New York, 1944.

1564 HOLBROOK, Stewart H. *Holy Old Mackinaw: A Natural History of the American Lumberjack.* New York, 1938. Repr. with new title, *The American Lumberjack.* New York, 1962.

1565 HOUGH, Franklin B. *Report upon Forestry.* Washington, D.C., 1878.

1566 HOWD, Cloice R. *Industrial Relations in the West Coast Lumber Industry.* (USDL, Bur of Lab Stats, *Bull* 349). Washington, D.C., 1924.

1567 HUGHSON, Oliver G. "When We Logged the Columbia." *Ore Hist Q,* LX (1959), 173–209.

1568 HUTCHINSON, William H. *California Heritage: A History of Northern California Lumbering.* Chico, Calif., 1958. Repr. Santa Cruz, Calif., 1974. †

1569 HYMAN, Harold M. *Soldiers and Spruce: Origins of the Loyal Legion of Loggers and Lumbermen.* Los Angeles, 1963.

1570 *Idaho Yesterdays,* VI (Winter 1962). Special issue on forestry in the Pacific Northwest.

1571 ISE, John, *The United States Forest Policy.* New Haven, Conn., 1920. Repr. New York, 1972.

1572 JENSEN, Vernon H. *Lumber and Labor.* New York, 1945. Repr. New York, 1971.

1573 KIRKLAND, Herbert D., III. "The American Forests, 1864–1898: A Trend toward Conservation." Doctoral dissertation, Florida State University, 1971.

1574 KORTUM, Karl and Roger OLMSTEAD. "... *it is a dangerous-looking place":* *Sailing Days on the Redwood Coast.* San Francisco, 1971. Photographs and text of the coastal lumber trade.

1575 LABBE, John T. and Vernon GOE. *Railroads in the Woods.* Berkeley, Calif., 1961. Western lumber roads.

1576 LUCIA, Ellis. *The Big Woods.* Garden City, N.Y., 1975.

1577 MCCONNELL, Grant. "The Multiple-Use Concept in Forest Service Policy." *Sierra Club Bull,* XLIV (1959), 14–28.

1578 MCCULLOCH, Walter F. *Woods Words: A Comprehensive Dictionary of Loggers Terms.* Portland, Ore., 1958. †

1579 MASON, David T. *Timber Ownership and Lumber Production in the Inland Empire.* Portland, Ore., 1920.

1580 MEAD, Walter J. *Competition and Oligopsony in the Douglas Fir Lumber Industry (Pubs Bur Bus & Econ Res,* UCLA). Berkeley and Los Angeles, 1966.

1581 MEANY, Edmond S., Jr. "The History of the Lumber Industry in the Pacific Northwest to 1917." Doctoral dissertation, Harvard University, 1935.

1582 MELENDY, H. Brett. "One Hundred Years of the Redwood Lumber Industry, 1850–1950." Doctoral Dissertation, Stanford University, 1952.

1583 MELENDY, H. Brett. "Two Men and a Mill: John Dolbeer, William Carson, and the Redwood Lumber Industry in California." *Calif Hist Soc Q,* XXXVIII (1959), 59–71.

1584 MELTON, William Ray. *The Lumber Industry in Washington.* Olympia, Wash., 1941. Mimeographed.

1585 MORGAN, George T., Jr. "The Fight Against Fire: Development of Cooperative Forestry in the Pacific Northwest." *Idaho Yes,* VI (Winter 1962), 20–30.

1586 MORGAN, George T., Jr. "The Fight Against Fire: Development of Cooperative Forestry in the Pacific Northwest, 1900–1950." Doctoral dissertation, University of Oregon, 1964.

1587 MORGAN, George T., Jr. *William B. Greeley: A Practical Forester, 1879–1955.* St. Paul, Minn., 1961.

1588 MUNNS, E. N. *The Distribution of Important Forest Trees of the United States (USDA, Misc Pub* no. 287). Washington, D.C., 1938.

1589 MUNNS, E. N. *A Selected Bibliography of North American Forestry* (USDA, *Misc Pub* no. 364). 2 vols, Washington, D.C., 1940.

1590 NICHOLS, Claude W., Jr., "Brotherhood in the Woods: The Loyal Legion of Loggers and Lumbermen, a Twenty-Year Attempt at Industrial Cooperation." Doctoral dissertation, University of Oregon, 1959.

1591 O'CALLAGHAN, Jerry A. *The Disposition of the Public Domain in Oregon.* See 1503.

1592 PEATTIE, Donald C. *A Natural History of Western Trees.* Boston, 1953.

1593 PETERSON, Charles S. "Small Holding Land Patterns and the Problem of Forest Watershed Management." *For Hist,* XVII (1973), 4–13.

1594 PINCHOT, Gifford. *The Training of a Forester.* Philadelphia, 1914. Rev. ed., 1937.

1595 PUTER, Stephen A. D., in collab. with Horace STEVENS. *Looters of the Public Domain: Embracing a Complete Exposure of the Fraudulent System of Acquiring Titles to the Public Lands of the United States.* Portland, Ore., 1908. Repr. New York, 1972.

1596 RADER, Benjamin G. "The Montana Lumber Strike of 1917." *Pac Hist Rev,* XXXVI (1967), 189–207.

1597 RAKESTRAW, Lawrence. "Uncle Sam's Forest Reserves." *Pac N W Q,* XLIV (1953), 145–151.

1598 ROBERTS, Paul H. *Hoof Prints on Forest Ranges: The Early Years of National Forest Range Administration.* San Antonio, Tex., 1963.

1599 RODGERS, Andrew D., III. *Bernhard Eduard Fernow: A Story of North American Forestry.* Princeton, N.J., 1951.

1600 RUTLEDGE, Peter J., and Richard H. TOOKER. "Steam Power for Loggers: Two Views of the Dolbeer Donkey." *For Hist,* XIV (1970), 18–29.

1601 SARGENT, Charles S. *Report on the Forests of North America (Tenth Census, 1880, Vol. IX),* Washington, D.C., 1884.

1602 SCHIFF, Ashley L. *Fire and Water: Scientific Heresy in the Forest Service.* Cambridge, Mass., 1962.

1603 SCHREPFER, Susan R. "A Conservation Reform: Saving the Redwoods, 1917 to 1940." Doctoral dissertation, University of California, Riverside, 1971.

1604 SHARP, Paul F. "The Tree Farm Movement: Its Origin and Development." *Ag Hist,* XXIII (1949), 41–45.

1605 SHIDELER, James H. "Opportunities and Hazards in Forest History Research." *For Hist,* VII (1963), 10–14.

1606 SMITH, David C. "The Logging Frontier." *J For Hist,* XVIII (1974), 96–106.

1607 SPENCER, Betty G. *The Big Blowup.* Caldwell, Idaho, 1956. Giant Northwest forest fire of 1910.

1608 STANGER, Frank M. *Sawmills in the Redwoods: Logging on the San Francisco Peninsula, 1849–1967.* San Mateo, Calif., 1967.

1609 STEER, Henry B., comp. *Lumber Production in the United States, 1799–1946.* (USDA, *Misc Pub* 669). Washington, D.C., 1948. Statistics.

1610 TATTERSALL, James N. "The Economic Development of the Pacific Northwest to 1920." Doctoral dissertation, University of Washington, 1960.

1611 TODES, Charlotte. *Labor and Lumber.* New York, 1931.

1612 TOOLE, K. Ross, and Edward BUTCHER. "Timber Depredations on the Montana Public Domain, 1885–1918." *J W,* VII (1968), 351–362.

1613 TYLER, Robert L. *Rebels of the Woods: The IWW in the Pacific Northwest.* Eugene, Ore., 1967.

1614 WEINSTEIN, Robert A. "Lumber Ships at Puget Sound." *Am W,* II (Fall 1965), 50–63.

1615 WINKENWERDER, Hugo. *Forestry in the Pacific Northwest.* Washington, D.C., 1928.

1616 WINTERS, Robert K., ed. *Fifty Years of Forestry in the U.S.A.* Washington, D.C., 1950.

XVII. Oil in the West

1617 ANDREANO, Ralph L. "The Emergence of New Competition in the American Petroleum Industry Before 1911." Doctoral dissertation, Northwestern University, 1960.

1618 ANDREANO, Ralph L. "The Structure of the California Petroleum Industry, 1895–1911." *Pac Hist Rev,* XXXIX (1970), 171–192.

1619 BADEN, Anne L., comp. *The Petroleum Industry: A Selected List of Recent References.* Washington, D.C., 1942.

1620 BAIN, Joe S. *The Economics of the Pacific Coast Petroleum Industry.* 3 vols. Berkeley, Calif., 1944–1947.

1621 BARNES, Robert J. "Novels of the Oil Industry in the Southwest." *S W Am Lit,* II (1972), 74–82

1622 BARTLEY, Ernest R. *The Tidelands Oil Controversy: A Legal and Historical Analysis.* Austin, Tex., 1953.

1623 BATES, J. Leonard. *The Origins of Teapot Dome: Progressives, Parties and Petroleum, 1909–1921.* Urbana, Ill., 1963.

1624 BEATON, Kendall. *Enterprise in Oil: A History of Shell in the United States.* New York, 1957.

1625 BOATRIGHT, Mody C. *Folklore of the Oil Industry.* Dallas, Tex., 1963.

1626 BOATRIGHT, Mody C. *Gib Morgan: Minstrel of the Oil Fields.* Dallas, Tex., 1945, 1965.

1627 CLARK, James A. *The Chronological History of the Petroleum and Natural Gas Industries.* Houston, Tex., 1963.

1628 CLARK, James A., and Michael T. HALBOUTY. *Spindletop.* New York, 1952.

1629 DE GOLYER, Everette L., and Harold VANCE, comps. *Bibliography on the Petroleum Industry.* College Station, Tex., 1944.

1630 FORBES, Gerald. *Flush Production: The Epic of Oil in the Gulf-Southwest.* Norman, Okla., 1942.

1631 GIBB, George S., and Evelyn H. KNOWLTON. *History of Standard Oil Company (New Jersey): The Resurgent Years, 1911–1927.* New York, 1956.

1632 GRESSLEY, Gene M. "The French, Belgians, and Dutch Come to Salt Creek." *Bus Hist Rev,* XLIV (1970), 498–519.

1633 HARDWICKE, Robert E., comp. *Petroleum and Natural Gas Bibliography.* Austin, Tex., 1937. Includes section on history.

1634 HIDY, Ralph W. "Some Implications of the Recent Literature on the History of the Petroleum Industry." *Bus Hist Rev,* XXX (1956), 329–346.

1635 HIDY, Ralph W., and Muriel E. HIDY. *History of the Standard Oil Company (New Jersey): Pioneering in Big Business, 1882–1911.* New York, 1955.

1636 HUTCHINSON, William H. *Oil, Land, and Politics: The California Career of Thomas Robert Bard.* 2 vols. Norman, Okla., 1965.

1637 ISE, John. *The United States Oil Policy.* New Haven, Conn., 1926. Repr. New York, 1972.

1638 JOHNSON, Arthur M. "California and the Natural Oil Industry." *Pac Hist Rev,* XXXIX (1970), 155–169.

1639 JOHNSON, Arthur M. *Petroleum Pipelines and Public Policy, 1906–1959.* Cambridge, Mass., 1967.

1640 KNOWLES, Ruth S. *The Greatest Gamblers: The Epic of American Oil Exploration.* New York, 1959.

1641 LARSON, Henrietta M., and Kenneth W. PORTER. *History of Humble Oil and Refining Company: A Study in Industrial Growth.* New York, 1959.

1642 LOGAN, Leonard M. *Stabilization of the Petroleum Industry.* Norman, Okla., 1930.

1643 MCLAUGHLIN, R. P. *The Tenderfoot Comes West: Half a Century of Progress in California and the Petroleum Industry.* New York, 1968.

1644 MATHEWS, John J. *Life and Death of an Oilman: The Career of E. W. Marland.* Norman, Okla., 1951.

1645 MINER, H. Craig. "The Cherokee Oil and Gas Co., 1889–1902: Indian Sovereignty and Economic Change." *Bus Hist Rev,* XLVI (1972), 45–66.

1646 MOORE, Richard R. "The Impact of the Oil Industry in West Texas." Doctoral dissertation, Texas Technological College, 1965.

1647 NASH, Gerald D. "Oil in the West: Reflections on the Historiography of an Unexplored Field." *Pac Hist Rev,* XXXIX (1970), 193–204.

1648 NASH, Gerald D. *United States Oil Policy, 1890–1964: Business and Government in Twentieth Century America.* Pittsburgh, Pa., 1968.

1649 NOGGLE, Burl. *Teapot Dome: Oil and Politics in the 1920's.* Baton Rouge, Louis., 1962. †

1650 NORDHAUSER, Norman. "Origins of Federal Oil Regulation in the 1920's." *Bus Hist Rev,* XLVII (1973), 53–71.

1651 O'CONNOR, Richard. *The Oil Barons: Men of Greed and Grandeur.* Boston, 1971.

1651A OWEN, Edgar W. *Trek of the Oil Finders: A History of Exploration for Petroleum.* Tulsa, Okla, 1975. A massive history of the petroleum industry as well as of oil finding.

1652 "The Petroleum Industry." *Pac Hist Rev,* XXXIX (May 1970). Special issue on oil in the West.

1653 REDWOOD, Boverton. *Petroleum: A Treatise on the Geographical Distribution and Geological Occurrence of Petroleum and Natural Gas . . . and a Bibliography.* 4th ed., 3 vols., London, 1922. The bibliography, III, pp. 1155–1317, lists 8804 entries from all over the world.

1654 RISTER, Carl C. *Oil! Titan of the Southwest.* Norman, Okla., 1949.

1655 ROBERTS, Harold. *Salt Creek, Wyoming: The Story of a Great Oil Field.* Denver, Colo., 1956.

1656 ROSS, William M. *Oil Pollution as an International Problem: A Study of Puget Sound and the Strait of Georgia.* Seattle, Wash., 1973.

1657 ROSTOW, Eugene V. *A National Policy for the Oil Industry.* New Haven, Conn., 1947.

1658 RUNDELL, Walter, Jr., comp. "Centennial Bibliography: Annotated Selections on the History of the Petroleum Industry in the United States." *Bus Hist Rev,* XXXII (1959), 429–447.

1659 RUNDELL, Walter, Jr. "Texas Petroleum History: A Selective Annotated Bibliography." *S W Hist Q,* LXVII (1963), 267–278.

1660 SCHRUBEN, Francis W. "The Kansas State Refinery Law of 1905." *Kan Hist Q,* XXXIV (1968), 299–324.

1661 SCHRUBEN, Francis W. *Wea Creek to El Dorado: Oil in Kansas, 1860–1920.* Columbia, Mo., 1972.

1662 SCHWARZMAN, Richard C. "The Pinal Dome Oil Company: An Adventure in Business, 1901–1917." Doctoral dissertation, University of California, Los Angeles, 1967.

1663 SNIDER, Luther C. *Oil and Gas in the Mid-Continent Fields.* Oklahoma City, Okla., 1920. "History," pp. 139–154.

1664 SPRATT, John S. *The Road to Spindletop: Economic Change in Texas, 1875–1901.* Dallas, Tex., 1955. †

1665 STRATTON, David H. "Behind Teapot Dome: Some Personal Insights." *Bus Hist Rev,* XXXI (1957), 385–402.

1666 SWANSON, Edward B., comp. *A Century of Oil and Gas in Books: A Descriptive Bibliography.* New York, 1960.

1667 TAIT, Samuel W., Jr. *The Wildcatters: An Informal History of Oil-Hunting in America.* Princeton, N.J., 1946.

1668 TOMPKINS, Walker A. *Little Giant of Signal Hill: An Adventure in American Enterprise.* Englewood Cliffs, N.J. 1964.

1669 VAGNERS, Juris, ed. *Oil on Puget Sound: An Interdisciplinary Study in Systems Engineering.* Seattle, Wash., 1972.

1670 WARNER, Charles A. *Texas Oil and Gas Since 1543.* Houston, Tex., 1939.

1671 WELTY, Earl M., and Frank J. TAYLOR. *Black Bonanza.* New York, 1956.

1672 WHITE, Gerald T. "California's Other Mineral." *Pac Hist Rev,* XXXIX (1970), 135–154.

1673 WHITE, Gerald T. *Formative Years in the Far West: A History of Standard Oil Company of California and Predecessors Through 1919.* New York, 1962.

1674 WHITE, Gerald T. *Scientists in Conflict: The Beginnings of the Oil Industry in California.* San Marino, Calif., 1968.

1675 WILLIAMSON, Harold F., and Arnold R. DAUM. *The American Petroleum Industry: The Age of Illumination, 1859–1899.* Evanston, Ill., 1959.

1676 WILLIAMSON, Harold F., et al. *The American Petroleum Industry: The Age of Energy, 1899–1959.* Evanston, Ill., 1963.

1677 ZIMMERMANN, Erich W. *Conservation in the Production of Petroleum: A Study in Industrial Control.* New Haven, Conn., 1957.

XVIII. Transportation and Communication

1. The Great Trails

1678 ANDREWS, Thomas F. "The Ambitions of Lansford W. Hastings: A Study in Western Myth-Making." *Pac Hist Rev,* XXXIX (1970), 473–491.

1679 ANDREWS, Thomas F. "The Controversial Hastings Overland Guide: A Reassessment." *Pac Hist Rev,* XXXVII (1968), 21–34.

1680 BELL, James C., Jr. *Opening a Highway to the Pacific, 1838–1846.* New York, 1921.

1681 BOWEN, William A. "Migration and Settlement on a Far Western Frontier: Oregon to 1850." Doctoral dissertation, University of California, Berkeley, 1972.

1682 DUFFUS, Robert L. *The Santa Fe Trail.* New York, 1930. Repr. New York, 1936. †

1683 EATON, Herbert. *The Overland Trail to California in 1852.* New York, 1974. †

1684 FAULK, Odie B. *Destiny Road: The Gila Trail and the Opening of the Southwest.* New York, 1973.

1685 FIELD, Matthew C. *Matt Field on the Santa Fe Trail.* Collected by Clyde and Mae Reed Porter. Ed. John E. Sunder. Norman, Okla., 1960.

1686 GHENT, W. J. *The Road to Oregon: A Chronicle of the Great Emigrant Trail.* New York, 1929.

1687 GREGG, Josiah. *Commerce of the Prairies: Or the Journal of a Santa Fe Trader during Eight Expeditions across the Great Western Prairies. . . .* 2 vols. New York, 1844. Ed. Max L. Moorhead, Norman, Okla., 1954. †

1688 HAMMOND, George P., and Edward H. HOWES, eds. *Overland to California on the Southwestern Trail, 1849: Diary of Robert Eccleston.* Berkeley, Calif., 1950.

1689 HASTINGS, Lansford Warren. *The Emigrants' Guide to Oregon and California. . . .* Cincinnati, 1845.

1690 HILL, Joseph J. "The Old Spanish Trail." *His-Am Hist Rev,* IV (1921), 444–473.

1691 HUSBAND, Michael B. "To Oregon in 1843: The Backgrounds and Organization of the 'Great Migration.'" Doctoral dissertation, University of New Mexico, 1970.

1692 INMAN, Colonel Henry. *The Old Santa Fé Trail: The Story of a Great Highway.* New York, 1897.

1693 LAVENDER, David. *Westward Vision: The Story of the Oregon Trail.* New York, 1963. †

1694 MATTES, Merrill J. *The Great Platte River Road: The Covered Wagon Mainline via Fort Kearny to Fort Laramie.* Lincoln, Neb., 1969.

1695 MATTES, Merrill J. "The Jumping-Off Places on the Overland Trail." *The Frontier Re-examined.* Ed. John Francis McDermott. Urbana, Ill., 1967.

1696 MATTES, Merrill J. "New Horizons on the Old Oregon Trail." *People of the Plains and Mountains: Essays in the History of the West Dedicated to Everett Dick.* Ed. Ray Allen Billington. Westport, Conn., 1973.

1697 MONAGHAN, Jay. *The Overland Trail.* Indianapolis, Ind., 1937.

1698 MOORHEAD, Max L. *New Mexico's Royal Road: Trade and Travel on the Chihuahua Trail.* Norman, Okla., 1958.

1699 MORGAN, Dale L., ed. *Overland in 1846: Diaries and Letters of the California-Oregon Trail.* 2 vols. Georgetown, Calif., 1963.

1700 MORGAN, Dale L., ed. *The Overland Diary of James A. Pritchard from Kentucky to California in 1849.* Denver, Colo., 1959. Catalogs all known diaries of the South Pass route in 1849.

1701 *Oregon Historical Society Quarterly,* I, no. 4 (December 1900). Special issue on the Oregon Trail; includes Jesse Applegate's famous "A Day with the Cow Column in 1843."

1702 PADEN, Irene D. *The Wake of the Prairie Schooner.* New York, 1943. †

1703 PARKMAN, Francis. *The California and Oregon Trail: Being Sketches of Prairie and Rocky Mountain Life.* New York, 1849. Ed. E. N. Feltskog. Madison, Wis.,1969.

1704 RITTENHOUSE, Jack D., comp. *The Santa Fe Trail: A Historical Bibliography.* Albuquerque, N.M., 1971.

1705 STEGNER, Wallace. *The Gathering of Zion: The Story of the Mormon Trail.* See 1007.

1706 STEWART, George R. *The California Trail: An Epic with Many Heroes.* New York, 1962. †

1707 STEWART, George R. *Ordeal by Hunger: The Story of the Donner Party.* Rev. ed. Boston, 1960. †

1708 WAGNER, Henry R., and Charles L. CAMP. *The Plains and the Rockies.* See 119.

2. Pre-Railroad: Teamsters, Stagecoaches, Express Companies, Pony Express, Wagon Roads, and Steamboats

1709 BARSNESS, Richard W. "Los Angeles' Quest for Improved Transportation, 1846–1861." *Calif Hist Soc Q,* XLVI (1967), 291–306.

1710 CHAPMAN, Arthur. *The Pony Express: The Record of a Romantic Adventure in Business.* New York, 1932.

1711 CHITTENDEN, Hiram M. *History of Early Steamboat Navigation on the Missouri River; Life and Adventures of Joseph La Barge.* 2 vols. New York, 1903.

1712 CONKLING, Roscoe P., and Margaret P. CONKLING. *The Butterfield Overland Mail, 1857–1869....* 3 vols. Glendale, Calif., 1947.

1713 CONNELLY, Thomas L. "The American Camel Experiment: A Reappraisal." *S W Hist Q,* LXIX (1966), 442–462.

1714 DUNBAR, Seymour. *A History of Travel in America.* . . . 4 vols. Indianapolis, 1915. Repr. New York, 1937; Westport, Conn., 1968.

1715 EGGENHOFER, Nick. *Wagons, Mules and Men: How the Frontier Moved West.* New York, 1961. Good illustrations and descriptions.

1716 FOWLER, Harlan D. *Camels to California: A Chapter in Western Transportation.* Stanford, Calif., 1950.

1717 FREDERICK, James V. *Ben Holladay, The Stagecoach King: A Chapter in the Development of Transcontinental Transportation.* Glendale, Calif., 1940.

1718 FREEMAN, Otis W. "Early Wagon Roads in the Inland Empire." *Pac N W Q,* XLV (1954), 125–130.

1719 GILL, Frank B., and Dorothy O. JOHANSEN. "A Chapter in the History of the Oregon Steam Navigation Company." *Ore Hist Q,* XXXVIII (1937), 1–43, 300–322, 398–410; XXXIX (1938), 50–64.

1720 HAFEN, Le Roy R. "Handcarts to Utah, 1856–1860." *Utah Hist Q,* XXIV (1956), 309–317.

1721 HAFEN, Le Roy R. *The Overland Mail, 1849–1869: Promoter of Settlement, Precursor of Railroads.* Cleveland, Ohio, 1926.

1722 HUNGERFORD, Edward. *Wells Fargo: Advancing the American Frontier.* New York, 1949.

1723 HUNTER, Louis C. *Steamboats on the Western Rivers: An Economic and Technological History.* Cambridge, Mass. 1949.

1724 JACKSON, W. Turrentine. "A Look at the Wells Fargo, Stagecoaches and the Pony Express." *Calif Hist Soc Q,* XLV (1966), 291–324.

1725 JACKSON, W. Turrentine. *Wagon Roads West: A Study of Federal Surveys and Construction in the Trans-Mississippi West. 1846–1869.* Berkeley, Calif., 1952. Repr. New Haven, Conn., 1965.

1726 JACKSON, W. Turrentine. "Wells Fargo: Symbol of the Wild West?" *W Hist Q,* (1972), 179–196.

1727 JACKSON, W. Turrentine. "Wells Fargo's Pony Expresses." *J W,* XI (1972), 405–436.

1728 JOHANSEN, Dorothy O. "Capitalism on the Far Western Frontier: The Oregon Steam Navigation Company." Doctoral dissertation, University of Washington, 1941.

1729 JOHANSEN, Dorothy O. "The Oregon Steam Navigation Company: An Example of Capitalism on the Frontier." *Pac Hist Rev,* X (1941). 179–188.

1730 *Kansas Quarterly,* V (Spring 1973). Western trails and transportation issue.

1731 LASS, William E. *From the Missouri to the Great Salt Lake: An Account of Overland Freighting.* Lincoln, Neb., 1972.

1732 LASS, William E. *A History of Steamboating on the Upper Missouri River.* Lincoln, Neb., 1962.

1733 LEAVITT, Francis H. "Steam Navigation on the Colorado River." *Calif Hist Soc Q,* XXII (1943), 1–25, 151–174.

1734 MACMULLEN, Jerry. *Paddle-Wheel Days in California.* Stanford, Calif. 1944. Illustrated essay on steamboats.

1735 MAJORS, Alexander. *Seventy Years on the Frontier....* Chicago, 1893. Autobiography of the famous freighter.

1736 MASON, Philip P. "The League of American Wheelmen and the Good Roads Movement, 1880–1905." Doctoral dissertation, University of Michigan, 1957.

1737 MILLS, Randall V. *Sternwheelers Up the Columbia: A Century of Steamboating in the Oregon Country.* Palo Alto, Calif., 1947.

1738 MOODY, Ralph. *Stagecoach West.* New York, 1967.

1739 ORMSBY, Waterman L. *The Butterfield Overland Mail.* Ed. Lyle H. Wright and Josephine M. Bynum. San Marino, Calif., 1942.

1740 SETTLE, Raymond W., and Mary L. SETTLE. "The Early Careers of William Bradford Waddell and William Hepburn Russell: Frontier Capitalists." *Kan Hist Q,* XXVI (1960), 355–382.

1741 SETTLE, Raymond W., and Mary L. SETTLE. *Empire on Wheels: The Story of Russell Majors and Waddell.* Stanford, Calif., 1949.

1742 SETTLE, Raymond W., and Mary L. SETTLE. *Saddles and Spurs: The Pony Express Saga.* Harrisburg, Pa., 1955. †

1743 SETTLE, Raymond W., and Mary L. SETTLE. *War Drums and Wagon Wheels: The Story of Russell, Majors, and Waddell.* San Francisco, Calif., 1961. Rev. ed. Lincoln, Neb., 1966.

1744 SHUMWAY, George, Edward DURRELL, and Howard C. FREY. *Conestoga Wagon, 1750–1850: Freight Carrier for 100 Years of America's Westward Expansion.* York, Pa., 1964. 2d ed., York, Pa., 1966.

1745 SPRING, Agnes W. *The Cheyenne and Black Hills Stage and Express Routes.* Glendale, Calif., 1949. †

1746 TAYLOR, Morris F. *First Mail West: Stagecoach Lines on the Santa Fe Trail.* Albuquerque, N.M., 1971.

1746A WALKER, Henry P., comp. "Pre-Railroad Transportation in the Trans-Mississippi West: An Annotated Bibliography." *Ariz W,* XVIII (1976), 53–80.

1747 WALKER, Henry P. "Wagon Freighting in Arizona." *Smoke Sig,* XXVIII (1973), 182–202.

1748 WALKER, Henry P. *The Wagonmasters: High Plains Freighting from the Earliest Days of the Santa Fe Trail to 1880.* Norman, Okla., 1966.

1749 WILTSEE, Ernest A. *The Pioneer Miner and the Pack Mule Express.* San Francisco, 1931.

1750 WINTHER, Oscar O. *Express and Stagecoach Days in California from the Gold Rush to the Civil War.* Stanford, Calif., 1936.

1751 WINTHER, Oscar O. *The Old Oregon Country: A History of Frontier Trade, Transportation, and Travel.* Stanford, Calif., 1950; Bloomington, Ind., 1950. Repr. Lincoln, Neb., 1969.

1752 WINTHER, Oscar O. "Pack Animals for Transportation in the Pacific Northwest." *Pac N W Q,* XXXIV (1943), 131–146.

1753 WINTHER, Oscar O. "The Persistence of Horse-Drawn Transportation in the Trans-Mississippi West, 1865–1900." *Probing the American West.* Ed. K. Ross Toole, *et al.* Santa Fe, N.M., 1962.

1754 WINTHER, Oscar O. "The Place of Transportation in the Early History of the Pacific Northwest." *Pac Hist Rev,* XI (1942), 383–396.

1755 WINTHER, Oscar O. *The Transportation Frontier: Trans-Mississippi West, 1865–1890.* New York, 1964. †

1756 WINTHER, Oscar O. *Via Western Express and Stagecoach.* Stanford, Calif., 1945. †

1757 WYMAN, Walker D. "Freighting: A Big Business on the Santa Fe Trail." *Kan Hist Q,* I (1931), 17–27.

1758 WYMAN, Walker D. "Military Phase of Santa Fe Freighting, 1846–1865." *Kan Hist Q,* I (1932), 415–428.

3. Railroads, Interurban Lines, and Highways

1759 ANDERSON, George L. *General William J. Palmer: A Decade of Colorado Railroad Building, 1870–1880.* Colorado Springs, Colo., 1936.

1760 ANDERSON, George L. *Kansas West.* San Marino, Calif., 1963.

1761 ARRINGTON, Leonard J. "The Transcontinental Railroad and the Development of the West." *Utah Hist Q,* XXXVII (1969), 3–15.

1762 ATHEARN, Robert G. "Railroad Renaissance in the Rockies." *Utah Hist Q,* XXV (1957), 1–26.

1763 ATHEARN, Robert G. *Rebel of the Rockies: A History of the Denver and Rio Grande Western Railroad.* New Haven, Conn., 1962.

1764 ATHEARN, Robert G. *Union Pacific Country.* Chicago, 1971. †

1765 BEAL, Merrill D. *Intermountain Railroads: Standard and Narrow Gauge.* Caldwell, Idaho, 1962.

1766 BOYD, William H. "The Holladay-Villard Transportation Empire in the Pacific Northwest, 1868–1893." *Pac Hist Rev,* XV (1946), 379–389.

1767 CLARK, Ira G. *Then Came the Railroads: The Century form Steam to Diesel in the Southwest.* Norman, Okla. 1958.

1768 CLINCH, Thomas A. "The Northern Pacific and Montana's Mineral Lands." *Pac Hist Rev,* XXXIV (1965), 323–335.

1769 COCHRAN, John S. "Economic Importance of Early Transcontinental Railroads: Pacific Northwest." *Ore Hist Q,* LXXI (1970), 26–98.

1770 COCHRAN, Thomas C. *Railroad Leaders, 1845–1890: The Business Mind in Action.* Cambridge, Mass., 1953.

1771 COTRONEO, Ross R. "Western Land Marketing by the Northern Pacific Railway." *Pac Hist Rev,* XXXVII (1968), 299–320.

1772 DAGGETT, Stuart. *Chapters on the History of the Southern Pacific.* New York, 1922.

1773 FAHEY, John. *Inland Empire: D. C. Corbin and Spokane.* Seattle, Wash., 1965.

1774 FARNHAM, Wallace D. "Grenville Dodge and the Union Pacific: A Study of Historical Legends." *J Amer Hist,* LI (1965), 632–650.

1775 FARNHAM, Wallace D. "Railroads in Western History: The View from the Union Pacific." *The American West: A Reorientation.* Ed. Gene M. Gressley. Laramie, Wyo.,1966.

1776 FOGEL, Robert W. *Railroads and American Economic Growth: Essays in Econometric History.* Baltimore, Md., 1964. † A controversial thesis that has stirred fierce debate.

1777 FOGEL, Robert W. *The Union Pacific Railroad: A Case Study in Premature Enterprise.* Baltimore, 1960.

1778 GOODWIN, Herbert M. "California's Growing Freeway System." Doctoral dissertation, University of California, Los Angeles, 1969.

1779 GREEVER, William S. *Arid Domain: The Santa Fe Railroad and Its Western Land Grant.* Stanford, Calif., 1954.

1780 GREEVER, William S. "Railroad Development in the Southwest." *N M Hist Rev,* XXXII (1957), 151–203.

1781 GRODINSKY, Julius. *Jay Gould: His Business Career, 1867–1892.* Philadelphia, 1957.

1782 HEDGES, James B. *Henry Villard and the Railways of the Northwest.* New Haven, Conn., 1930.

1783 HILTON, George W., and John F. DUÉ. *The Electric Interurban Railways in America.* Stanford, Calif., 1960.

1784 HIRSHSON, Stanley P. *Grenville M. Dodge: Soldier, Politician, Railroad Pioneer.* Bloomington, Ind., 1967.

1785 JOHNSON, Arthur M., and Barry E. SUPPLE. *Boston Capitalists and Western Railroads: A Study in the Nineteenth Century Railroad Investment Process.* Cambridge, Mass., 1967.

1786 KEMBLE, John Haskell. "The Transpacific Railroads, 1869–1915." *Pac Hist Rev,* XVIII (1949), 331–343.

1787 KNOWLTON, Ezra C. *History of Highway Development in Utah.* [Salt Lake City, Utah, 1962?]

1788 KOLKO, Gabriel. *Railroads and Regulation, 1877–1916.* Princeton, N.J., 1965. †

1789 LABBE, John T., and Vernon GOE. *Railroads in the Woods.* See 1575.

1790 LAVENDER, David. *The Great Persuader.* Garden City N.Y., 1970. A biography of Collis P. Huntington.

1791 LEONARD, William N. *Railroad Consolidation under the Transportation Act of 1920.* New York, 1946.

1792 LEWIS, Oscar. *Big Four: The Story of Huntington, Stanford, Hopkins, and Crocker, and of the Building of the Central Pacific.* New York, 1938. †

1793 MCAFEE, Ward M. "A Constitutional History of Railroad Rate Regulation in California, 1879–1911." *Pac Hist Rev,* XXXVII (1968), 265–279.

1794 MCAFEE, Ward M. "Local Interests and Railroad Regulation in California During the Granger Decade." *Pac Hist Rev,* XXXVII (1968), 51–66.

1795 MCCAGUE, James. *Moguls and Iron Men: The Story of the First Transcontinental Railroad.* New York, 1964.

1795A MARTIN, Albro. *James J. Hill and the Opening of the Northwest.* New York, 1976.

1796 MYERS, Rex C. "Trolleys of the Treasure State." *Mont: Mag W Hist,* XXII (1972), 34–47.

1797 NESBIT, Robert C. *"He Built Seattle": A Biography of Judge Thomas Burke.* Seattle, Wash., 1961. Burke was an important figure in northwestern railroad development, especially in regard to the Great Northern.

1798 O'CONNOR, Richard. *Iron Wheels and Broken Men: The Railroad Barons and the Plunder of the West.* New York, 1973.

1799 OVERTON, Richard C. *Burlington Route: A History of the Burlington Lines.* New York, 1965.

1800 OVERTON, Richard C. *Burlington West: A Colonization History of the Burlington Railroad.* Cambridge, Mass., 1941.

1801 OVERTON, Richard C. *Gulf to Rockies: The Heritage of the Fort Worth and Denver-Colorado and Southern Railways, 1861–1898.* Austin, Tex., 1953.

1802 "The Pacific Railroad, 1869–1969: A Centennial Issue." *Am W,* VI (May 1969).

1803 PAXSON, Frederic L. "The Highway Movement, 1916–1935." *Amer Hist Rev,* LI (1946), 236–253.

1804 POST, Robert C. "The Fair Fare Fight: An Episode in Los Angeles History." *S Calif Q,* LII (1970), 275–298.

1805 QUIETT, Glenn C. *They Built the West: An Epic of Rails and Cities,* New York, 1934.

1806 RIEGEL, Robert E. *The Story of Western Railroads.* New York, 1926.

1807 RUSSEL, Robert R. *Improvement of Communication with the Pacific Coast as an Issue in American Politics, 1783–1864.* Cedar Rapids, Iowa, 1948.

1808 SCAMEHORN, Lee. "The Development of Air Transportation in the West." *The American West: An Appraisal.* Ed. Robert G. Ferris. Santa Fe, N.M., 1963.

1809 STOVER, John F. *American Railroads.* Chicago, 1961. †

1810 STOVER, John F. *The Life and Decline of the American Railroad.* New York, 1970.

1811 TRAXLER, Ralph N., Jr. "Collis P. Huntington and the Texas and Pacific Land Grant." *N M Hist Rev,* XXXIV (1959), 117–133.

1812 TROTTMAN, Nelson. *History of the Union Pacific: A Financial and Economic Survey.* New York, 1923.

1813 *Utah Historical Quarterly,* XXXVII (Winter 1969). Centennial issue on the joining of the Union Pacific and the Central Pacific.

1814 UTLEY, Robert M. "The Dash to Promontory." *Utah Hist Q,* XXIX (1961), 99–117.

1815 WATERS, Lawrence L. *Steel Trails to Santa Fe.* Lawrence, Kan., 1950. The Atchison, Topeka and Santa Fe Railroad.

1816 WHITE, John H., Jr. "The Railroad Reaches California: Men, Machines, and Culture Migration." *Calif Hist Q,* LII (1973), 131–144.

4. Mail and Telegraph

1817 FULLER, Wayne E. *RFD: The Changing Face of Rural America.* Bloomington, Ind., 1964.

1818 THOMPSON, Robert L. *Wiring a Continent: The History of the Telegraph Industry in the United States, 1832–1866.* Princeton, N.J., 1947.

XIX. Western Cities and Towns

1819 ABBOTT, Carl. "Boom State and Boom City: Stages in Denver's Growth." *Colo Mag,* L (1973), 207–230.

1820 ALLEN, James B. "The Company-Owned Mining Town in the West: Exploitation or Benevolent Paternalism?" *Reflections of Western Historians.* Ed. John A. Carroll. Tucson, Ariz., 1969.

1821 Allen, James B. *The Company Town in the American West.* Norman, Okla., 1966.

1822 ATHERTON, Lewis E. *Main Street on the Middle Border.* Bloomington, Ind., 1954. †

1823 ATHERTON, Lewis E. "The Midwestern Country Town—Myth and Reality." *Ag Hist,* XXVI (1952), 73–80.

1824 AVERBACH, Alvin. "San Francisco's South of Market Street District, 1858–1958: The Emergence of a Skid Row." *Calif Hist Q,* LII (1973), 196–223.

1825 BARTH, Gunther. *Instant Cities: Urbanization and the Rise of San Francisco and Denver.* New York, 1975.

1826 BARTH, Gunther. "Metropolitanism and Urban Elites in the Far West." *The Age of Industrialism in America. . . .* Ed. Frederick C. Jaher. New York, 1968.

1827 BINNS, Archie. *Northwest Gateway: The Story of the Port of Seattle.* Garden City, N.Y., 1941.

1828 BOSKIN, Joseph, and Victor PILSON, "The Los Angeles Riot of 1965: A Medical Profile of an Urban Crisis." *Pac Hist Rev,* XXXIX (1970), 353–365.

1829 BULLOCK, Paul, ed. *Watts: The Aftermath—An Inside View of the Ghetto, by the People of Watts.* New York, [1969]. †

1829A CAUGHEY, John W., and La Ree CAUGHEY. *Los Angeles: Biography of a City.* Berkeley, Calif., 1976. An anthology.

1830 CHAFFEE, Eugene B. "Boise: The Founding of a City." *Idaho Yes,* VII (1963), 2–7.

1831 CHAPMAN, Berlin B. "Oklahoma City, From Public Land to Private Property." *Chron Okla,* XXXVII (1959–60), 211–237, 330–353, 440–479.

1832 CLARK, Norman H. *Mill Town: A Social History of Everett, Washington. . . .* See 1539.

1833 DE ARMOND, R. N. *The Founding of Juneau.* See 1045.

1834 DEBO, Angie. *Prairie City: The Story of an American Community.* New York, 1944.

1835 DEBO, Angie. *Tulsa: From Creek Town to Oil Capital.* Norman, Okla., 1943.

1836 DE GRAAF, Lawrence B. "The City of Black Angels: Emergence of the Los Angeles Ghetto, 1890–1930." *Pac Hist Rev,* XXXIX (1970), 323–352.

1837 DE GRAAF, Lawrence B. "Negro Migration to Los Angeles, 1930–1950." Doctoral dissertation, University of California at Los Angeles, 1962.

1838 DYKSTRA, Robert R. *The Cattle Towns.* See 1154.

1839 ELAZAR, Daniel J. *Cities of the Prairie: The Metropolitan Frontier and American Politics.* New York, 1970.

1840 ELLIOTT, Russell R. *Nevada's Twentieth-Century Mining Boom: Tonopah, Goldfield, Ely.* See 1046.

1841 FAHEY, John. "The Million-Dollar Corner: The Development of Downtown Spokane, 1890–1920." *Pac N W Q,* LXII (1971), 77–85.

1842 FARGO, Lucile F. *Spokane Story.* New York, 1950.

1843 FATOUT, Paul. *Meadow Lake: Gold Town.* Bloomington, Ind., 1969. †

1844 FAULK, Odie B. *Tombstone: Myth and Reality.* New York, 1972.

1845 FOGELSON, Robert M. *The Fragmented Metropolis: Los Angeles, 1850–1930.* Cambridge, Mass., 1967.

1846 FOGELSON, Robert M., comp. *The Los Angeles Riots.* New York, 1969.

1846A FOSTER, Mark S. "The Model-T, The Hard Sell, and Los Angeles' Urban Growth: The Decentralization of Los Angeles during the 1920s." *Pac Hist Rev,* XLIV (1975), 459–484.

1847 GARRETT, Julia K. *Fort Worth: A Frontier Triumph.* Austin, Tex., 1972.

1848 GLAAB, Charles N. "Visions of Metropolis: William Gilpin and Theories of City Growth in the American West." *Wis Mag Hist,* LXV (1961), 21–31.

1849 GREENLEAF, Cameron, and Andrew WALLACE. "Tucson: Pueblo, Presidio, and American City: A Synopsis of Its History." *Ariz,* III (1962), 18–27.

1850 GUEST, Francis F. "Municipal Government in Spanish California." *Calif Hist Soc Q,* XLVI (1967), 307–335.

1851 HARRIS, Chauncy D. "Salt Lake City, A Regional Capital." Doctoral dissertation, University of Chicago, 1940.

1852 HESS, Leland E. "The Coming of Urban Redevelopment and Urban Renewal to Oregon, 1949–1963: A Study in Democracy." Doctoral dissertation, University of Chicago, 1968.

1853 HICKS, John D. "The Significance of the Small Town in American History." *Reflections of Western Historians.* Ed. John A. Carroll, Tucson, Ariz., 1969.

1854 HILL, Burton S. "Buffalo—Ancient Cow Town: A Wyoming Saga." *Ann Wyo,* XXXV (1963), 125–154.

1855 HINE, Robert V. *California's Utopian Colonies.* San Marino, Calif., 1953; New Haven, Conn., [1966]. †

1856 HOWARD, James K. "An Economic and Social History of Dallas, Texas." Doctoral dissertation, Harvard University, 1955–1956.

1857 JACKSON, W. Turrentine. *Treasure Hill: Portrait of a Silver Mining Camp.* See 1064.

1858 *Journal of the West,* XIII (July 1974). Special issue on western urbanization.

1859 KLIEWER, Waldo O. "The Foundations of Billings, Montana." *Pac N W Q,* XXXI (1940), 255–283.

1860 KNIGHT, Oliver. "Toward an Understanding of the Western Town." *W Hist Q,* IV (1973), 28–42.

1861 LA FARGE, Oliver. *Santa Fe: The Autobiography of a Southwestern Town.* Norman, Okla., 1959.

1862 LARSEN, Lawrence H., and Robert L. BRANYAN. "The Development of an Urban Civilization on the Frontier of the American West." *Societas,* I (1971), 33–50.

1863 LEADER, Leonard J. "Los Angeles and the Great Depression." Doctoral dissertation, University of California at Los Angeles, 1972.

1864 LOTCHIN, Roger W. *San Francisco, 1846–1856: From Hamlet to City.* New York, 1974.

1865 LUCKINGHAM, Bradford. "The City in the Westward Movement—A Bibliographical Note." *W Hist Q,* V (1974), 295–306.

1866 MCCOMB, David G. *Houston, the Bayou City.* Austin, Tex., 1969.

1867 MACDONALD, Norbert. "Population Growth and Change in Seattle and Vancouver, 1880–1960." *Pac Hist Rev,* XXXIX (1970), 297–321.

1868 MANN, Ralph E., II. "Decade after the Gold Rush." See 1079.

1869 MANN, Ralph E., II. "The Social and Political Structure of Two California Gold Towns." Doctoral dissertation, Stanford University, 1970.

1870 MARTIN, Robert L. *The City Moves West: Economic and Industrial Growth in Central West Texas.* Austin, Tex., 1969.

1871 MARTIN, Walter T. "Continuing Urbanization on the Pacific Coast." *Am J Soc,* LXII (1956), 320–328.

1872 MERRIAM, Paul G. "Portland, Oregon, 1840–1890: A Social and Economic History." Doctoral dissertation, University of Oregon, 1971.

1872A MERRIAM, Paul G. "Urban Elite in the Far West: Portland, Oregon, 1870–1890." *Ariz W,* XVIII (1976), 41–52.

1873 MILLER, Zane L. *The Urbanization of Modern America: A Brief History.* New York, 1973. †

1874 MOORE, Joan W., and Frank G. MITTELBACH. *Residential Segregation in the Urban Southwest: A Comparative Study.* Los Angeles, 1966.

1875 MORGAN, Dale L. "The Changing Face of Salt Lake City." *Utah Hist Q,* XXVII (1959), 209–232.

1876 MORGAN, Murray. *Skid Road: An Informal Portrait of Seattle.* New York, 1951. Rev. ed., 1960. †

1877 NADEAU, Remi. *City-Makers: The Men Who Transformed Los Angeles from Village to Metropolis . . . 1868–76.* Garden City. N.Y., 1948.

1878 NADEAU, Remi. *Los Angeles: From Mission to Modern City.* New York, 1960.

1879 NELSON, Lowry. *The Mormon Village: A Pattern and Technique of Land Settlement.* See 992.

1880 NESBIT, Robert C. *"He Built Seattle": A Biography of Judge Thomas Burke.* See 1797.

1880A NICHOLS, Roger. "A Miniature Venice: Florence, Arizona, 1866–1910." *J Ariz Hist,* XVI (1975), 335–356.

1880B NUNIS, Doyce B., Jr., comp. *Los Angeles and Its Environs in the Twentieth Century: A Bibliography of a Metropolis.* Los Angeles, 1973. Nearly 10,000 entries.

1881 PEARSON, John E. "Urban Housing and Population Changes in the Southwest, 1940–1960." *S W Soc Sci Q,* XLIV (1964), 357–366.

1882 PERRIGO, Lynn I. "A Condensed History of Boulder, Colorado." *Colo Mag,* XXVI (1949), 37–49.

1883 POMEROY, Earl. *In Search of the Golden West: The Tourist in Western America.* New York, 1957.

1884 POMEROY, Earl. "The Urban Frontier of the Far West." *The Frontier Challenge: Responses to the Trans-Mississippi West.* Ed. John G. Clark. Lawrence, Kan., 1971.

1885 REPS, John W. *Town Planning in Frontier America.* Princeton, N.J., 1969. †

1886 ROBBINS, William G. "Opportunity and Persistence in the Pacific Northwest: A Quantitative Study of Early Roseburg, Oregon." *Pac Hist Rev,* XXXIX (1970), 279–296.

1887 ROBINSON, W. W. *Los Angeles: A Profile.* Norman, Okla., 1968.

1887A SALE, Roger. *Seattle, Past and Present.* Seattle, Wash., 1976.

1888 SCHNELL, J. Christopher, and Katherine B. CLINTON. "The New West: Themes in Nineteenth Century Urban Promotion, 1815–1880." *Mo Hist Soc Bull,* XXX (1974), 75–88.

1889 SCHNELL, J. Christopher, and Patrick E. MCLEAR. "Why the Cities Grew: A Historiographical Essay on Western Urban Growth, 1850–1880." *Mo Hist Soc Bull,* XXVIII (1972), 162–177.

1890 SMITH, Duane A. *Rocky Mountain Mining Camps.* See 1104

1891 STELTER, Gilbert A. "The Birth of a Frontier Boom Town: Cheyenne in 1867." *Ann Wyo,* XXXIX (1967), 5–33.

1892 STELTER, Gilbert A. "The City and Western Expansion: A Western Case Study." *W Hist Q,* IV (1973), 187–202.

1893 TELLING, Irving, Jr. "New Mexican Frontiers: A Social History of the Gallup Area, 1881–1901." Doctoral dissertation, Harvard University, 1952–1953.

1894 VAN ORMAN, Richard A. *A Room for the Night: Hotels of the Old West.* Bloomington, Ind., 1966.

1895 VAN ORMAN, Richard A. "San Francisco: Hotel City of the West." *Reflections of Western Historians.* Ed. John A. Carroll. Tucson, Ariz., 1969.

1896 WADE, Richard C. *The Urban Frontier.* See 303.

1897 WADE, Richard C. "Urban Life in Western America, 1790–1830." *Am Hist Rev,* LXIV (1958), 14–30.

1898 WEST, Elliott. "Cleansing the Queen City: Prohibition and Urban Reform in Denver." *Ariz W,* XIV (1972), 331–346.

1899 WEST, Ray B., ed. *Rocky Mountain Cities.* New York, 1949.

1900 WHEELER, Kenneth W. *To Wear a City's Crown: The Beginnings of Urban Growth in Texas, 1836–1865.* Cambridge, Mass., 1968.

1901 WILSON, William H. "The Founding of Anchorage: Federal Town Building on the Last Frontier." *Pac N W Q,* LVIII (1967), 130–141.

1902 WINTHER, Oscar O. "The Colony System of Southern California." *Ag Hist,* XXVII (1953), 94–103.

XX. Merchants, Investors, Speculators, and the Economy

1903 ANDERSON, George L. "Banks, Mails, and Rails, 1880–1915." *The Frontier Challenge: Responses to the Trans–Mississippi West.* Ed. John G. Clark. Lawrence, Kan., 1971.

1904 ARRINGTON, Leonard J. *The Changing Economic Structure of the Mountain West, 1850–1950.* Logan, Utah, 1963.

1904A ARRINGTON, Leonard J. *David Eccles: Pioneer Western Industrialist.* Logan, Utah, 1975.

1905 ARRINGTON, Leonard J. "From Panning Gold to Nuclear Fission: Idaho's Economic Development, 1860–1960." *Idaho Yes,* VI (Summer 1962), 2–10.

1906 ARRINGTON, Leonard J. *Great Basin Kingdom.* See 934.

1907 ARRINGTON, Leonard J., and Thomas G. ALEXANDER. *A Dependent Commonwealth: Utah's Economy from Statehood to the Great Depression.* Provo, Utah, 1974. †

1908 ATHERTON, Lewis E. *The Frontier Merchant in Mid-America.* Columbia, Mo., 1971.

1909 BAKER, Abner. "Economic Growth in Portland in the 1880s." *Ore Hist Q,* LXVII (1966), 105–123.

1910 BARNETT, Paul S. "Colorado Domestic Business Corporations, 1859–1900." Doctoral dissertation, University of Illinois, 1966.

1911 BERGE, Wendell. *Economic Freedom for the West.* Lincoln, Neb., 1946.

1912 BLACKFORD, Mansel G. "Banking and Bank Legislation in California, 1890–1915." *Bus Hist Rev,* XLVII (1973), 482–507.

1913 BLACKFORD, Mansel G. *The Politics of Business in California, 1890–1920.* Columbus, Ohio, 1976.

1914 BUTT, Paul D. *Branch Banking and Economic Growth in Arizona and New Mexico.* Albuquerque, N.M., 1960.

1915 CARRIKER, Robert C. *Fort Supply, Indian Territory: Frontier Outpost on the Plains.* Norman, Okla., 1970.

1916 CARSTENSEN, Vernon. "The Fisherman's Frontier on the Pacific Coast: The Rise of the Salmon-Canning Industry." *The Frontier Challenge: Responses to the Trans-Mississippi West.* Ed. John G. Clark. Lawrence, Kan., 1971.

1917 CLARKE, Dwight L. *William Tecumseh Sherman: Gold Rush Banker.* San Francisco, 1969.

1918 COHN, Edwin J., Jr. *Industry in the Pacific Northwest and the Location Theory.* New York, 1954.

1919 DODDS, Gordon B. *The Salmon King of Oregon: R. D. Hume and the Pacific Fisheries.* Chapel Hill, N.C., 1959, 1963.

1920 FIERMAN, Floyd S. "Jewish Pioneering in the Southwest: A Record of the Freudenthal-Lesinsky-Solomon Families." *Ariz W,* II (1960), 54–72.

1921 FIERMAN, Floyd S., ed. "Samuel J. Freudenthal: Southwestern Merchant and Civic Leader." *Am Jew Hist Q,* LVII (1968), 353–435. An edited version of Freudenthal's reminiscences.

1922 FIERMAN, Floyd S. "The Spiegelbergs: Pioneer Merchants and Bankers in the Southwest." *Am Jew Hist Q,* LVI (1967), 371–451.

1923 FRITZSCHE, Bruno. "'On Liberal Terms': The Boston Hide-Merchants in California." *Bus Hist Rev,* XLII (1968), 467–481.

1924 GARNSEY, Morris E. *America's New Frontier: The Mountain West.* New York, 1950.

1925 GATES, Charles M. "Boom Stages in American Expansion." *Bus Hist Rev,* XXXIII (1959), 32–42. Economic growth in the Pacific Northwest.

1926 HAKOLA, John W. "Samuel T. Hauser and the Economic Development of Montana: A Case Study in Nineteenth Century Frontier Capitalism." Doctoral dissertation, Indiana University, 1961.

1927 HALL, Linda. "Neiman-Marcus: The Beginning." *W States Jew Hist Q,* VII (1975), 138–150.

1928 HALVORSON, Ora J. "Charles E. Conrad of Kalispell: Merchant Prince with Gentle Touch." *Mont: Mag W Hist,* XXI (Spring 1971), 56–67.

1929 HINCKLEY, Ted C. *The Americanization of Alaska, 1867–1897.* See 54. Includes discussion of the Alaska Commercial Company monopoly.

1929A JACKSON, W. Turrentine. *The Enterprising Scot.* See 1062.

1929B KELSEY, Harry E., Jr. *Frontier Capitalist: The Life of John Evans.* [Denver] 1969.

1930 KNIGHT, Oliver. "An Oklahoma Indian Trader as a Frontiersman of Commerce." *J S Hist,* XXIII (1957), 203–219.

1931 LAVENDER, David. *Nothing Seemed Impossible: William C. Ralston and Early San Francisco.* See 1071.

1932 LEVINSON, Robert E. "Julius Basinski: Jewish Merchant in Montana." *Mont: Mag W Hist,* XXII (January 1972), 60–68.

1933 MACDONALD, Alexander Norbert. "The Business Leaders of Seattle, 1880–1910." *Pac N W Q,* L (1959), 1–13.

1934 MACDONALD, Alexander Norbert. "Seattle's Economic Development, 1880–1910." Doctoral dissertation, University of Washington, 1959.

1934A MARTIN, Albro. *James J. Hill and the Opening of the Northwest.* See 1795A.

1935 MILLER, Ronald L. "Henry Delano Fitch: A Yankee Trader in California, 1826–1849." Doctoral dissertation, University of Southern California, 1972.

1936 NASH, Gerald D. "Bureaucracy and Reform in the West: Notes on the Influence of a Neglected Interest Group." *W Hist Q,* II (1971), 295–305.

1937 NASH, Gerald D. "Research in Western Economic History—Problems and Opportunities." *The American West: An Appraisal.* Ed. Robert G. Ferris. Santa Fe, N.M., 1963.

1938 NASH, Gerald D. "Western Economic History as a Field of Research." *W Econ J,* III (1964), 86–98.

1939 NORTH, Douglass C. "International Capital Flows and the Development of the American West." *J Econ Hist,* XVI (1956), 493–505.

1940 NORTH, Douglass C. "Location Theory and Regional Economic Growth." *J Pol Econ,* LXIII (1955), 243–258.

1941 OGDEN, Adele. *The California Sea Otter Trade, 1784–1848.* Berkeley, Calif., 1941, 1975.

1942 OGDEN, Adele. "Hides and Tallow: McCulloch, Hartnell and Company, 1822–1828." *Calif Hist Soc Q,* VI (1927), 254–264.

1943 *Oregon Historical Quarterly,* LXVII (June 1966). Special issue entitled "Impact of the Transcontinentals" (i.e., railroads), with articles on Portland, sheep and wool, cattle, and lumber.

1944 OVIATT, Alton B. "Pacific Coast Competition for the Gold Camp Trade of Montana." *Pac N W Q,* XLVI (1965), 168–176.

1945 PALMER, William R. "Early Merchandising in Utah." *Utah Hist Q,* XXXI (1963), 36–50.

1946 PARISH, William J. *The Charles Ilfeld Company: A Study of the Rise and Decline of Mercantile Capitalism in New Mexico.* Cambridge, Mass., 1961.

1947 QUINN, Larry D. *Politicians in Business: A History of the Liquor Control System in Montana.* Missoula, Mont., 1970.

1948 RIDGE, Martin. "Why They Went West: Economic Opportunity on the Trans-Mississippi Frontier." *Am W,* I (Summer 1964), 40–57.

1948A SCAMEHORN, H. Lee *Pioneer Steelmaker in the West.* Boulder, Colo., 1976.

1949 SHARP, Paul F. *Whoop-Up Country.* See 76.

1950 SLOSS, Frank H., and Richard A. PIERCE. "The Hutchinson, Kohl Story." *Pac N W Q,* LXII (1971), 1–6. The evolution of a dominant trading firm in Alaska.

1951 SMITH, Alice E. *James Duane Doty, Frontier Promoter.* Madison, Wis., 1950.

1951A SPENCE, Clark C. *British Investments and the American Mining Frontier.* See 1108.

1952 TATTERSALL, James N. "The Economic Development of the Pacific Northwest to 1920." Doctoral dissertation, University of Washington, 1960.

1953 THROCKMORTON, Arthur L. *Oregon Argonauts: Merchant Adventurers on the Western Frontier.* Portland, Ore., 1961.

1954 WALTER, Paul A. F. "New Mexico's Pioneer Bank and Bankers." *N M Hist Rev,* XXI (1946), 209–225.

1955 WINTHER, Oscar O. *Old Oregon Country.* See 1751.

XXI. Labor in the West

See also: Agriculture; Mining; Lumbering; Chinese and Japanese; Spanish-Speaking Peoples

1956 ALLEN, James B. *The Company Town in the American West.* See 1821.

1957 BARNES, Donald M. "The Ideology of the Industrial Workers of the World, 1905–1921." Doctoral dissertation, Washington State University, 1962.

1958 BAYARD, Charles J. "The 1927–28 Colorado Coal Strike." *Pac Hist Rev,* XXXII (1963), 235–250.

1959 BECHTOL, Paul T., Jr. "The 1880 Labor Dispute in Leadville." *Colo Mag,* XLVII (1970), 312–325.

1960 BRINLEY, John E., Jr. "The Western Federation of Miners." Doctoral dissertation, University of Utah, 1972.

1961 BRISSENDEN, Paul F. *The I.W.W.: A Study of American Syndicalism.* New York, 1919.

1962 BROWN, Giles T. "The West Coast Phase of the Maritime Strike of 1921." *Pac Hist Rev,* XIX (1950), 385–396.

1963 CASH, Joseph H. *Working the Homestake.* See 1039.

1964 *The Centralia Case: Three Views of the Armistice Day Tragedy at Centralia, Washington, November 11, 1919.* New York, 1971. Contemporary briefs and reports by Ralph Chaplin, Ben Hur Lampman, and the Federal Council of Churches.

1965 CHAPLIN, Ralph. *Wobbly: The Rough-and-Tumble Story of an American Radical.* Chicago, 1948. Repr. New York, 1972.

1966 CHIU, Ping. *Chinese Labor in California, 1850–1880: An Economic Study.* Madison, Wis., 1963.

1967 CLARK, Norman H. *Mill Town: A Social History of Everett, Washington.* See 1539.

1968 CLINCH, Thomas A. "Coxey's Army in Montana." *Mont: Mag W Hist,* XV (1965), 2–11.

1969 CONLIN, Joseph R. *Big Bill Haywood and the Radical Union Movement.* Syracuse, N.Y., 1969.

1970 CONLIN, Joseph R. *Bread and Roses Too: Studies of the Wobblies.* Westport, Conn., 1969.

1971 CROSS, Ira B. *A History of the Labor Movement in California.* Berkeley, Calif., 1935, 1974.

1972 DAVIES, J. Kenneth. "Mormonism and the Closed Shop." *Labor Hist,* III (1962), 169–187.

1973 DAVIES, J. Kenneth. "Utah Labor Before Statehood." *Utah Hist Q,* XXXIV (1966), 202–217.

1974 DUBOFSKY, Melvyn. "The Leadville Strike of 1896–1897: An Appraisal." *Mid-Amer,* XLVIII (1966), 99–118.

1975 DUBOFSKY, Melvyn. "The Origins of Western Working Class Radicalism, 1890–1905." *Labor Hist,* VII (1966), 131–154.

1976 DUBOFSKY, Melvyn. *We Shall Be All: A History of the Industrial Workers of the World.* Chicago, 1969. †

1977 EARL, Phillip I. "Nevada's Italian War . . . July-September 1879." *Nev Hist Soc Q,* XII (1969), 47–87.

1978 ELLIOTT, Russell R. *Radical Labor in the Nevada Mining Booms.* See 1047.

1979 FAHEY, John. "Coeur d' Alene Confederacy." *Idaho Yes,* XII (1968), 2–7.

1980 FEARIS, Donald F. "The California Farm Worker, 1930–1942." Doctoral dissertation, University of California, Davis, 1971.

1981 FODELL, Beverly, comp. *Cesar Chavez and the United Farm Workers.* See 885.

1982 FONER, Philip S. *History of the Labor Movement in the United States.* 4 vols. New York, 1947–1965. †

1983 FRIEDHEIM, Robert L. *The Seattle General Strik:.* Seattle, Wash., 1964.

1984 FROST, Richard H. *The Mooney Case.* Stanford, Calif., 1968.

1985 GABOURY, William J. "From Statehouse to Bull Pen: Idaho Populism and the Coeur d' Alene Troubles of the 1890s." *Pac N W Q,* LVIII (1967), 14–22.

1986 GARNEL, Donald. *The Rise of Teamster Power in the West.* Berkeley, Calif., 1972.

1987 GENTRY, Curt. *Frame-up: The Incredible Case of Tom Mooney and Warren Billings.* New York, 1967.

1988 GORDON, Margaret S. *Employment Expansion and Population Growth: The California Experience, 1900–1950.* Berkeley, Calif., 1954.

1989 GROVER, David H. *Debaters and Dynamiters: The Story of the Haywood Trial.* Corvallis, Ore., 1964. †

1990 HAYWOOD, William D. *Bill Haywood's Book: The Autobiography of William D. Haywood.* New York, 1929. Repr. New York, 1966.

1991 HOLBROOK, Stewart H. *The Rocky Mountain Revolution.* New York, 1956. Harry Orchard, the dynamiter.

1992 HOUGH, Merrill. "Leadville and the Western Federation of Miners." *Colo Mag,* XLIX (1972), 19–34.

1993 HYMAN, Harold M. *Soldiers and Spruce: Origins of the Loyal Legion of Loggers and Lumbermen.* Los Angeles, 1963.

1994 JENSEN, Vernon H. *Heritage of Conflict.* See 1065.

1995 JENSEN, Vernon H. *Lumber and Labor.* See 1572.

1996 JENSEN, Vernon H. *Nonferrous Metals Industry Unionism, 1932–1954: A Story of Leadership Controversy.* Ithaca, N.Y., 1954.

1997 KNIGHT, Robert E. L. *Industrial Relations in the San Francisco Bay Area, 1900–1918.* Berkeley, Calif., 1960.

1998 LARROWE, Charles P. *Harry Bridges: The Rise and Fall of Radical Labor in the United States.* New York, 1972. †

1999 LASLETT, John H. M. *Labor and the Left: A Study of Socialist and Radical Influences in the American Labor Movement, 1881–1924.* New York, 1970.

2000 LE WARNE, Charles P. "On the Wobbly Train to Fresno." *Labor Hist,* XIV (1973), 264–289.

2001 LINGENFELTER, Richard E. *The Hardrock Miners.* See 1075.

2002 LONSDALE, David L. "The Fight for an Eight-Hour Day." *Colo Mag,* XLIII (1966), 339–353.

2003 LONSDALE, David L. "The Movement for an Eight-Hour Law in Colorado, 1893–1913." Doctoral dissertation, University of Colorado, 1963.

2004 MCMURRY, Donald L. *Coxey's Army: A Study of the Industrial Army Movement of 1894.* Boston, 1929.

2005 MCWILLIAMS, Carey. *Factories in the Field: The Story of Migratory Farm Labor in California,* See 1318.

2006 MCWILLIAMS, Carey. *Ill Fares the Land: Migrants and Migratory Labor in the United States.* See 1319.

2007 NASH, Gerald D. "The Influence of Labor on State Policy, 1860–1920: The Experience of California." *Calif Hist Soc Q,* XLII (1963), 241–257.

2008 NICHOLS, Claude W., Jr., "Brotherhood in the Woods: The Loyal Legion of Loggers and Lumbermen, A Twenty Year Attempt at 'Industrial Cooperation.' " See 1590.

2009 NORQUEST, Carrol. *Rio Grande Wetbacks: Migrant Mexican Workers.* See 912.

2010 PAPANIKOLAS, Helen Z. "Unionism, Communism, and the Great Depression: The Carbon County Coal Strike of 1933." *Utah Hist Q,* XLI (1973), 254–300.

2011 PAWAR, Sheelwant B. "The Structure and Nature of Labor Unions in Utah, An Historical Perspective, 1890–1920." *Utah Hist Q,* XXXV (1967), 236–255.

2012 PELLING, Henry. *American Labor.* Chicago, 1960. †

2013 PERRY, Louis B., and Richard S. PERRY. *A History of the Los Angeles Labor Movement, 1911–1941.* Berkeley, Calif., 1963.

2014 RADER, Benjamin G., "The Montana Lumber Strike of 1917." *Pac Hist Rev,* XXXVI (1967), 189–207.

2015 RAYBACK, Joseph G. *A History of American Labor.* New York, 1959. †

2016 REESE, James V. "The Worker in Texas, 1821–1876." Doctoral dissertation, University of Texas, 1964.

2017 RENSHAW, Patrick. *The Wobblies: The Story of Syndicalism in the United States.* Garden City, N.Y., 1967. †

2018 ROBINSON, Robert M. "San Francisco Teamsters at the Turn of the Century." *Calif Hist Soc Q,* XXXV (1956), 59–69, 145–153.

2019 SAXTON, Alexander P. *The Indispensable Enemy: Labor and the Anti-Chinese Movement in California.* Berkeley, Calif., 1971. †

2020 SAXTON, Alexander P. "San Francisco Labor and the Populist and Progressive Insurgencies." *Pac Hist Rev,* XXXIV (1965), 421–438.

2021 SCRUGGS, Otey M. "Evolution of the Mexican Farm Labor Agreement of 1942." See 919.

2022 SCRUGGS, Otey M. "The First Mexican Farm Labor Program." See 920.

2023 SIMS, Robert C. "Idaho's Criminal Syndicalism Act: One State's Response to Radical Labor." *Labor Hist,* XV (1974), 511–527.

2024 SLOBODEK, Mitchell. *A Selective Bibliography of California Labor History.* Los Angeles, 1964.

2025 SMITH, Gibbs M. *Joe Hill.* Salt Lake City, Utah, 1969.

2026 SMITH, Robert W. *The Coeur d'Alene Mining War of 1892: A Case Study of an Industrial Dispute.* Corvallis, Ore., 1961.

2027 STIMSON, Grace H. *The Rise of the Labor Movement in Los Angeles.* Berkeley, Calif., 1955

2028 STONE, Harry W. "Beginning of Labor Movement in the Pacific Northwest." *Ore Hist Q,* XLVII (1946), 155–164.

2029 SUGGS, George G., Jr. *Colorado's War on Militant Unionism.* See 1110.

2030 SUGGS, George G., Jr. "Militant Western Labor Confronts the Hostile State: A Case Study." *W Hist Q,* II (1971), 385–400.

2031 TAFT, Philip. "The Bisbee Deportation." *Labor Hist,* XIII (1972), 3–40.

2032 TAFT, Philip. "The IWW in the Grain Belt." *Labor Hist,* I (1960), 53–67.

2033 TAFT, Philip. *Labor Politics American Style: The California State Federation of Labor.* Cambridge, Mass., 1968.

2034 TAYLOR, Paul S. *Mexican Labor in the United States.* 2 vols. in 3. Berkeley, Calif., 1928–1934. Repr. 2 vols. New York, 1970.

2035 TAYLOR, Paul S. *The Sailors' Union of the Pacific.* New York, 1923.

2036 TOBIE, Harvey E. "Oregon Labor Disputes, 1919–23. . . ." *Ore Hist Q,* XLVIII (1947), 7–24, 195–213, 309–321.

2037 TYLER, Robert L. *Rebels of the Woods: The IWW.* See 1613

2038 VOELTZ, Herman C. "Coxey's Army in Oregon, 1894." *Ore Hist Q,* LXV (1964), 263–295.

2039 WATKINS, T. H. "Requiem for the Federation." *Am W,* III (Winter 1966), 4–12, 91–95.

2040 WELLS, Merle W. "The Western Federation of Miners." *J W,* XII (1973), 18–35.

2041 WHITTEN, Woodrow S. "The Wheatland Episode." *Pac Hist Rev,* XVII (1948), 37–42.

2042 WINN, Charles C. "Mexican-Americans in the Texas Labor Movement." Doctoral dissertation, Texas Christian University, 1972.

2043 WOLF, Jerome. "The Imperial Valley as an Index of Agricultural Labor Relations in California." Doctoral dissertation, University of Southern California, 1964.

2044 WOLLENBERG, Charles. "Race and Class in Rural California: The El Monte Berry Strike of 1933." *Calif Hist Q,* LI (1972), 155–164.

2045 WYMAN, Mark. "The Underground Miner, 1860–1910: Labor and Industrial Change in the Northern Rockies." Doctoral dissertation, University of Washington, 1971.

XXII. Chinese and Japanese Immigrants, Their Descendants, and Treatment of Them

2046 ARRINGTON, Leonard J. *The Price of Prejudice: The Japanese-American Relocation Center in Utah during World War II.* Logan, Utah, 1962.

2047 BAILEY, Thomas A. *Theodore Roosevelt and the Japanese-American Crises: An Account of the International Complications Arising from the Race Problem on the Pacific Coast.* Stanford, Calif., 1934.

2048 BARTH, Gunther. *Bitter Strength: A History of the Chinese in the United States, 1850–1870.* Cambridge, Mass., 1964.

2049 BOSWORTH, Allan R. *America's Concentration Camps.* New York, 1967.

2050 CARRANCO, Lynwood. "Chinese Expulsion from Humboldt County." *Pac Hist Rev,* XXX (1961), 329–340.

2051 CHEN, Wen-Hui Chang. "Changing Socio-Cultural Patterns of the Chinese Community of Los Angeles." Doctoral dissertation, University of Southern California, 1952.

2052 CHIU, Ping. *Chinese Labor in California, 1850–1880: An Economic Study.* Madison, Wis., 1963.

2053 CHOY, Philip P. "Golden Mountain of Lead: The Chinese Experience in California." *Calif Hist Q,* L (1971), 267–276.

2054 CHU, George. "Chinatowns in the Delta: The Chinese in the Sacramento-San Joaquin Delta, 1870–1960." *Calif Hist Soc Q,* XLIX (1970), 21–37.

2055 CONN, Stetson. "Japanese Evacuation from the West Coast." *Guarding the United States and its Outposts (The United States Army in World War II: The Western Hemisphere).* Ed. Stetson Conn, *et al.* Washington, D.C., 1964.

2056 CONRAT, Maisie, and Richard CONRAT. *Executive Order 9066: The Internment of 110,000 Japanese Americans.* San Francisco, 1972. † Vivid pictorial record with captions.

2057 COOLIDGE, Mary R. *Chinese Immigration.* New York, 1909. Repr. New York, 1969.

2058 CRANE, Paul, and T. A. LARSON. "The Chinese Massacre." *Ann Wyo,* XII (1940), 47–55, 153–161.

2059 DANIELS, Roger. "The Asian American Experience." *The Reinterpretation of American History and Culture.* Ed. William H. Cartwright and Richard L. Watson, Jr. Washington, D.C., 1973. Includes brief bibliography.

2060 DANIELS, Roger. *Concentration Camps, USA: Japanese Americans and World War II.* New York, 1971.

2061 DANIELS, Roger. *The Politics of Prejudice: The Anti-Japanese Movement in California and the Struggle for Japanese Exclusion.* New York, 1962.

2062 DANIELS, Roger. "Westerners from the East: Oriental Immigrants Reappraised." *Pac Hist Rev,* XXXV (1966), 373–383.

2063 DERIG, Betty. "Celestials in the Diggings." *Idaho Yes,* XVI (1972), 2–23.

2064 GIRDNER, Audrie, and Anne LOFTIS. *The Great Betrayal: The Evacuation of the Japanese-Americans during World War II.* New York, 1969.

2065 GRODZINS, Morton. *Americans Betrayed: Politics and the Japanese Evacuation.* Chicago, 1949. †

2066 HALE, Robert M. "The United States and Japanese Immigration." Doctoral dissertation, University of Chicago, 1945.

2067 HANSEN, Gladys C., and William F. HEINTZ, comps. *The Chinese in California: A Brief Bibliographic History.* Portland, Ore., 1970.

2068 HATA, Donald T., Jr., " 'Undesirables': Unsavory Elements among the Japanese in America prior to 1893 and Their Influence on the First Anti-Japanese Movement in California." Doctoral dissertation, University of Southern California, 1970.

2069 HOSOKAWA, Bill. *Nisei: The Quiet Americans.* New York, 1969. †

2070 HOUSTON, Jeanne Wakatsuki, and James D. HOUSTON. *Farewell to Manzanar.* Boston, 1973. †

2071 HSU, Frances L. K. *The Challenge of the American Dream: The Chinese in the United States.* Belmont, Calif., 1971. †

2072 HUNDLEY, Norris, Jr., ed. *The Asian American: Essays from the Pacific Historical Review.* Santa Barbara, Calif., 1976. Reprints essays on Chinese, Japanese, Filipinos, Koreans, East Indians, and East Asians.

2073 ICHIHASHI, Yamato. *Japanese in the United States: A Critical Study of the Problems of the Japanese Immigrants and Their Children.* Stanford, Calif., 1932.

2074 IGA, Mamoru. "Acculturation of the Japanese Population in Davis County, Utah." Doctoral dissertation, University of Utah, 1955.

2075 IWATA, Masakazu. "The Japanese Immigrants in California Agriculture." *Ag Hist,* XXXVI (1962), 25–37.

2076 KACHI, Teruko O. "The Treaty of 1911 and the Immigration and Alien Land Law Issue between the United States and Japan, 1911–1913." Doctoral dissertation, University of Chicago, 1957.

2077 KARLIN, Jules A. "The Anti-Chinese Outbreak in Tacoma, 1885." *Pac Hist Rev,* XXIII (1954), 271–283.

2078 KARLIN, Jules A. "The Anti-Chinese Outbreaks in Seattle, 1885–1886." *Pac N W Q,* XXXIX (1948), 103–130.

2079 KIKUCHI, Charles. *The Kikuchi Diary: Chronicle from an American Concentration Camp.* Ed. John Modell. Urbana, Ill., 1973.

2080 KITAGAWA, Daisuke. *Issei and Nisei: The Internment Years.* New York, 1967. †

2081 KITANO, Harry L. *The Japanese Americans: The Evolution of a Subculture.* Englewood Cliffs, N.J., 1969. †

2082 KONVITZ, Milton R. *The Alien and the Asiatic in American Law.* Ithaca, N.Y., 1946.

2083 KUNG, Shien-woo. *Chinese in American Life: Some Aspects of Their History, Status, Problems, and Contributions.* Seattle, Wash., 1962.

2084 LEE, Rose Hum. *The Chinese in the United States of America.* Hong Kong, 1960.

2085 LEIGHTON, Alexander H. *The Governing of Men: General Principles and Recommendations Based on Experience at a Japanese Relocation Camp.* Princeton, N.J., 1945. Report by a psychiatrist who had previous experience in studying Navajo and Eskimo communities.

2086 LOCKLEAR, William R. "The Celestials and the Angels: A Study of the Anti-Chinese Movement in Los Angeles to 1882." *S Calif Q,* XLII (1960), 239–256.

2087 LOFTIS, Anne. *California—Where the Twain DID Meet.* New York, 1973.

2088 LYMAN, Stanford M. *The Asian in the West* Reno, Nev., 1970,

2089 LYMAN, Stanford M. "The Structure of Chinese Society in Nineteenth Century America." Doctoral dissertation, University of California, Berkeley, 1961.

2090 MCCLELLAN, Robert. *The Heathen Chinee: A Study of American Attitudes toward China, 1890–1905.* [Columbus, Ohio], 1971.

2091 MCKENZIE, R. D. *Oriental Exclusion: The Effect of American Immigration Laws, Regulations, and Judicial Decisions upon the Chinese and Japanese on the American Pacific Coast.* Chicago, 1928. A sociologist reports on the operation of the Immigration Act of 1924.

2092 MCLEOD, Alexander. *Pigtails and Gold Dust: A Panorama of Chinese Life in Early California.* Caldwell, Idaho, 1947.

2093 MCWILLIAMS, Carey. *Prejudice; Japanese Americans: Symbol of Racial Intolerance.* Boston, 1944.

2094 MATTHEWS, Fred H. "White Community and 'Yellow Peril'." *Miss Val Hist Rev,* L (1964), 612–633.

2095 MELENDY, H. Brett. *The Oriental Americans.* New York, 1972 †

2096 MILLER, Stuart C. *The Unwelcome Immigrant: The American Image of the Chinese, 1785–1882.* Berkeley, Calif., 1969. †

2097 MILLIS, H. A. *The Japanese Problem in the United States.* New York, 1915. Under the sponsorship of the Federal Council of Churches, this economist studied the occupations, homes, and communities of Japanese-Americans.

2098 MIYAMOTO, S. Frank. "The Japanese Minority in the Pacific Northwest." *Pac N W Q,* LIV (1963), 143–149.

2099 MODELL, John. "The Japanese of Los Angeles: A Study in Growth and Accommodation, 1900–1946." Doctoral dissertation, Columbia University, 1969.

2100 MODELL, John. "Tradition and Opportunity: The Japanese Immigrant in America." *Pac Hist Rev,* XL (1971), 163–182.

2101 MYER, Dillon S. *Uprooted Americans: The Japanese Americans and the War Relocation Authority during World War II.* Tucson, Ariz., 1971. † Myer was the director of the War Relocation Authority.

2102 NESBIT, Robert C. *"He Built Seattle": A Biography of Judge Thomas Burke.* See 1797. Chap. VII: "Law and Order" (describes anti-Chinese outbreak).

2103 NORTH, Hart H. "Chinese and Japanese Immigration to the Pacific Coast." *Calif Hist Soc Q,* XXVIII (1949), 343–350.

2104 NORTH, Hart H. "Chinese Highbinder Societies in California." *Calif Hist Soc Q,* XXVII (1948), 19–31.

2105 OKIMOTO, Daniel K. *American in Disguise.* New York, 1971.

2106 OKUBO, Miné. *Citizen 13660.* New York, 1946.

2107 OLIN, Spencer C., Jr. "European Immigrant and Oriental Alien: Acceptance and Rejection by the California Legislature of 1913." *Pac Hist Rev,* XXXV (1966), 303–315.

2108 OURADA, Patricia K. "The Chinese in Colorado." *Colo Mag,* XXIX (1952), 273–284.

2109 PAUL, Rodman W. *The Abrogation of the Gentlemen's Agreement.* Cambridge, Mass., 1936. Diplomacy and politics of ending Japanese immigration.

2110 PAUL, Rodman W. "The Origin of the Chinese Issue in California." *Miss Val Hist Rev,* XXV (1938), 181–196.

2111 PURSINGER, Marvin G. "Oregon's Japanese in World War II: A History of Compulsory Relocation." Doctoral dissertation, University of Southern California, 1961.

2112 QUINN, Larry D. " 'Chink Chink Chinaman': The Beginning of Nativism in Montana." *Pac N W Q,* LVIII (1967), 82–89.

2113 ROSTOW, Eugene V. "Our Worst Wartime Mistake." *Harp,* CXCI (1945), 193–201. Wartime internment of the Japanese-Americans.

2114 SAKODA, James M. "Minidoka: An Analysis of Changing Patterns of Social Interaction." Doctoral dissertation, University of California, Berkeley, 1949.

2115 SANDMEYER, Elmer C. *The Anti-Chinese Movement in California.* Urbana, Ill., 1939. †

2116 SAXTON, Alexander. *The Indispensable Enemy: Labor and the Anti-Chinese Movement in California.* Berkeley, Calif., 1971. †

2117 SEAGER, Robert, II. "Some Denominational Reactions to Chinese Immigration to California, 1856–1892." *Pac Hist Rev,* XXVIII (1959), 49–66.

2118 SMITH, Bradford. *Americans from Japan.* Philadelphia, 1948.

2119 SPICER, Edward H., *et al. Impounded People: Japanese-Americans in the Relocation Centers.* Tucson, Ariz., 1969.

2120 SPOEHR, Luther W. "Sambo and the Heathen Chinee: Californians' Racial Stereotypes in the Late 1870s." *Pac Hist Rev,* XLII (1973), 185–204.

2121 STRONG, Edward K., Jr., *Japanese in California.* Stanford, Calif., 1933. A psychologist's statistical study of age, sex, size of family, education, occupation, and religious affiliation.

2122 STRONG, Edward K., Jr. *The Second-Generation Japanese Problem.* Stanford, Calif., 1933. A psychologist studies the adjustment of the second-generation Japanese-Americans to life in California.

2123 SUNG, Betty Lee. *Mountain of Gold: The Story of the Chinese in America.* New York, 1967.

2124 THOMAS, Dorothy S., *et. al. Japanese-American Evacuation and Resettlement.* 3 vols. Berkeley, 1946–1954. The three volumes have, respectively, these titles: *The Spoilage; The Salvage;* and *Prejudice, War and the Constitution.* †

2125 THOMPSON, Richard A. "The Yellow Peril, 1890–1924." Doctoral dissertation, University of Wisconsin, 1957.

2126 TURNER, Albert B. "The Origins and Development of the War Relocation Authority." Doctoral dissertation, Duke University, 1967.

2127 WYNNE, R. E. "Reaction to the Chinese in the Pacific Northwest and British Columbia, 1850–1910." Doctoral dissertation, University of Washington, 1964.

XXIII. Black Americans in the West

2128 ABAJIAN, James de T., comp. *Blacks and their Contributions to the American West: A Bibliography and Union List of Library Holdings through 1970.* Boston, 1974. By far the biggest bibliography published so far, with over 4,000 entries. Well indexed.

2129 ANDREWS, Thomas F. "Freedmen in Indian Territory: Post-Civil War Dilemma." *J W,* IV (1965), 367–376.

2130 BAKEWELL, Dennis C., comp. *The Black Experience in the United States.* Northridge, Calif., 1970. One of the larger recent bibliographies on Blacks in the West.

2131 BEASLEY, Delilah L. *The Negro Trail Blazers of California.* Los Angeles, 1919.

2132 BELLER, Jack. "Negro Slaves in Utah." *Utah Hist Q,* II (1929), 122–126.

2133 BELOUS, Russell E., ed. *America's Black Heritage.* Los Angeles, 1969. Black people in California.

2134 BERWANGER, Eugene H. *The Frontier Against Slavery: Western Anti-Negro Prejudice and the Slavery Extension Controversy.* Urbana, Ill., 1967. †

2135 BERWANGER, Eugene H. "Reconstruction on the Frontier: The Equal Rights Struggle in Colorado, 1865–1867." *Pac Hist Rev,* XLIV (1975), 313–329.

2136 BITTLE, William E., and Gilbert L. GEIS. "Racial Self-Fulfillment and the Rise of An All-Negro Community in Oklahoma." *The Making of Black America.* Eds. August Meier and Elliott M. Rudwick. Vol. I. New York, 1969. †

2137 BONTEMPS, Arna, and Jack CONROY. *Anyplace but Here.* New York, 1966. † A "revised and expanded version" of a book published in 1945 as *They Seek a City,* a study of Black migration and individual careers.

2138 BULLOCK, Paul, ed. *Watts: The Aftermath—An Inside View of the Ghetto, by the People of Watts.* New York, [1969]. †

2139 CARROLL, John M., ed. *The Black Military Experience in the American West.* New York, 1971. Abr. ed. New York, 1973. † A profusely illustrated anthology.

2140 CARROLL, John M., ed. *Buffalo Soldiers West.* Fort Collins, Colo., 1971. Primarily pictorial.

2141 COHEN, Jerry, and William S. MURPHY. *Burn, Baby, Burn! The Los Angeles Race Riot, August, 1965.* New York, 1966. Two journalists give a first-hand report.

2142 CONOT, Robert. *Rivers of Blood, Years of Darkness.* New York, 1967. † Vivid and informative account of the outburst at Watts.

2143 CORNISH, Dudley T. *The Sable Arm: Negro Troops in the Union Army, 1861–1865.* New York, 1956. †

2144 DAVIS, Lenwood G., comp. *Blacks in the American West: A Working Bibliography.* Monticello, Ill., 1974.

2145 DAVIS, Lenwood G., comp. *Blacks in the Pacific Northwest, 1788–1972: A Bibliography of Published Works and of Unpublished Source Materials on the Life and Contributions of Black People.* Monticello, Ill., 1972.

2146 DE GRAAF, Lawrence B. "The City of Black Angels: Emergence of the Los Angeles Ghetto, 1890–1930." *Pac Hist Rev,* XXXIX (1970), 323–352.

2147 DE GRAAF, Lawrence B. "Negro Migration to Los Angeles, 1930–1950." Doctoral dissertation, University of California at Los Angeles, 1962.

2148 DE GRAAF, Lawrence B. "Recognition, Racism, and Reflections on the Writing of Western Black History." *Pac Hist Rev,* XLIV (1975), 22–51.

2149 DROTNING, Philip T. *A Guide to Negro History in America.* Garden City, N.Y., 1968.

2150 DURHAM, Philip, and Everett L. JONES. *The Negro Cowboys.* New York, 1965.

2151 FISHER, James A. "A History of the Political and Social Development of the Black Community in California, 1850–1950." Doctoral dissertation, State University of New York at Stony Brook, 1972.

2152 FISHER, James A. "The Political Development of the Black Community in California, 1850–1950." *Calif Hist Q,* L (1971), 256–266.

2153 FISHER, James A. "The Struggle for Negro Testimony in California, 1851–1863." *S Calif Q,* LI (1969), 313–324.

2153A FLETCHER, Marvin E. *The Black Soldier and Officer in the United States Army.* See 704A

2154 FLIPPER, Henry O. *Negro Frontiersman: The Western Memoirs of Henry O. Flipper, First Negro Graduate of West Point.* Ed. Theodore D. Harris. El Paso, Tex., 1963.

2155 FOGELSON, Robert M., comp. *The Los Angeles Riots.* New York, 1969.

2156 FORBES, Jack D. *Afro-Americans in the Far West: A Handbook for Educators.* Berkeley, Calif., 1966.

2157 FOWLER, Arlen L. *The Black Infantry in the West, 1869–1891.* Westport, Conn., 1971.

2158 FRANCE, Edward. "Some Aspects of the Migration of the Negro to the San Francisco Bay Area Since 1940." Doctoral dissertation, University of California at Los Angeles, 1962.

2159 FRANKLIN, William E. "The Archy Case: The California Supreme Court Refuses to Free a Slave." *Pac Hist Rev,* XXXII (1963), 137–154.

2160 GARVIN, Roy. "Benjamin, or 'Pap,' Singleton and His Followers." *J Neg Hist,* XXXIII (1948), 7–23. Deals with the "Great Exodus" to Kansas.

2161 GLASRUD, Bruce A. *Black Texans, 1900–1930: A History.* Lubbock, Tex., 1969.

2162 GOODE, Kenneth G. *California's Black Pioneers: A Brief Historical Survey.* Santa Barbara, Calif., 1973. †

2163 HARVEY, James R. "Negroes in Colorado." *Colo Mag,* XXVI (1949), 165–176.

2164 HILL, D. G. "The Negro as a Political and Social Issue in the Oregon Country." *J Neg Hist,* XXXIII (1948), 130–145.

2165 HOGG, Thomas C. "Black Man in White Town." *Pac N W Q,* LXIII (1972), 14–21. Deals with Eugene, Oregon.

2166 JENSEN, Joan M. "Apartheid: Pacific Coast Style." *Pac Hist Rev.* XXXVIII (1969), 335–340.

2167 KATZ, William L. *The Black West.* Garden City, N.Y., 1971. Rev ed. Garden City, N.Y., 1973. A collection of pictures, documents, and historical and biographical summaries.

2168 LAPP, Rudolph M. *Archy Lee, A California Fugitive Slave.* San Francisco, 1969.

2169 LAPP, Rudolph M. "The Negro in Gold Rush California." *J Neg Hist,* XLIX (1964), 81–98.

2170 LAPP, Rudolph M. "Negro Rights Activities in Gold Rush California." *Calif Hist Soc Q,* XLV (1966), 3–20.

2171 LECKIE, William H. *The Buffalo Soldiers: A Narrative of the Negro Cavalry in the West.* Norman, Okla., 1967.

2172 LYTHGOE, Dennis L. "Negro Slavery in Utah." *Utah Hist Q,* XXXIX (1971), 40–54.

2173 MONTESANO, Philip M. "San Francisco Black Churches in the Early 1860's: Political Pressure Group." *Calif Hist Q,* LII (1973), 145–152.

2174 MONTESANO, Philip M. *Some Aspects of the Free Negro Question in San Francisco, 1849–1870.* San Francisco, 1973. †

2175 MOTHERSHEAD, Harmon. "Negro Rights in the Colorado Territory (1859–1867)." *Colo Mag,* XL (1963), 212–223.

2176 MULLER, William G. *The Twenty-Fourth Infantry: Past and Present.* [n. p., 1923]. New ed. Fort Collins, Colo., c. 1972.

2177 NANKIVELL, John H., ed. *History of the Twenty-Fifth Regiment, United States Infantry, 1869–1926.* Denver, 1927. New ed. Fort Collins, Colo., c. 1972.

2178 NASH, A. E. Keir. "The Texas Supreme Court and Trial Rights of Blacks, 1845–1860." *J Am Hist,* LVIII (1971), 622–642.

2179 PETTIT, Arthur G. "Mark Twain's Attitude Toward the Negro in the West, 1861–1867." *W Hist Q,* I (1970), 51–62.

2180 PORTER, Kenneth Wiggins. "Negroes and the Fur Trade." See 560.

2181 PORTER, Kenneth Wiggins. *The Negro on the American Frontier.* New York, 1971. A collection of essays; the best source on this topic.

2182 RICE, Lawrence D. *The Negro in Texas, 1874–1900.* Baton Rouge, La., 1971.

2182A SAVAGE, W. Sherman. *Blacks in the West.* Westport, Conn., 1976.

2183 SAVAGE, W. Sherman. "The Negro in the History of the Pacific Northwest." *J Neg Hist,* XIII (1928), 255–264.

2184 SAVAGE, W. Sherman. "The Negro in the Westward Movement." *J Neg Hist,* XXV (1940), 531–539.

2185 SAVAGE, W. Sherman. "The Negro on the Mining Frontier." *J Neg Hist,* XXX (1945), 30–46.

2186 SAVAGE, W. Sherman. "The Role of Negro Soldiers in Protecting the Indian Frontier from Intruders." *J Neg Hist,* XXXVI (1951), 25–34.

2187 SCHOEN, Harold. "The Free Negro in the Republic of Texas." *S W Hist Q,* XXXIX (1936), 292–308; XL (1936), 26–34, 85–113, 169–199, 267–289; XLI (1937), 83–108.

2188 SCHOENBERGER, Dale T. "The Black Man in the American West." *Neg Hist Bull,* XXXII (1969), 7–11.

2189 SCHUBERT, Frank N. "The Suggs Affray: The Black Cavalry in the Johnson County War." *W Hist Q,* IV (1973), 57–68.

2190 SMITH, T. Lynn. "The Redistribution of the Negro Population of the United States, 1910–1960." *J Neg Hist,* LI (1966), 155–173. Note especially pp. 166–167 on "The Movement to West-Coast Cities."

2191 SMURR, J. W. "Jim Crow Out West." *Historical Essays on Montana and the Northwest....* Eds. J. W. Smurr and K. Ross Toole. Helena, Mont., 1957.

2192 *Southwestern Historical Quarterly,* LXXVI (April 1973). Special issue on Blacks in Texas.

2193 SPOEHR, Luther W. "Sambo and the Heathen Chinee." See 2120.

2194 TALMADGE, Marian, and Iris GILMORE. *Barney Ford, Black Baron.* New York, 1973. A Colorado success story.

2195 THOMPSON, Erwin N. "The Negro Soldiers on the Frontier: A Fort Davis Case Study." *J W,* VII (1968), 217–235.

2196 THURMAN, Sue Bailey, *Pioneers of Negro Origin in California.* San Francisco, [1952].

2197 TOLL, William, "Du Bois and Turner." See 206.

2198 TOLSON, Arthur, "The Negro in Oklahoma Territory, 1889–1907: A Study in Racial Discrimination." Doctoral dissertation, University of Oklahoma, 1966.

2199 U.S. Bureau of the Census, *Negro Population, 1790–1915.* Washington, D.C., 1918. A massive statistical study important for its negative evidence of showing how small was the Black population in the West prior to the First World War.

2200 U.S. National Advisory Commission on Civil Disorders. *Report.* Washington, D.C., 1968. Also published simultaneously New York, 1968, with intro. by Tom Wicker. Essential for understanding western urban conditions and especially the violence at Watts.

2201 VAN DEUSEN, John G. "The Exodus of 1879." *J Neg Hist,* XXI (1936), 111–129. The "Exodus" was to Kansas.

2201A WAYNE, George H. "Negro Migration and Colonization in Colorado—1870–1930." *J W,* XV (1976), 102–120.

2202 Wilson, Elinor. *Jim Beckworth: Black Mountain Man and War Chief of the Crows.* Norman, Okla., 1972.

2203 WOOLFOLK, George R. "Turner's Safety Valve and Free Negro Westward Migration." See 212.

XXIV. European Ethnic Groups

2204 ARESTAD, Sverre. "The Norwegians in the Pacific Coast Fisheries." *Pac N W Q,* XXXIV (1943), 3–17.

2205 ARESTAD, Sverre. "Research Suggestions: Bibliography on the Scandinavians of the Pacific Coast." *Pac N W Q,* XXVI (1945), 269–278.

2206 BASKAUSKAS, Liucija. "An Urban Enclave: Lithuanian Refugees in Los Angeles." Doctoral dissertation, University of California, Los Angeles, 1971.

2207 BOHME, Frederick G. "A History of Italians in New Mexico." Doctoral dissertation, University of New Mexico, 1958.

2208 BOHME, Frederick G. "The Portuguese in California." *Calif Hist Soc Q,* XXXV (1956), 233–252.

2209 BRECK, Allen duPont. *The Centonnial History of the Jews of Colorado, 1859–1959.* Denver, Colo., 1960.

2210 BROOKS, Juanita. *History of the Jews in Utah and Idaho.* Salt Lake City, Utah, 1973.

2211 CROWDER, David L. "Moses Alexander, Idaho's Jewish Governor, 1914–1918." Doctoral dissertation, University of Utah, 1972.

2212 DAHLIE, Jorgen. "Old World Paths in the New: Scandinavians Find Familar Home in Washington." *Pac N W Q,* LXI (1970), 65–71.

2213 DAHLIE, Jorgen. "A Social History of Scandinavian Immigration, Washington State, 1895–1910." Doctoral dissertation, Washington State University, 1967.

2214 DORSETT, Lyle W. "The Ordeal of Colorado's Germans During World War I." *Colo Mag,* LI (1974), 277–293.

2215 DOUGLASS, William A. "The Basques of the American West: Preliminary Historical Perspectives." *Nev Hist Soc Q,* XIII (1970), 12–25.

2216 DWYER, Robert J. "The Irish in the Building of the Intermountain West." *Utah Hist Q,* XXV (1957), 221–235.

2217 EARL, Phillip. "Nevada's Italian War." See 1977.

2218 ETULAIN, Richard W. "Basque Beginnings in the Pacific Northwest." *Idaho Yes,* XVIII (1974), 26–32.

2219 GLANZ, Rudolph. *The Jews of California, From the Discovery of Gold until 1880.* New York, 1960.

2220 HUDSON, Estelle. *Czech Pioneers of the Southwest.* Dallas, Tex., 1934.

2221 JORDAN, Terry G. *German Seed in Texas Soil: Immigrant Farmers in Nineteenth-Century Texas.* Austin, Tex., 1966.

2222 LA PIERE, Richard T. "The Armenian Colony in Fresno County, California: A Study in Social Psychology." Doctoral dissertation, Stanford University, 1930.

2223 LEDER, Hans H. "Cultural Persistence in a Portuguese-American Community." Doctoral dissertation, Stanford University, 1968. San Francisco area.

2224 LEVINSON, Robert E. "American Jews in the West." *W Hist Q,* V (1974), 285–294.

2225 LEVINSON, Robert E. "The Jews in the California Gold Rush." Doctoral dissertation, University of Oregon, 1968.

2226 LUCAS, Henry S. *Netherlanders in America: Dutch Immigration to the United States and Canada, 1789–1950.* Ann Arbor, Mich., 1955.

2227 LUEBKE, Frederick C. *Immigrants and Politics: The Germans of Nebraska, 1800–1900.* Lincoln, Neb., 1969.

2228 OLIN, Spencer C., Jr. "European Immigrant and Oriental Alien." See 2107.

2229 PALMER, Hans C. "Italian Immigration and the Development of California Agriculture." Doctoral dissertation, University of California, Berkeley, 1965.

2230 PAPANIKOLAS, Helen Z. "Toil and Rage in a New Land: The Greek Immigrants in Utah." *Utah Hist Q,* XXXVIII (1970), 99–203.

2231 PATTERSON, George J. "The Unassimilated Greeks of Denver." Doctoral dissertation, University of Colorado, 1969.

2232 RICARDS, Sherman L., and George M. BLACKBURN. "The Sydney Ducks: a Demographic Analysis." *Pac Hist Rev,* XLII (1973), 20–31. An Australian group that was a favorite target for criticism and hostility during the Gold Rush and the Vigilance Committee of 1851.

2233 ROLLE, Andrew F. *The Immigrant Upraised: Italian Adventurers and Colonists in an Expanding America.* Norman, Okla., 1968. †

2234 ROWSE, A. L. *The Cousin Jacks: The Cornish in America.* New York, 1969.

2235 SHEPPERSON, Wilbur S. *Restless Strangers: Nevada's Immigrants and Their Interpreters.* Reno, Nev., 1970.

2236 STERN, Norton B. *California Jewish History; A Descriptive Bibliography: Over Five Hundred Fifty Works for the Period Gold Rush to Post-World War I.* Glendale, Calif., 1967.

2237 VORSPAN, Max, and Lloyd P. GARTNER. *History of the Jews of Los Angeles.* San Marino, Calif., 1970.

2238 WALLIS, Wilson D. *Fresno Armenians to 1919.* Ed. with intro. by Nectar Davidian. Lawrence, Kan., 1965.

2239 WINTHER, Oscar O. "English Migration to the American West, 1865–1900." *Hunt Lib Q,* XXVII (1964), 159–173.

2240 WYLLYS, Rufus K. "The French of California and Sonora." *Pac Hist Rev,* I (1932), 337–359.

XXV. Racism, Nativism, and Ethnicity

2241 BRACK, Gene M. "Mexican Opinion, American Racism, and the War of 1846." See 599.

2242 *California Historical Quarterly,* L (September 1971). Special issue on ethnic experiences in California.

2243 DANIELS, Roger, and Harry H. L. KITANO. *American Racism: Exploration of the Nature of Prejudice.* Englewood Cliffs, N.J., 1970. †

2244 DANIELS, Roger, and Spencer C. OLIN, Jr. *Racism in California: A Reader in the History of Oppression.* New York, 1972. †

2245 DE GRAAF, Lawrence B. "Recognition, Racism, and Reflections on . . . Black History." See 2148.

2246 FRAKES, George E., and Curtis B. SOLBERG, eds. *Minorities in California History.* New York, 1971. †

2247 GOSSETT, Thomas F. *Race: The History of an Idea in America.* Dallas, Tex., 1963. Rev. ed. New York, 1965. †

2248 GUZMAN, Ralph. "The Function of Anglo-American Racism in the Political Development of Chicanos." See 896.

2249 HEIZER, Robert F., and Alan J. ALMQUIST. *The Other Californians: Prejudice and Discrimination Under Spain, Mexico, and the United States to 1920.* Berkeley, Calif., 1971.

2250 *Journal of Arizona History,* XIV (Winter 1973). Special issue on minorities of the Southwest.

2251 LARSON, Robert W. "The White Caps of New Mexico." See 902.

2252 LOFTIS, Anne. *California—Where the Twain Did Meet.* See 2087.

2253 MELDRUM, George W. "The History of the Treatment of Foreign and Minority Groups in California, 1830–1860." Doctoral dissertation, Stanford University, 1949.

2254 MERRIAM, H. G. "Ethnic Settlement of Montana." *Pac Hist Rev,* XII (1943), 157–168.

2255 METZGAR, Joseph V. "Ethnic Sensibility of Spanish New Mexicans." See 907.

2256 OLMSTED, Roger, and Charles WOLLENBERG, eds. *Neither Separate Nor Equal: Race and Racism in California.* San Francisco, Calif., 1971.

2257 PITT, Leonard. "The Beginnings of Nativism in California." *Pac Hist Rev,* XXX (1961), 23–38.

2258 QUINN, Larry D. " 'Chink Chink Chinaman': The Beginning of Nativism in Montana." See 2112.

2259 RISCHIN, Moses. "Beyond the Great Divide: Immigration and the Last Frontier." *J Am Hist,* LV (1968), 42–53.

2260 RISCHIN, Moses. "Immigration, Migration, and Minorities in California: A Reassessment." *Pac Hist Rev,* XLI (1972), 71–90.

2261 SPOEHR, Luther W. "Sambo and the Heathen Chinee." See 2120.

2262 VECOLI, Rudolph J. "Ethnicity: A Neglected Dimension of American History." *The State of American History.* Ed. Herbert J. Bass. Chicago, 1971.

2263 WALDRON, Gladys H. "Antiforeign Movements in California, 1919–1929." Doctoral dissertation, University of California, Berkeley, 1945.

2264 WOLLENBERG, Charles, comp. *Ethnic Conflict in California History.* Los Angeles, 1970.

2265 WOLLENBERG, Charles. "Ethnic Experiences in California History: An Impressionistic Survey." *Calif Hist Q,* L (1971), 221–233.

XXVI. Vigilantism, Violence, and Extra-Legal Government

2266 ADAMS, Ramon F. *A Fitting Death for Billy the Kid.* Norman, Okla., 1960.

2267 ADAMS, Ramon F., comp. *Six Guns and Saddle Leather: A Bibliography of Books and Pamphlets on Western Outlaws and Gunmen.* Norman, Okla., 1954. Rev. ed., 1969.

2268 ALEXANDER, Charles C. *The Ku Klux Klan in the Southwest.* Lexington, Ken., 1965. †

2269 BALL, Larry D. "The Office of the United States Marshal in the Arizona and New Mexico Territories, 1851–1912." Doctoral dissertation, University of Colorado, 1970.

2270 BANCROFT, Hubert H. *Works.* The two volumes entitled *Popular Tribunals.* See 1.

2271 BELL, William G. "Frontier Lawman." *Am W,* I (Summer 1964), 4–13, 78.

2272 BETENSON, Lula P. (as told to Dora FLACK). *Butch Cassidy, My Brother.* Provo, Utah, 1975.

2273 BIRNEY, Hoffman. *Vigilantes.* Philadelphia, 1929. The Plummer gang in Montana.

2274 BLEW, Robert W. "Vigilantism in Los Angeles, 1835–1874." *S Calif Q,* LIV (1972), 11–30.

2275 BOGUE, Allan G. "The Iowa Claim Clubs: Symbol and Substance." *The Public Lands: Studies in the History of the Public Domain.* Ed. Vernon Carstensen. See 1443.

2276 BROWN, Richard Maxwell. "Historical Patterns of Violence in America," and "The American Vigilante Tradition." *Violence in America: Historical and Comparative Perspectives: A Report Submitted to the National Commission on the Causes and Prevention of Violence.* Eds. Hugh D. Graham and Ted R. Gurr. New York, 1969.

2277 BROWN, Richard Maxwell. "Pivot of American Vigilantism: The San Francisco Vigilance Committee of 1856." *Reflections of Western Historians.* Ed. John A. Carroll, Tucson, Ariz., 1969.

2277A BROWN, Richard Maxwell. *Strain of Violence: Historical Studies of American Violence and Vigilantism.* New York, 1975.

2278 BURG, B. Richard. "Vigilantes in Lawless Denver: The City of the Plains." *Great Plains J,* VI (1967), 68–84.

2279 CARRANCO, Lynwood. "Chinese Expulsion from Humboldt County." See 2050.

2280 CAUGHEY, John W. *Their Majesties, the Mob.* Chicago, 1960.

2281 CAWELTI, John G. "The Gunfighter and Society." *Am W,* V (March 1968), 30–35, 76–78.

2282 CONOT, Robert. *Rivers of Blood.* See 2142.

2283 CRANE, Paul, and T. A. LARSON, "The Chinese Massacre." See 2058.

2284 CUNNINGHAM, Eugene. *Triggernometry: A Gallery of Gunfighters.* Caldwell, Idaho, 1941.

2285 DAVIS, James H. "Colorado under the Klan." *Colo Mag,* XLII (1965), 93–108.

2286 DIMSDALE, Thomas J. *The Vigilantes of Montana, or Popular Justice in the Rocky Mountains.* Virginia City, Mont., 1866. New ed. with intro. by E. De Golyer. Norman, Okla., 1953.

2287 DYKSTRA, Robert R. *The Cattle Towns.* See 1154.

2288 FAULK, Odie B. *Tombstone: Myth and Reality.* See 1844.

2289 FOGELSON, Robert M., comp. *The Los Angeles Riots.* See 2155.

2290 FRANTZ, Joe B. "The Frontier Tradition: An Invitation to Violence." *Violence in America: Historical and Comparative Perspectives: A Report Submitted to the National Commission on the Causes and Prevention of Violence.* Eds. Hugh D. Graham and Ted R. Gurr. New York, 1969.

2291 GARD, Wayne. *Frontier Justice.* Norman, Okla., 1949. Repr. Norman, Okla., 1968.

2292 GARDNER, Richard M. *Grito! Reies Tijerina and the New Mexico Land Grant War.* See 889.

2293 GARNETT, Porter, ed. *Papers of the San Francisco Committee of Vigilance of 1851.* 3 vols. Berkeley, Calif., 1910–1919.

2294 GATES, Paul W. *History of Public Land Law Development.* On squatter's claims organizations. See 1467.

2295 GOULD, Lewis L. "A. S. Mercer and the Johnson County War: A Reappraisal." *Ariz W,* VII (1965), 5–20.

2296 GOWER, Calvin W. "Vigilantes." *Colo Mag,* XLI (1964), 93–104.

2297 GROVER, David H. *Diamondfield Jack: A Study in Frontier Justice.* Reno, Nev., 1968.

2298 GUNNS, Albert F. "Civil Liberties and Crisis: The Status of Civil Liberties in the Pacific Northwest, 1917–1940." Doctoral Dissertation, University of Washington, 1971.

2299 HENDRICKS, George D. *The Bad Man of the West.* Rev. ed. San Antonio, Tex., 1959.

2300 HICKS, Jimmie. "The Frontier and American Law." *Great Plains J,* VI (1967), 53–67.

2301 HOLDEN, W. C. "Law and Lawlessness on the Texas Frontier, 1875–1890." *S W Hist Q,* XLIV (1940), 188–203.

2302 HOLLON, W. Eugene. *Frontier Violence: Another Look.* New York, 1974.

2303 HUTTON, Harold. *Doc Middleton: Life and Legends of the Notorious Plains Outlaw.* Chicago, 1974.

2304 JENSEN, Vernon H. *Heritage of Conflict.* On labor strife. See 1065.

2305 JORDAN, Philip D. "Frontier Law and Order." *N Dak Hist,* XXXIX (1972), 6–12.

2306 JORDAN, Philip D. *Frontier Law and Order: Ten Essays.* Lincoln, Neb., 1970.

2307 JORDAN, Philip D. "The Town Marshal and the Police." *People of the Plains and Mountains. . . .* Ed. Ray Allen Billington. Westport, Conn., 1973.

2308 *Journal of Arizona History,* XIV (Autumn 1973). Special issue on frontier law and lawlessness.

2309 KARLIN, Jules A. "Anti-Chinese Outbreak in Tacoma," and "Anti-Chinese Outbreaks in Seattle." See 2077. 2078.

2310 KELEHER, William A. *Violence in Lincoln County, 1869–1881.* Albuquerque, N.M., 1957. †

2311 LAKE, Stuart N. *Wyatt Earp: Frontier Marshal.* Boston, 1931.

2312 LANGFORD, Nathaniel P. *Vigilante Days and Ways; The Pioneers of the Rockies: The Makers and Making of Montana, Idaho, Oregon, Washington, and Wyoming.* 2 vols. Boston, 1890. Repr. New York, n.d.

2313 LANGUM, David J. "Pioneer Justice on the Overland Trails." *W Hist Q,* V (1974) 421–439.

2314 LARSON, Robert W. "The White Caps of New Mexico." See 902.

2315 LEVI, Steven C. "San Francisco's Law and Order Committee, 1916." *J W,* XII (1973), 53–70.

2316 LINGENFELTER, Richard E. *The Hardrock Miners.* On labor strife. See 1075.

2317 MERCER, Asa S. *Banditti of the Plains; or, The Cattlemen's Invasion of Wyoming in 1892.* Cheyenne, Wyo., 1894. Repr. with foreword by William H. Kittrell. Norman, Okla., 1954.

2318 METZ, Leon C. *Pat Garrett: The Story of a Western Lawman.* Norman, Okla., 1974.

2319 MILLER, Nyle H., and Joseph W. SNELL. *Great Gunfighters of the Kansas Cowtowns, 1867–1886.* Lincoln, Neb., 1963. †

2320 MOORE, Waddy W. "Some Aspects of Crime and Punishment on the Arkansas Frontier." *Ark Hist Q,* XXIII (1964), 50–64.

2321 MULLIN, Robert N. "The Boyhood of Billy the Kid." *S W Stud,* V (1967), 5–26.

2322 NESBIT, Robert C. *"He Built Seattle": A Biography of Judge Thomas Burke.* See 1797. Chap. VII: "Law and Order" (describes anti-Chinese outbreak).

2323 NUNIS, Doyce, ed. *The San Francisco Vigilance Committee of 1856: Three Views: William T. Coleman, William T. Sherman, James O'Meara.* Los Angeles, Calif., 1971. (Los Angeles Westerners Publication no. 103)

2324 O'CONNOR, Richard. *Bat Masterson.* Garden City, N.Y., 1957. †

2325 OLSEN, Barton C. "Lawlessness and Vigilantes in America: An Historical Analysis Emphasizing California and Montana." Doctoral dissertation, University of Utah, 1968.

2326 OSGOOD, Ernest S. *Day of the Cattleman.* On cattlemen's associations. See 1199.

2327 PAUL, Rodman W. *Mining Frontiers of the Far West.* On miners' codes, courts, and self-government. See 1090.

2328 PAUL, Rodman W. "'Old Californians' in British Gold Fields." *Hunt Lib Q,* XVII (1954), 161–172. Compares experience of mining camps under American and British rule.

2329 PAUL, Rodman W. "Origin of the Chinese Issue in California." See 2110.

2330 PERRIGO, Lynn L. "Law and Order in Early Colorado Camps." See 1091.

2331 PRASSEL, Frank R. *The Western Peace Officer: A Legacy of Law and Order.* Norman, Okla., 1972.

2332 RICARDS, Sherman L., and George M. BLACKBURN. "The Sydney Ducks." See 2232.

2333 ROBERTS, Gary L. "The West's Gunmen." *Am W,* VIII (January 1971), 10–15, 64; (March 1971), 18–23, 61–62.

2334 ROSA, Joseph G. *The Gunfighter: Man or Myth?* Norman, Okla., 1969.

2335 ROSA, Joseph G. *Wild Bill: The Life and Adventures of James Butler Hickok.* 2d ed., rev. and enl. Norman, Okla., 1974.

2336 SAXTON, Alexander. *The Indispensable Enemy.* See 2116.

2337 SCHERER, James A. B. *The Lion of the Vigilantes: William T. Coleman and the Life of Old San Francisco.* Indianapolis, Ind., 1939.

2338 SLOTKIN, Richard. *Regeneration through Violence.* See 294.

2339 SMITH, Helena H. *The War on Powder River.* New York, 1966. †

2340 SMITH, Robert W. *The Coeur d'Alene Mining War.* See 1106.

2341 SMURR, John W. "Afterthoughts on the Vigilantes." *Mont: Mag W Hist,* VIII (April 1958), 8–20.

2342 SONNICHSEN, C. L. *The Texas Feuds.* Rev. ed. Albuquerque, N.M., 1971. †

2343 STECKMESSER, Kent L. *The Western Hero in History and Legend.* Norman, Okla., 1965.

2344 STEWART, George R. *Committee of Vigilance: Revolution in San Francisco, 1851.* Boston, 1964.

2345 TAYLOR, Morris F. "The Coe Gang: Rustlers of 'Robbers' Roost.' " *Colo Mag,* LI (1974), 199–215.

2346 THOMSON, George. "The History of Penal Institutions in the Rocky Mountain West, 1846–1900." Doctoral dissertation, University of Colorado, 1965.

2347 TRIMBLE, William J. *Mining Advance into the Inland Empire.* On law and government in American territories and British Columbia. See 1119.

2348 TYLER, Robert L. *Rebels of the Woods: The IWW.* See 1613.

2349 VALENTINE, Alan C. *Vigilante Justice.* New York, 1956.

2350 WARD, James R. "The Texas Rangers, 1919–1935: A Study in Law Enforcement." Doctoral dissertation, Texas Christian University, 1972.

2351 WEBB, Walter Prescott. *The Texas Rangers: A Century of Frontier Defense.* Boston, 1935. Rev. ed. Austin, Tex., 1965.

2352 WEST, John O. "To Die Like a Man: The 'Good' Outlaw Tradition in the American Southwest." Doctoral dissertation, University of Texas, 1964.

2353 WILLIAMS, Mary F. *History of the San Francisco Committee of Vigilance of 1851: A Study of the Social Control on the California Frontier in the Days of the Gold Rush.* Berkeley, Calif., 1921.

XXVII. State and Territorial Government and Politics in the Nineteenth Century

2354 ALBRIGHT, Robert E. "Politics and Public Opinion in the Western Statehood Movement of the 1880's." *Pac Hist Rev,* III (1934), 296–306.

2355 ATHEARN, Robert G. "Early Territorial Montana: A Problem in Colonial Administration." *Mont: Mag W Hist,* I (1951), 15–35.

2356 BAKKEN, Gordon M. "The English Common Law in the Rocky Mountain West." *Ariz W,* XI (1969), 109–128.

2357 BAKKEN, Gordon M. "Rocky Mountain Constitution-Making, 1850–1912." Doctoral dissertation, University of Wisconsin, 1970.

2358 BARR, Alwyn, *Reconstruction to Reform: Texas Politics, 1876–1906.* Austin, Tex., 1971.

2359 BERKHOFER, Robert F. "Jefferson, the Ordinance of 1784, and the Origins of the American Territorial System." *Wm Mar Q,* XXIX (1972), 231–262.

2360 BLOEDEL, Richard Henry. "The Alaska Statehood Movement." Doctoral dissertation, University of Washington, 1974.

2361 BLOOM, John P., ed. *The American Territorial System.* Athens, Ohio, 1973. An especially important volume that includes papers and proceedings of the Conference on the History of Territories, November 3–4, 1969.

2362 CARTER, Clarence E., and John P. BLOOM, eds. *The Territorial Papers of the United States.* Washington, D.C., 1934–; New York, 1973–

2363 COOLEY, Everett L. "Carpetbag Rule: Territorial Government in Utah." *Utah Hist Q,* XXVI (1958), 107–129.

2364 DEUTSCH, Herman J. "The Evolution of Territorial and State Boundaries in the Inland Empire of the Pacific Northwest." *Pac N W Q,* LI (1960), 115–131.

2365 EBLEN, Jack E. *The First and Second United States Empires: Governors and Territorial Government, 1784–1912.* Pittsburgh, Pa., 1968.

2366 EBLEN, Jack E. "Status, Mobility, and Empire: The Territorial Governors, 1869–1890." *Pac N W Q,* LX (1969), 145–153.

2367 ELLISON, Joseph. *California and the Nation, 1850–1869: A Study of the Relations of a Frontier Community with the Federal Government.* Berkeley, Calif., 1927.

2368 ELLISON, William H. *A Self-Governing Dominion: California, 1849–1860.* Berkeley, Calif., 1950.

2369 FISCHER, LeRoy H., ed. "The Governors of Oklahoma Territory." *Chron Okla,* LIII (1975), 3–144. A collection of essays.

2370 FRANKLIN, William E., Jr. "The Political Career of Peter Hardeman Burnett." Doctoral dissertation, Stanford University, 1954.

2371 FREDMAN, L. E. "Broderick: A Reassessment." *Pac Hist Rev,* XXX (1961), 39–46.

2372 GOODWIN, Cardinal L. *The Establishment of State Government in California, 1846–1850.* New York, 1914.

2373 GOULD, Lewis L. *Wyoming: A Political History, 1868–1896.* New Haven, Conn., 1968.

2374 GOWER, Calvin W. "Gold Rush Governments." *Colo Mag,* LXII (1965), 115–132.

2375 GRESSLEY, Gene M. *West by East: The American West in the Gilded Age.* Provo, Utah, 1972. †

2376 GUICE, John D. W. *The Rocky Mountain Bench: The Territorial Supreme Courts of Colorado, Montana, and Wyoming, 1861–1890.* New Haven, Conn., 1972.

2377 HENDRICKSON, James E. *Joe Lane of Oregon: Machine Politics and the Sectional Crisis, 1849–1861.* New Haven, Conn., 1967.

2378 HENSEL, Donald W. "A History of the Colorado Constitution in the Nineteenth Century." Doctoral dissertation, University of Colorado, 1957.

2379 HINCKLEY, Ted C. *The Americanization of Alaska.* On government, politics, and relations with Washington. See 54.

2380 HOGAN, William R. *The Texas Republic: A Social and Economic History.* Norman, Okla., 1946. †

2381 HURT, Peyton. "The Rise and Fall of the 'Know Nothings' in California." *Calif Hist Soc Q,* IX (1930), 16–49, 99–128.

2382 JACKSON, W. Turrentine. "The Governorship of Wyoming, 1885–1889: A Study in Territorial Politics." *Pac Hist Rev,* XIII (1944), 1–11.

2383 JOHANNSEN, Robert W. *Frontier Politics and the Sectional Conflict: The Pacific Northwest on the Eve of the Civil War.* Seattle, Wash., 1955. Repr. with abbreviated title, Seattle, Wash., 1966.

2384 JOHANSEN, Dorothy O. "A Tentative Appraisal of Territorial Government in Oregon." *Pac Hist Rev,* XVIII (1949), 485–499.

2385 KAPLAN, Mirth T. "Courts, Counselors and Cases: The Judiciary of Oregon's Provisional Government." *Ore Hist Q,* LXII (1961), 117–163.

2386 LAIN, Bobby Dave. "North of Fifty-Three: Army, Treasury Department, and Navy Administration of Alaska, 1867–1884." Doctoral dissertation, University of Texas, 1974.

2387 LAMAR, Howard R. *Dakota Territory, 1861–1889: A Study of Frontier Politics.* New Haven, Conn., 1956.

2388 LAMAR, Howard R. *The Far Southwest, 1846–1912: A Territorial History.* New Haven, Conn., 1966.†

2389 LARSON, Gustive O. *The 'Americanization' of Utah for Statehood.* See 977.

2390 LARSON, Robert W. *New Mexico's Quest for Statehood, 1846–1912.* Albuquerque, N.M., 1968.

2391 LIMBAUGH, Ronald H. "The Idaho Spoilsmen: Federal Administrators and Idaho Territorial Politics, 1863–1890." Doctoral dissertation, University of Idaho, 1967.

2392 MARLEY, Bert W. "Alaska: Its Transition to Statehood." Doctoral dissertation, University of Utah, 1970.

2393 MORGAN, Dale L. "The State of Deseret." See 988.

2394 NEIL, William M. "The American Territorial System Since the Civil War: A Summary Analysis." *Ind Mag Hist,* LX (1964), 219–240.

2395 NEIL, William M. "The Territorial Governor in the Rocky Mountain West." Doctoral dissertation, University of Chicago, 1951.

2396 NICHOLS, Roy F. "The Territories: Seedbeds of Democracy." *Neb Hist,* XXXV (1954), 159–172.

2397 OWENS, Kenneth N. "Frontier Governors: A Study of the Territorial Executives in the History of Washington, Idaho, Montana, Wyoming, and Dakota Territories." Doctoral dissertation, University of Minnesota, 1959.

2398 OWENS, Kenneth N. "Patterns and Structure in Western Territorial Politics." *W Hist Q,* I (1970), 373–392.

2399 OWENS, Kenneth N. "Research Opportunities in Western Territorial History." *Ariz W,* VIII (1966), 7–18.

2400 POLL, Richard D. "The Political Reconstruction of Utah Territory, 1866–1890." See 1000.

2401 POMEROY, Earl. "California, 1846–1860: Politics of a Representative Frontier State." *Calif Hist Soc Q,* XXXII (1953), 291–302.

2402 POMEROY, Earl. *The Territories and the United States, 1861–1890: Studies in Colonial Administration.* Philadephia, 1947. Repr. Seattle, Wash., 1970. †

2403 RICHARDS, Kent D. "The American Colonial System in Nevada." *Nev Hist Soc Q,* XIII (1970), 29–39.

2404 ROTHMAN, David J. *Politics and Power: The United States Senate, 1869–1901.* Cambridge, Mass., 1966. †

2405 SHINN, Charles H. *Mining-Camps: A Study in American Frontier Government.* New York, 1885. Repr., ed. by Rodman W. Paul. New York, 1965.

2406 SIEGEL, Stanley. *A Political History of the Texas Republic, 1836–1845.* Austin, Tex., 1956.

2407 SMURR, John W. "Territorial Constitutions: A Legal History of the Frontier Governments Erected by Congress in the American West, 1787–1900." Doctoral dissertation, Indiana University, 1960.

2408 SPENCE, Clark C. "Beggars to Washington: Montana's Territorial Delegates." *Mont: Mag W Hist,* XXIV (Winter 1974), 2–13.

2409 SPENCE, Clark C. *Territorial Politics and Government in Montana: 1864–89.* Urbana, Ill., 1975.

2410 SWISHER, Carl B. *Motivation and Political Technique in the California Constitutional Convention, 1878–79.* Claremont, Calif., 1930.

2411 WAGONER, Jay J. *Arizona Territory, 1863–1912: A Political History.* Tucson, Ariz., 1970.

2412 WELLS, Merle W. "The Creation of the Territory of Idaho." *Pac N W Q,* XL (1949), 106–123.

2413 WELLS, Merle W. "The Idaho Admission Movement, 1888–1890." *Ore Hist Q,* LVI (1955), 27–46.

2414 WELLS, Merle W. "Territorial Government in the Inland Empire." *Pac N W Q,* XLIV (1953), 80–87.

2415 WESTPHALL, Victor, *Thomas Benton Catron and his Era.* Tucson, Ariz., 1973.

2416 WHITE, Lonnie J. *Politics on the Southwestern Frontier: Arkansas Territory, 1819–1836.* Memphis, Tenn., 1964.

2417 WILLIAMS, David A. "California Democrats of 1860: Division, Description, Defeat." *S Calif Q,* LV (1973), 239–252.

2418 WILLIAMS, David A. *David C. Broderick: A Political Portrait.* San Marino, Calif., 1969.

2419 WILLIAMS, R. Hal. *The Democratic Party and California Politics, 1880–1896.* Stanford, Calif., 1973.

XXVIII. Western Politics and Reform Movements since 1890

2420 *Agricultural History,* XXXIX (April 1965). Special issue on Populism. Includes articles by Norman Pollack, Oscar Handlin, Irwin Unger, and comments by J. Rogers Hollingsworth.

2421 ALLEN, Howard W. "Miles Poindexter and the Progressive Movement." *Pac N W Q,* LIII (1962), 114–122.

2422 ARRINGTON, Leonard J. "The New Deal in the West: A Preliminary Statistical Inquiry." *Pac Hist Rev,* XXXVIII (1969), 311–316.

2423 ASHBY, LeRoy. *The Spearless Leader: Senator Borah and the Progressive Movement in the 1920's.* Urbana, Ill., 1972.

2424 BATES, J. Leonard. "Politics and Ideology: Thomas J. Walsh and the Rise of Populism." *Pac N W Q,* LXV (1974), 49–56.

2425 BEAN, Walton E. *Boss Ruef's San Francisco: The Story of the Union Labor Party, and the Graft Prosecution.* Berkeley, Calif., 1952. †

2426 BEAN, Walton E. "Ideas of Reform in California." *Calif Hist Q,* LI (1972), 213–226.

2427 BICHA, Karel D. "Jerry Simpson: Populist Without Principles." *J Am Hist,* LIV (1967), 291–306.

2428 BLACKFORD, Mansel G. "Reform Politics in Seattle During the Progressive Era, 1902–1916." *Pac N W Q,* LIX (1968), 177–185.

2429 BLACKORBY, Edward C. *Prairie Rebel: The Public Life of William Lemke.* Lincoln, Neb., 1963.

2430 BLANKENSHIP, Warren M. "Progressives and the Progressive Party in Oregon, 1906–1916." Doctoral dissertation, University of Oregon, 1966.

2431 BRAMMER, Clarence L. "Thomas J. Walsh: Spokesman for Montana." Doctoral dissertation, University of Missouri, 1972.

2432 BRENNAN, John. *Silver and the First New Deal.* Reno, Nev., 1969.

2433 BRODHEAD, Michael J. *Persevering Populist: The Life of Frank Doster.* Reno, Nev., 1969.

2434 BUCK, Solon J. *The Agrarian Crusade: A Chronicle of the Farmer in Politics.* New Haven, Conn. 1920.

2435 BUCK, Solon J. *The Granger Movement.* See 1274.

2436 BULLOCK, Paul. " 'Rabbits and Radicals': Richard Nixon's 1946 Campaign Against Jerry Voorhis." *S Calif Q,* LV (1973), 319–359.

2437 BURBANK, Garin. "Agrarian Radicals and Their Opponents: Political Conflict in Southern Oklahoma, 1910–1924." *J Am Hist,* LVIII (1971), 5–23.

2438 BURKE, Robert E. *Olson's New Deal for California.* Berkeley, Calif., 1953.

2439 BURTON, Robert E. *Democrats of Oregon: The Pattern of Minority Politics, 1900–1956.* Eugene, Ore., 1970.

2439A CHAN, Loren B. *Sagebrush Statesman: Tasker L. Oddie of Nevada.* Reno, Nev., 1973.

2440 CLANTON, O. Gene. *Kansas Populism: Ideas and Men.* Lawrence, Kan., 1969.

2441 CLARK, Norman H. *The Dry Years: Prohibition and Social Change in Washington.* Seattle, Wash., 1965.

2442 CLINCH, Thomas A. *Urban Populism and Free Silver in Montana: A Narrative of Ideology in Political Action.* Missoula, Mont., 1970.

2443 COLE, Robert L. "The Democratic Party in Washington State, 1919–1933: Barometer of Social Change." Doctoral dissertation, University of Washington, 1972.

2444 COLETTA, Paolo E. *William Jennings Bryan.* 3 vols. Lincoln, Neb., 1964, 1969.

2445 COOMBS, F. Alan. "Joseph Christopher O'Mahoney: The New Deal Years." Doctoral dissertation, University of Illinois, 1968.

2446 DE GRAZIA, Alfred. *The Western Public, 1952 and Beyond.* Stanford, Calif., 1954.

2447 DELMATIER, Royce D. "The Rebirth of the Democratic Party in California, 1928–1938." Doctoral dissertation, University of California, Berkeley, 1955.

2448 DONNELLY, Thomas C., ed. *Rocky Mountain Politics.* Albuquerque, N.M., 1940.

2449 ELLIS, Elmer. *Henry Moore Teller, Defender of the West.* Caldwell, Idaho, 1941.

2450 EVANS, Tony H. "Oregon Progressive Reform, 1902–1914." Doctoral dissertation, University of California, Berkeley, 1966.

2451 FITE, Gilbert C. *Peter Norbeck: Prairie Statesman.* Columbia, Mo., 1948.

2452 GABOURY, William J. "Dissension in the Rockies: A History of Idaho Populism." Doctoral dissertation, University of Idaho, 1966.

2453 GABOURY, William J. "From Statehouse to Bullpen: Idaho Populism and the Coeur d' Alene Troubles of the 1890's." *Pac N W Q,* LVIII (1967), 14–22.

2454 GLAD, Paul W. *The Trumpet Soundeth: William Jennings Bryan and His Democracy, 1896–1912.* Lincoln, Neb., 1960. †

2455 GLASS, Mary Ellen. *Silver and Politics in Nevada, 1892–1902.* Reno, Nev., 1969.

2456 GOULD, Lewis L. *Progressives and Prohibitionists: Texas Democrats in the Wilson Era.* Austin, Tex., 1973.

2457 GOULD, Lewis L. "Western Range Senators and the Payne-Aldrich Tariff." *Pac N W Q,* LXIV (1973), 49–56.

2458 GRASSMAN, Curtis E. "Prologue to California Reform: The Democratic Impulse, 1886–1898." *Pac Hist Rev,* XLII (1973), 518–536.

2459 GRIFFITHS, David B. "Far Western Populism: The Case of Utah, 1893–1900." *Utah Hist Q,* XXXVII (1969), 396–407.

2460 GRIFFITHS, David B. "Far-Western Populist Thought: A Comparative Study of John R. Rogers and Davis H. Waite." *Pac N W Q,* LX (1969), 183–192.

2461 GRIFFITHS, David B. "Populism in the Far West, 1890–1900." Doctoral dissertation, University of Washington, 1967.

2462 HARVEY, Richard B. "Governor Earl Warren of California: A Study in 'Non-Partisan' Republican Politics." *Calif Hist Soc Q*, XLVI (1967), 33–51.

2463 HENDERSON, Lloyd R. "Earl Warren and California Politics." Doctoral dissertation, University of California, Berkeley, 1965.

2464 HENDERSON, Richard B. *Maury Maverick: A Political Biography*. Austin, Tex., 1970.

2465 HENNINGS, Robert E. "California Democratic Politics in the Period of Republican Ascendancy." *Pac Hist Rev*, XXXI (1962), 267–280.

2466 HENNINGS, Robert E. "James D. Phelan and the Wilson Progressives of California." Doctoral dissertation, University of California, 1961.

2467 HICKS, John D. *The Populist Revolt: A History of the Farmers' Alliance and the People's Party*. Minneapolis, Minn., 1931. Repr. Lincoln, Neb., 1961. †

2468 HOLMES, Jack E. *Politics in New Mexico*. Albuquerque, N.M. 1967.

2469 ISRAEL, Fred L. *Nevada's Key Pittman*. Lincoln, Neb., 1963.

2470 JOHNSON, Claudius O. *Borah of Idaho* New York, 1936; Seattle, 1967. †

2471 JONAS, Frank H., ed. *Bibliography on Western Politics: Selected, Annotated, with Introductory Essays*. Salt Lake City, Utah, 1958. Supplement to *W Pol Q*, XI, no. 4 (December 1958). Has a separate essay and bibliography for each western state.

2472 JONAS, Frank H., ed. *Politics in the American West*. Salt Lake City, Utah, 1969. Has a separate essay on each western state, including Alaska and Hawaii. The bibliography, pp. 499–528, brings up to date Jonas' previous bibliography, see 2471.

2472A KARLIN, Jules A. *Joseph M. Dixon of Montana*. 2 vols. Missoula, Mont., 1974.

2473 KERR, William T., Jr. "The Progressives of Washington, 1910–1912." *Pac N W Q*, LV (1964), 16–27.

2474 KOEPPLIN, Leslie W. "A Relationship of Reform: Immigrants and Progressives in the Far West." Doctoral dissertation, University of California, Los Angeles, 1971.

2475 LARSON, Robert W. *New Mexico Populism: A Study of Radical Protest in a Western Territory*. Boulder, Colo., 1974.

2476 LARSON, T. A. "The New Deal in Wyoming." *Pac Hist Rev*, XXXVIII (1969), 249–273.

2477 LINK, Arthur S., and William M. LEARY, Jr., comps. *The Progressive Era and the Great War, 1896–1920*. New York, 1969. †

2478 LOWER, Richard C. "Hiram Johnson: The Making of an Irreconcilable." *Pac Hist Rev*, XLI (1972), 505–526.

2479 LOWITT, Richard. *George W. Norris: The Making of a Progressive, 1861–1912*. Syracuse, N.Y., 1963; *George W. Norris: The Persistence of a Progressive, 1913–1933*. Urbana, Ill., 1971.

2479A MCCARTHY, G. Michael. "Colorado's Populist Party and the Progressive Movement." *J W*, XV (1976), 54–75.

2480 MCCARTHY, G. Michael. "The People's Party in Colorado: A Profile of Populist Leadership." *Ag Hist*, XLVII (1973), 146–155.

2481 MCCLINTOCK, Thomas C. "J. Allen Smith, A Pacific Northwest Progressive." *Pac N W Q,* LIII (1962), 49–59.

2482 MCCOY, Donald R. *Landon of Kansas.* Lincoln, Neb., 1966.

2483 MCKENNA, Marian. *Borah.* Ann Arbor, Mich., 1961.

2484 MALONE, Michael P. *C. Ben Ross and the New Deal in Idaho.* Seattle, Wash., 1970.

2485 MALONE, Michael P. "Montana Politics and the New Deal." *Mont: Mag W Hist,* XXI (1971), 2–11.

2486 MOODY, Eric N. "Nevada's Bull Moose Progressives: The Formation and Function of a State Political Party in 1912." *Nev Hist Soc Q,* XVI (1973), 157–179.

2487 MORRIS, John R. "Davis Hanson Waite: The Ideology of a Western Populist." Doctoral dissertation, University of Colorado, 1965.

2488 MOWRY, George. *The California Progressives.* Berkeley, Calif., 1951. †

2489 MURRAY, Keith A. "Issues and Personalities of Pacific Northwest Politics, 1889–1950." *Pac N W Q,* XLI (1950), 213–233.

2490 NUGENT, Walter T. K. "Some Parameters of Populism." *Ag Hist,* XL (1966), 255–270.

2491 NUGENT, Walter T. K. *The Tolerant Populists: Kansas Populism and Nativism.* Chicago, 1963.

2492 NYE, Russel B. *Midwestern Progressive Politics: A Historical Study of Its Origins and Development, 1870–1950.* East Lansing, Mich., 1951.

2493 OLIN, Spencer C. *California's Prodigal Sons: Hiram Johnson and the Progressives, 1911–1917.* Berkeley, Calif., 1968.

2494 OSTRANDER, Gilman M. *The Prohibition Movement in California, 1848–1933.* Berkeley, Calif., 1957.

2495 PARSONS, Stanley B. *The Populist Context: Rural versus Urban Power on a Great Plains Frontier.* Westport, Conn., 1973.

2496 PATTERSON, James T. "The New Deal and the States." *Am Hist Rev,* LXXIII (1967), 70–84.

2497 PATTERSON, James T. "The New Deal in the West." *Pac Hist Rev,* XXXVIII (1969), 317–327.

2498 PETERSON, F. Ross. *Prophet Without Honor: Glen H. Taylor and the Fight for American Liberalism.* Lexington, Ken., 1974.

2499 "Politics in the West." *Journal of the West,* XIII (October 1974). Special issue.

2500 POLLACK, Norman. *The Populist Response to Industrial America: Midwestern Populist Thought.* Cambridge, Mass., 1962. †

2501 PUTNAM, Jackson K. *Old-Age Politics in California: From Richardson to Regan.* Stanford, Calif., 1970.

2502 ROEDER, Richard B. "Montana in the Early Years of the Progressive Period." Doctoral dissertation, University of Pennsylvania, 1971.

2503 ROGIN, Michael P., and John L. SHOVER. *Political Change in California: Critical Elections and Social Movements, 1890–1966.* Westport, Conn., 1970. †

2504 ROSE, Alice. "The Rise of California Insurgency: Origins of the League of Lincoln-Roosevelt Republican Clubs, 1900–1907." Doctoral dissertation, Stanford University, 1942.

2505 ROWLEY, William D. "Francis G. Newlands: A Westerner's Search for a Progressive and White America." *Nev Hist Soc Q,* XVII (1974), 69–79.

2506 RUETTEN, Richard T. "Burton K. Wheeler of Montana: A Progressive Between Wars." Doctoral dissertation, University of Oregon, 1961.

2507 RUETTEN, Richard T. "Senator Burton K. Wheeler and Insurgency in the 1920's." *The American West: A Reorientation.* Ed. Gene M. Gressley. Laramie, Wyo., 1966.

2508 SALOUTOS, Theodore. "The Professors and the Populists." *Ag Hist,* XL (1966), 235–254.

2509 SALOUTOS, Theodore, and John D. HICKS. *Agricultural Discontent in the Middle West, 1900–1939.* Madison, Wis., 1951. Repr. with new title, *Twentieth Century Populism.* Lincoln, Neb., 1964.

2510 SAXTON, Alexander. "San Francisco Labor and the Populist and Progressive Insurgencies." *Pac Hist Rev,* XXXIV (1965), 421–438.

2511 SCHRUBEN, Francis W. *Kansas in Turmoil, 1930–1936.* Columbia, Mo., 1969.

2512 SCOTT, George W. "Arthur B. Langlie: Republican Governor in a Democratic State." Doctoral dissertation, University of Washington, 1971.

2513 SMITH, A. Robert. *The Tiger in the Senate: The Biography of Wayne Morse.* Garden City, N.Y., 1962.

2514 SPRITZER, Donald E. "B. K. Wheeler and Jim Murray: Senators in Conflict." *Mont: Mag W Hist,* XXIII (1973), 16–33.

2515 STEDMAN, Murray S., Jr., and Susan W. STEDMAN. *Discontent at the Polls: A Study of Farmer and Labor Parties, 1827–1948.* New York, 1950. An analysis done chiefly through statistics and graphs.

2516 STRATTON, David H. "Two Western Senators and Teapot Dome: Thomas J. Walsh and Albert B. Fall." *Pac N W Q,* LXV (1974), 57–65.

2517 TINSLEY, James A. "The Progressive Movement in Texas." Doctoral dissertation, University of Wisconsin, 1954.

2518 TRASK, David S. "The Nebraska Populist Party: A Social and Political Analysis." Doctoral dissertation, University of Nebraska, 1971.

2519 TYSON, Carl. "A Bibliographical Essay: Politics in the West." *J W,* XIII (1974), 117–122.

2520 WALSH, James P. "Abe Ruef Was No Boss: Machine Politics, Reform, and San Francisco." *Calif Hist Q,* LI (1972), 3–16.

2521 WALTERS, Donald E. "Populism in California, 1889–1900." Doctoral dissertation, University of California, Berkeley, 1952.

2522 WEINSTEIN, Allen. *Prelude to Populism: Origins of the Silver Issue, 1867–1878.* New Haven, Conn., 1970.

2523 WEISS, Stuart L. "Maury Maverick and the Liberal Bloc." *J Am Hist,* LVII (1971), 880–895.

2524 WELLS, Merle W. "Fred T. Dubois and the Idaho Progressives." *Idaho Yes,* IV (Summer 1960), 24–31. Includes comment by Robert E. Burke.

2525 WICKENS, James F. "The New Deal in Colorado." *Pac Hist Rev,* XXXVIII (1969), 275–291.

2526 WOODWARD, Robert C. "W. S. U'Ren and the Single Tax in Oregon." *Ore Hist Q,* LXI (1960), 46–63.

2527 WOODWARD, Robert C. "William S. U'Ren: A Progressive Era Personality." *Idaho Yes,* IV (Summer 1960), 4–10.

2528 WRIGHT, James E. *The Politics of Populism: Dissent in Colorado.* New Haven, Conn., 1974.

XXIX. Conservation and Concern for the Environment; the National Parks and the Wilderness

See also: Lumbering and Forestry; Cattle and Sheep

2529 BALDWIN, Donald N. "Wilderness: Concept and Change." *Colo Mag,* XLIV (1967), 224–240.

2530 BARTLETT, Richard A. *Nature's Yellowstone.* Albuquerque, N. M., 1974.

2531 BATES, J. Leonard. "Fulfilling American Democracy: The Conservation Movement, 1907–1921." *Miss Val Hist Rev,* XLIV (1957), 29–57.

2532 BATES, J. Leonard. "The Midwest Decision, 1915: A Landmark in Conservation History." *Pac N W Q,* LI (1960), 26–34. Upholding the president's power to withdraw and protect public lands, with special reference to California and Wyoming.

2533 BOX, Thadis W. "Range Deterioration in West Texas." *S W Hist Q,* LXXI (1967), 37–45.

2534 BUCHHOLTZ, Curtis W. "W. R. Logan and Glacier National Park." *Mont: Mag W Hist,* XIX (1969), 2–17.

2535 CART, Theodore W. " 'New Deal' for Wildlife: A Perspective on Federal Conservation Policy, 1933–1940." *Pac N W Q,* LXIII (1972), 113–120.

2536 CAUGHEY, John W. "The Californian and His Environment." *Calif Hist Q,* LI (1972) 195–204.

2537 CLEPPER, Henry, ed. *Origins of American Conservation.* New York, 1966.

2538 COMMONER, Barry. *The Closing Circle: Nature, Man and Technology.* New York, 1971. †

2539 COOLEY, Richard A. *Alaska: A Challenge in Conservation.* Madison, Wis., 1966. †

2540 COOLEY, Richard A., and Geoffrey WANDESFORDE-SMITH, eds. *Congress and the Environment.* Seattle, Wash., 1970. Case studies in legislative response.

2541 COWDREY, Albert E. "Pioneering Environmental Law: The Army Corps of Engineers and the Refuse Act." *Pac Hist Rev,* XLIV (1975), 331–349.

2542 COX, Thomas R. "Conservation by Subterfuge: Robert W. Sawyer and the Birth of the Oregon State Parks." *Pac N W Q*, LXIV (1973), 21–29.

2543 COX, Thomas R. "The Crusade to Save Oregon's Scenery." *Pac Hist Rev*, XXXVII (1968), 179–199.

2544 DE VOTO, Bernard. "Conservation: Down and on the Way Out." *Harp Mag*, CCIX (August 1954), 66–74.

2545 DODDS, Gordon B. "Artificial Propagation of Salmon in Oregon, 1875–1910: A Chapter in American Conservation." *Pac N W Q*, L (1959), 125–133.

2546 DODDS, Gordon B., ed. "Conservation and Reclamation in the Trans-Mississippi West: A Critical Bibliography." *Ariz W*, XIII (1971), 143–171.

2547 DODDS, Gordon B. "The Fight to Close the Rogue." *Ore Hist Q*, LX (1959), 461–474.

2548 DODDS, Gordon B. *Hiram Martin Chittenden: His Public Career.* Lexington, Ken., 1973.

2549 DODDS, Gordon B. "The Historiography of American Conservation: Past and Prospects." *Pac N W Q*, LVI (1965), 75–81.

2550 DODDS, Gordon B. "The Stream-Flow Controversy: A Conservation Turning Point." *J Am Hist*, LVI (1969), 59–69.

2551 ERISMAN, Fred. "The Environmental Crisis and Present-Day Romanticism." *Roc Mt Soc Sci J*, X (1973), 7–14.

2552 EVERHART, William C. *The National Park Service.* New York, 1972.

2553 FAHL, Ronald J., comp. *North American Forest and Conservation History.* See 1551.

2554 FAHL, Ronald J. "S. C. Lancaster and the Columbia River Highway: Engineer as Conservationist." *Ore Hist Q*, LXXIV (1973), 101–144.

2555 FLEMING, Donald. "Roots of the New Conservation Movement." *Per Am Hist*, VI (1972), 7–91.

2556 FOSS, Philip O. *Politics and Grass: Administration of Grazing.* See 1160.

2557 FROME, Michael. *Battle for the Wilderness.* New York, 1974. The history and philosophy of the movement that culminated in the Wilderness Act of 1964.

2558 HAYS, Samuel P. *Conservation and the Gospel of Efficiency: The Progressive Conservation Movement, 1890–1920.* Cambridge, Mass., 1959. †

2559 HUTH, Hans. *Nature and the American: Three Centuries of Changing Attitudes.* Berkeley, 1957. Repr. Lincoln, Neb., 1972. †

2560 ISE, John. *Our National Park Policy: A Critical History.* Baltimore, 1961.

2561 JACOBS, Wilbur R. "Frontiersmen, Fur Traders, and Other Varmints, An Ecological Appraisal of the Frontier in American History." *AHA News*, VIII (1970), 5–11.

2562 JARRETT, Henry, ed. *Perspectives on Conservation: Essays on America's Natural Resources.* Baltimore, Md., 1958. † Sponsored by Resources for the Future.

2563 JOHNSON, Ralph W. "Regulation of Commercial Salmon Fishermen: A Case of Confused Objectives." *Pac N W Q*, LV (1964), 141–145.

2564 JONES, Charles O. "From Gold to Garbage: A Bibliographical Essay on Politics and the Environment." *Am Pol Sci Rev*, LXVI (1972), 588–595.

2565 JONES, Holway R. *John Muir and the Sierra Club: The Battle for Yosemite.* San Francisco, 1965.

2566 LE DUC, Thomas. "The Historiography of Conservation." *For Hist,* IX (1965), 23–28.

2567 MCCARTHY, G. Michael. "Colorado Confronts the Conservation Impulse, 1891–1907." Doctoral dissertation, University of Denver, 1969.

2568 MCCLOSKEY, Michael. "Wilderness Movement at the Crossroads, 1945–1970." *Pac Hist Rev,* XLI (1972), 346–361.

2569 MCCONNELL, Grant. "The Conservation Movement—Past and Present." *W Pol Sci Q,* VII (1954), 463–478.

2570 MCGEARY, M. Nelson. *Gifford Pinchot, Forester—Politician.* Princeton, N.J., 1960.

2571 MCHENRY, Robert, and Charles VAN DOREN, eds. *A Documentary History of Conservation in America.* New York, 1972. †

2571A MCHUGH, Tom. *The Time of the Buffalo.* New York, 1972.

2572 MCKINLEY, Charles. *Uncle Sam in the Pacific Northwest: Federal Management of Natural Resources in the Columbia River Valley.* Berkeley, Calif., 1952.

2573 MCPHEE, John A. *Encounters with the Archdruid.* New York, 1971. Deals with Sierra Club leader David Brower.

2574 *Montana: The Magazine of Western History,* XXII (July 1972). Special issue on Yellowstone Park.

2575 NASH, Roderick, ed. *The American Environment: Readings in the History of Conservation.* Reading, Mass., 1968. †

2576 NASH, Roderick. "The American Invention of National Parks." *Am Q,* XXII (1970), 726–735.

2577 NASH, Roderick. "John Muir, William Kent, and the Conservation Schism." *Pac Hist Rev,* XXXVI (1967), 423–433.

2578 NASH, Roderick. *Wilderness and the American Mind.* New Haven, Conn., 1967. Rev. ed., 1973. †

2579 OGLESBY, Richard E. "Smoke Gets in Your Eyes." *Mo Hist Soc Bull,* XXVI (1970), 179–199.

2580 O'RIORDAN, Timothy. "The Third American Conservation Movement: New Implications for Public Policy." *J Am Stud,* V (1971), 155–171.

2581 *Pacific Historical Review,* XLI (August 1972). Special issue on environmental history.

2582 PENICK, James L., Jr. *Progressive Politics and Conservation: The Ballinger-Pinchot Affair.* Chicago, 1968.

2583 PINCHOT, Gifford. *Breaking New Ground.* New York, 1947. The autobiography of the forester who became the leader of the conservation movement.

2584 PINCHOT, Gifford. *The Fight for Conservation.* New York, 1910. Repr. with intro. by Gerald D. Nash. Seattle, Wash., 1967. †

2585 PINKETT, Harold T. *Gifford Pinchot: Private and Public Forester.* Urbana, Ill., 1970.

2586 POLENBERG, Richard. "Conservation and Reorganization: The Forest Service, 1937–38." *Ag Hist,* XXXIX (1965), 230–239.

2587 POLENBERG, Richard. "The Great Conservation Contest." *For Hist,* X (1967), 13–23.

2588 RAKESTRAW, Lawrence. "Before McNary: The Northwestern Conservationist, 1889–1913." *Pac N W Q,* LI (1960), 49–56.

2589 RAKESTRAW, Lawrence. "Conservation Historiography: An Assessment." *Pac Hist Rev,* XLI (1972), 271–288.

2590 RAKESTRAW, Lawrence. "A History of Forest Conservation in the Pacific Northwest, 1891–1913." Doctoral dissertation, University of Washington, 1955.

2591 RAKESTRAW, Lawrence. "Urban Influences on Forest Conservation." *Pac N W Q,* XLVI (1955), 108–113.

2592 RAKESTRAW, Lawrence. "The West, States' Rights, and Conservation: A Study of Six Public Land Conferences." *Pac N W Q,* XLVIII (1957), 89–99.

2593 REIGER, John F. "George Bird Grinnell and the Development of American Conservation, 1870–1901." Doctoral dissertation, Northwestern University, 1970.

2594 REINHARDT, Richard. "The Case of the Hard-Nosed Conservationists." *Am W,* IV (February 1967), 52–54, 85–90.

2595 RICHARDSON, Elmo R. "Conservation as a Political Issue: The Western Progressives' Dilemma, 1909–1912." *Pac N W Q,* XLIX (1958), 49–54.

2596 RICHARDSON, Elmo R. *Dams, Parks & Politics: Resource Development & Preservation in the Truman-Eisenhower Era.* Lexington, Ky., 1973.

2597 RICHARDSON, Elmo R. "Federal Park Policy in Utah: The Escalante National Monument Controversy of 1935–1940." *Utah Hist Q,* XXXIII (1965), 109–133.

2598 RICHARDSON, Elmo R. "The Interior Secretary as Conservation Villain: The Notorious Case of Douglas 'Giveaway' McKay." *Pac Hist Rev,* XLI (1972), 333–345.

2599 RICHARDSON, Elmo R. "Olympic National Park: Twenty Years of Controversy." *For Hist,* XII (1968), 6–15.

2600 RICHARDSON, Elmo R. *The Politics of Conservation: Crusades and Controversies, 1897–1913.* Berkeley, Calif., 1962.

2601 SALMOND, John A. *The Civilian Conservation Corps, 1933–1942: A New Deal Case Study.* Durham, N.C., 1967.

2602 SAUNDERSON, Mont H. *Western Land and Water Use.* Norman, Okla., 1950. A comprehensive survey by an agricultural economist.

2603 SCHEFFER, Victor B. "The Sea Otter on the Washington Coast." *Pac N W Q,* XXXI (1940), 371–388.

2604 SCHMITT, Peter J. *Back to Nature: The Arcadian Myth in Urban America.* New York, 1969.

2605 SMITH, Frank E. *The Politics of Conservation.* New York, 1966. †

2606 STEGNER, Wallace. *The Sound of Mountain Water.* Garden City, N.Y., 1969.

2607 STOUT, Joe A., Jr. "Cattlemen, Conservationists, and the Taylor Grazing Act." *N M Hist Rev,* XLV (1970), 311–332.

2608 STRONG, Douglas H. *The Conservationists.* Menlo Park, Calif., 1971 † Thoreau, Olmsted, Marsh, Pinchot, Muir, Roosevelt, Udall.

2609 STRONG, Douglas H. "The Sierra Forest Reserve: The Movement to Preserve the San Joaquin Valley Watershed." *Calif Hist Soc Q,* XLVI (1967), 3–17.

2610 SWAIN, Donald C. *Federal Conservation Policy, 1921–1933.* Berkeley, Calif., 1963.

2611 SWAIN, Donald C. "The National Park Service and the New Deal, 1933–1940." *Pac Hist Rev,* XLI (1972), 312–332.

2612 SWAIN, Donald C. "The Passage of the National Park Service Act of 1916." *Wis Mag Hist,* L (1966), 4–17.

2613 SWAIN, Donald C. *Wilderness Defender: Horace M. Albright and Conservation.* Chicago, 1970.

2614 THOMPSON, John T. "Governmental Responses to the Challenges of Water Resources in Texas." *S W Hist Q,* LXX (1966), 44–64.

2615 THOMPSON, Kenneth. "The Notions of Air Purity in Early California." *S Calif Q,* LIV (1972), 203–210.

2616 UDALL, Stewart L. *The Quiet Crisis.* New York, 1963. †

2617 *Utah Historical Quarterly,* XXXIX (Summer 1971). Special issue on natural resource development in Utah.

2618 VAN HISE, Charles R. *The Conservation of Natural Resources in the United States.* New York, 1910. Many later printings.

2618A WARNE, William E. *The Bureau of Reclamation.* New York, 1973.

2619 WILLIAMS, Donald A. "Conservation in the Future of the Great Plains." *Great Plains J,* I (1961), 1–5.

2620 WOLFE, Linne M. *Son of the Wilderness: The Life of John Muir.* New York, 1945.

2621 YEE, J. E., comp. *The Concern for Conservation in the United States: A Selected Bibliography* (U.S. Dept of the Interior, Library. Bibliography Series No. 13). Washington, D.C., 1969.

XXX. Women, the Family, and Women's Rights in the West

See also: Western Literature (for Mary Austin, Willa Cather); Drama; Music; Education; Religion. And see also 28.

2622 ALEXANDER, Thomas G. "An Experiment in Progressive Legislation: The Granting of Woman Suffrage in Utah in 1870." *Utah Hist Q,* XXXVIII (1970), 20–30.

2623 ALLEN, Martha M. "Women in the West: A Study of Book Length Travel Accounts by Women Who Traveled in the Plains and Rockies...." Doctoral dissertation, University of Texas, Austin, 1972.

2624 ARRINGTON, Leonard J. "Blessed Damozels: Women in Mormon History." *Dialogue,* VI (1971), 22–31.

2625 BALDWIN, Alice Blackwood. *An Army Wife on the Frontier: The Memoirs of Alice Blackwood Baldwin, 1867–1877.* Eds. Robert C. and Eleanor R. Carriker. Salt Lake City, Utah, 1975.

2626 BANNING, Evelyn I. *Helen Hunt Jackson.* New York, 1973.

2627 BLAKE, Nelson M. *The Road to Reno: A History of Divorce in the United States.* New York, 1962.

2628 BOARD, John C. "Jeannette Rankin: The Lady from Montana." *Mont: Mag W Hist,* XVII (July 1967), 2–17.

2629 BROWN, Dee. *The Gentle Tamers: Women of the Old Wild West.* New York, 1958. †

2629A BROWN, Mrs. Hugh [Marjorie Moore]. *Lady in Boomtown: Miners and Manners on the Nevada Frontier.* Palo Alto, Calif., 1968.

2630 BURKE, John. *The Legend of Baby Doe: The Life and Times of the Silver Queen of the West.* New York, 1974. †

2631 CANNON, Charles A. "The Awesome Power of Sex." See 947.

2632 CHITTENDEN, Elizabeth F. " 'By No Means Excluding Women': Abigail Scott Duniway, western pioneer in the struggle for equal voting rights." *Am W,* XII (March 1975), 24–27.

2633 CHRISTENSEN, Harold T. "Stress Points in Mormon Family Culture." See 948.

2634 CLAPP or CLAPPE, Louise A. K. S. (Dame Shirley, pseud.) *The Shirley Letters from California Mines in 1851–52: Being a Series of Twenty-Three Letters from Dame Shirley. . . . Reprinted from the Pioneer Magazine of 1854–55. . . .* San Francisco, Calif., 1922. With slightly varying title, ed. Carl I. Wheat, San Francisco, 1933; New York, 1949. †

2635 *Dialogue,* VI (Summer 1971). Special issue on women, chiefly Mormon women, with essays, photographs, poems, and interviews by women.

2636 DICK, Everett, "Sunbonnet and Calico, The Homesteader's Consort." *Neb Hist,* XLVII (1966), 3–13.

2637 DRAGO, Harry S. *Notorious Ladies of the Frontier.* New York, 1969.

2638 DRURY, Clifford. *First White Women Over the Rockies: Diaries, Letters, and Biographical Sketches of the Six Women of the Oregon Mission Who Made the Overland Journey in 1836 and 1838.* 3 vols. Glendale, Calif., 1963–66.

2639 DUNIWAY, Abigail Scott. *Path Breaking: An Autobiographical History of the Equal Suffrage Movement in Pacific Coast States.* Portland, Ore., 1914; New York, 1971. †

2639A DYSART, Jane. "Mexican Women in San Antonio." See 841A.

2640 ELLET, Elizabeth F. *Pioneer Women of the West.* New York, 1852.

2641 ELLSWORTH, S. George. *Dear Ellen: Two Mormon Women and Their Letters.* Salt Lake City, Utah, 1974.

2642 EWERS, John C. "Mothers of the Mixed-Bloods: The Marginal Woman in the History of the Upper Missouri." *Probing the American West.* Ed. K. Ross Toole, *et al.* Santa Fe, N.M., 1962.

2643 FOWLER, William W. *Woman on the American Frontier.* Hartford, Conn., 1877.

2644 GRIMES, Alan P. *The Puritan Ethic and Woman Suffrage.* New York, 1967.

2645 HAGAN, William T. "Squaw Men on the Kiowa, Comanche, and Apache Reservation: Advance Agents of Civilization or Disturbers of the Peace?" *The Frontier Challenge.* . . . Ed. John G. Clark. Lawrence, Kan., 1971.

2646 HARGREAVES, Mary W. "Homesteading and Homemaking on the Plains." See 1302.

2647 JENSEN, Billie Barnes. "Let the Women Vote." *Colo Mag,* XLI (1964), 13–25.

2648 JOSEPHSON, Hannah. *Jeannette Rankin, First Lady in Congress: A Biography.* Indianapolis, Ind., 1974.

2649 KANE, Elizabeth Wood. *Twelve Mormon Homes.* See 976.

2650 KAY, Margarita A. "Health and Illness in the Barrio: Women's Point of View." Doctoral dissertation, University of Arizona, 1972.

2651 KING, C. Richard. *Victorian Lady on the Texas Frontier: The Journal of Ann Raney Coleman.* Norman, Okla., 1971.

2652 KIZER, Benjamin H. "May Arkwright Hutton." *Pac N W Q,* LVII (1966), 49–56.

2653 LACY, James M. "New Mexican Women in Early American Writings." *N M Hist Rev,* XXXIV (1959), 41–51.

2654 LARSON, T. A. "Dolls, Vassals, and Drudges—Pioneer Women in the West." *W Hist Q,* III (1972), 5–16.

2655 LARSON, T. A. "Idaho's Role in America's Woman Suffrage Crusade." *Idaho Yes,* XVIII (Spring 1974), 2–15.

2656 LARSON, T. A. "Montana Women and the Battle for the Ballot: Women Suffrage in the Treasure State." *Mont: Mag W Hist,* XXIII (January 1973), 24–41.

2657 LARSON, T. A. "Woman Suffrage in Western America." *Utah Hist Q,* XXXVIII (1970), 7–19.

2658 LARSON, T. A. "Woman Suffrage in Wyoming." *Pac N W Q,* LVI (1965), 57–66.

2658A LARSON, T. A. "The Woman Suffrage Movement in Washington." *Pac N W Q,* LXVII (1976), 49–62.

2659 LARSON, T. A. "The Women's Rights Movement in Idaho." *Idaho Yes,* XVI (Spring 1972), 2–15, 18–19.

2660 LARSON, T. A. "Women's Role in the American West." *Mont: Mag W Hist,* XXIV (July 1974), 2–11.

2661 LOEWY, Jean. "Katherine Philips Edson and the California Suffragette Movement, 1919–1920." *Calif Hist Soc Q,* XLVII (1968), 343–350.

2662 MODELL, John. "The Japanese American Family: A Perspective for Future Investigators." *Pac Hist Rev,* XXXVII (1968), 67–81.

2663 MONTGOMERY, James W. *Liberated Woman: A Life of May Arkwright Hutton.* Spokane, Wash., 1974.

2664 MOYNIHAN, Ruth Barnes. "Children and Young People on the Overland Trail." *W Hist Q,* VI (1975), 279–294.

2665 O'MEARA, Walter. *Daughters of the Country: The Women of the Fur Traders and Mountain Men.* New York, 1968.

2666 PAUL, Rodman W. "In Search of 'Dame Shirley.'" *Pac Hist Rev*, XXXIII (1964), 127–146. The life and work of the author of the "Shirley Letters" from the California mines.

2667 PAUL, Rodman W., ed. *A Victorian Gentlewoman in the Far West: The Reminiscences of Mary Hallock Foote*. San Marino, Calif., 1972.

2667A PAUL, Rodman W. "When Culture Came to Boise: Mary Hallock Foote in Idaho." *Idaho Yes*, XX (Summer 1976), 2–12.

2668 RANDALL, Ruth (Painter). *I, Jessie. A Biography of the Girl Who Married John Charles Fremont, Famous Explorer of the West*. Boston, 1963.

2669 REID, Agnes Just. *Letters of Long Ago*. Ed. Brigham D. Madsen. Salt Lake City, Utah, 1973. Essentially the oral recollections of Emma Thompson Just, a pioneer settler in Idaho, as written down by her daughter.

2670 RHODEHAMEL, Josephine D., and Raymond F. WOOD. *Ina Coolbrith: Librarian and Laureate of California*. Provo, Utah, 1973.

2670A RICHEY, Elinor. *Eminent Women of the West*. Berkeley, Calif., 1975.

2671 RICHEY, Elinor. "The Flappers Were Her Daughters: The Liberated, Literary World of Gertrude Atherton." *Am W*, XI (July 1974), 4–10, 60–63.

2672 ROBBINS, Lynn A. "Blackfeet Families and Households." Doctoral dissertation, University of Oregon, 1971.

2673 ROSS, Nancy Wilson. *Westward the Women*. New York, 1944. † Essentially a long essay.

2674 ROYCE, Sarah Eleanor. *A Frontier Lady: Recollections of the Gold Rush and Early California*. Ed. Ralph Henry Gabriel. New Haven, Conn., 1932.

2674A SANFORD, Mollie D. *Mollie: The Journal of Mollie Dorsey Sanford in Nebraska and Colorado Territories, 1856–1866*. Lincoln, Neb., 1959. †

2675 SCHAFFER, Ronald. "The Montana Woman Suffrage Campaign, 1911–14." *Pac N W Q*, LV (1964), 9–15.

2675A SCHAFFER, Ronald. "The Problem of Consciousness in the Woman Suffrage Movement: A California Perspective." *Pac Hist Rev*, XLV (1976), 469–493.

2676 SHELTON, Emily J. "Lizzie E. Johnson: A Cattle Queen of Texas." *S W Hist Q*, L (1947), 349–366.

2677 SMITH, Page. *Daughters of the Promised Land: Women in American History*. Boston, 1970. †

2678 SPRAGUE, William F. *Women and the West: A Short Social History*. Boston, 1940.

2679 SUMMERHAYES, Martha. *Vanished Arizona: Recollections of My Army Life*. Philadelphia, Pa., 1908. 2d ed., Salem, Mass., 1911. Ed. Milo M. Quaife. Chicago, 1939. Ed. Ray Brandes. Tucson, Ariz., 1960.

2680 TANNER, Annie C. *A Mormon Mother*. See 1011.

2681 TERRELL, John U., and Donna M. TERRELL. *Indian Women of the Western Morning: Their Life in Early America*. New York, 1974.

2682 TRESSMAN, Ruth. "Home on the Range." *N M Hist Rev*. See 1218.

2683 TRULIO, Beverly. "Anglo-American Attitudes Toward New Mexican Women." *J W*, XII (1973), 229–239.

2684 UNDERHILL, Lonnie E., and Daniel F. LITTLEFIELD, Jr. "Women Home-seekers in Oklahoma Territory, 1889–1901." *Pac Hist Rev,* XVII (1973), 36–47.

2685 WHITE, Jean B. "Woman's Place Is in the Constitution: The Struggle for Equal Rights in Utah in 1895." *Essays on the American West, 1973–1974.* Ed. Thomas G. Alexander. Provo, Utah, 1975.

2686 WILLIAMS, Blaine T. "The Frontier Family: Demographic Fact and Historical Myth." *Essays on the American West.* Eds. Harold M. Hollingsworth and Sandra L. Myres. Austin, Tex., 1969.

2687 WILSON, Dorothy C. *Bright Eyes: The Story of Susette La Flesche, An Omaha Indian.* New York, 1974.

2688 "Women and the American West." *Mont: Mag W Hist,* XXIV (Summer 1974). Special topical issue.

2689 "Women in the West." *J W,* XII (April 1973). Special issue.

2690 "Women in Utah." *Utah Hist Q,* XXXVIII (Winter 1970).

XXXI. Western Literature and Literature about the West

2691 "Annual Bibliography of Studies in Western American Literature." *W Am Lit,* 1966–. Appears each year in the Winter issue.

2692 ASTRO, Richard, and Tetsumaro HAYASHI, eds. *Steinbeck: The Man and his Work.* Corvallis, Ore., 1971. A symposium.

2693 ATTEBERY, Louie W. "The American West and the Archetypal Orphan." *W Am Lit,* V (1970), 205–217.

2694 AUSTIN, Mary, *Earth Horizon: Autobiography.* Boston and New York, 1932.

2695 BARKER, Charles A. *Henry George.* New York, 1955.

2696 BOATRIGHT, Mody C. "The Beginnings of Cowboy Fiction." *S W Rev,* LI (1966), 11–28.

2697 Boise State University *Western Writers Series.* Boise, Idaho, 1972–. Five pamphlets appear each year; twenty have been published through 1975.

2698 BOYNTON, Percy H. *The Rediscovery of the Frontier.* Chicago, 1931.

2699 BROPHY, Robert J. *Robinson Jeffers: Myth, Ritual, and Symbol in his Narrative Poems.* Cleveland, Ohio, 1973.

2700 BROWN, E. K., completed by Leon EDEL. *Willa Cather: A Critical Biography.* New York, 1953.

2701 BUTLER, Michael D. "The Literary Landscape of the Trans-Mississippi West: 1826–1902." Doctoral dissertation, University of Illinois, Urbana, 1970.

2702 CARPENTER, Frederic I. *Robinson Jeffers.* New York, 1962.

2702A CAWELTI, John G. *Adventure, Mystery, and Romance: Formula Stories as Art and Popular Culture.* Chicago, 1976. Includes a major study of the "western."

2703 CAWELTI, John G. *The Six-Gun Mystique.* Bowling Green, Ohio, 1971.

2704 CLIFFORD, John. "Social and Political Attitudes of Fiction of Ranch and Range." Doctoral dissertation, University of Iowa, 1954.

2705 CLOUGH, Wilson O. *The Necessary Earth: Nature and Solitude in American Literature.* Austin, Tex., 1964.

2706 COFFIN, Arthur B. *Robinson Jeffers: Poet of Inhumanism.* Madison, Wis., 1971.

2707 DAVIS, David B. "Ten Gallon Hero." *Am Q,* VI (1954), 111–125.

2708 DE VOTO, Bernard. *Mark Twain's America.* Boston, 1932.

2709 DILLINGHAM, William B. *Frank Norris: Instinct and Art.* Lincoln, Neb., 1969. †

2710 DOBIE, J. Frank. *Guide to Life and Literature of the Southwest.* See 92.

2711 DONALD, David, and Frederick A. PALMER. "Toward a Western Literature, 1820–1860." *Miss Val Hist Rev,* XXXV (1948), 413–428.

2712 DONDORE, Dorothy Anne. *The Prairie and the Making of Middle America: Four Centuries of Description.* Cedar Rapids, Iowa, 1926.

2713 DUCKETT, Margaret. *Mark Twain and Bret Harte.* Norman, Okla., 1964.

2713A ETULAIN, Richard W. "The American Literary West and Its Interpreters: The Rise of a New Historiography." *Pac Hist Rev,* XLV (1976), 311–348.

2714 ETULAIN, Richard W. "The Historical Development of the Western." *J Pop Cult,* VII (1973), 75–84.

2715 ETULAIN, Richard W. "Literary Historians and the Western." *J Pop Cult,* IV (1970), 518–526.

2716 ETULAIN, Richard W. "Origins of the Western." *J Pop Cult,* V (1972), 799–805.

2717 ETULAIN, Richard W. "Research Opportunities in Western Literary History." *W Hist Q,* IV (1973), 263–272.

2718 ETULAIN, Richard W. *Western American Literature: A Bibliography of Interpretive Books and Articles.* Vermillion, S. D., 1972. †

2719 ETULAIN, Richard W. "Western American Literature: A Selective Annotated Bibliography." *Rendezvous,* VII (Winter 1972), 67–78.

2720 ETULAIN, Richard W., and Michael T. MARSDEN. *The Popular Western: Essays Toward a Definition.* Bowling Green, Ohio, 1974. Reprints *Journal of Popular Culture,* VII (Winter 1973), 645–753.

2721 FIEDLER, Leslie A. *The Return of the Vanishing American.* New York, 1968. †

2722 FOLSOM, James K. *The American Western Novel.* New Haven, Conn., 1966.

2723 FUSSELL, Edwin. *Frontier: American Literature and the American West.* Princeton, N.J., 1965. †

2724 GASTON, Edwin W., Jr. *The Early Novel of the Southwest.* Albuquerque, N.M., 1961.

2725 GOHDES, Clarence, comp. *Literature and Theater of the States and Regions of the U.S.A.: An Historical Bibliography.* Durham, N.C., 1967.

2726 GROSSMAN, James. *James Fenimore Cooper.* New York, 1949. †

2727 HASLAM, Gerald. "American Indians: Poets of the Cosmos." *W Am Lit,* V (1970), 15–29.

2728 HAZARD, Lucy L. *The Frontier in American Literature.* New York, 1927.

2729 HODGINS, Francis E., Jr. "The Literary Emancipation of a Region: The Changing Image of the American West in Fiction." Doctoral dissertation, Michigan State University, 1957.

2730 HOUSE, Kay S. *Cooper's Americans.* Columbus, O., 1965.

2731 HUNSAKER, Kenneth B. "The Twentieth Century Mormon Novel." See 971.

2732 "In-Depth: The Western." *J Pop Cult,* IV (1970), 453–526.

2733 *Interpretive Approaches to Western American Literature.* Pocatello, Idaho, 1972. Reprints *Rendezvous,* VII (Winter 1972).

2734 JACOBSON, Larry K. "Mythic Origins of the Western." Doctoral dissertation, University of Minnesota, 1973.

2735 JODY, Marilyn. "Alaska in the American Literary Imagination: A Literary History of Frontier Alaska with a Bibliographical Guide to the Study of Alaskan Literature." Doctoral dissertation, Indiana University, 1969.

2736 KAPLAN, Justin. *Mr. Clemens and Mark Twain: A Biography.* New York, 1966. †

2737 KAROLIDES, Nicholas J. *The Pioneer in the American Novel, 1900–1950.* Norman, Okla., 1967.

2738 LEE, Robert Edson. *From West to East: Studies in the Literature of the American West.* Urbana, Ill., 1966.

2739 LISCA, Peter. *The Wide World of John Steinbeck.* New Brunswick, N.J., 1958.

2740 MAJOR, Mabel, and T. M. PEARCE. *Southwest Heritage: A Literary History with Bibliographies.* 3d ed. Albuquerque, N.M., 1972. †

2741 MEYER, Roy W. *The Middle Western Farm Novel in the Twentieth Century.* Lincoln, Neb., 1965. †

2742 MILTON, John R. "The American West: A Challenge to the Literary Imagination." *W Am Lit,* I (1967), 267–284.

2743 MILTON, John R., ed. "The Western Novel—A Symposium." *S D Rev,* II (Autumn 1964), 3–35.

2744 MILTON, John R. "The Western Novel: Sources and Forms." *Chicago Rev,* XVI (Summer 1963), 74–100.

2745 NYE, Russel. *The Unembarrassed Muse: The Popular Arts in America.* New York, 1970. † Includes an important section on the historical development of the Western.

2746 O'CONNOR, Richard. *Jack London: A Biography.* Boston, 1964.

2746A *Pacific Historical Review,* XLV (August 1976). Special issue devoted to "Western Literary History."

2747 PAST, Raymond E. " 'Illustrated by the Author': A Study of Six Western-American Writer-Artists." Doctoral dissertation, University of Texas, 1950.

2748 PEARCE, Thomas M. *Mary Hunter Austin.* New York, 1965. †

2749 PETERSON, Martin S. *Joaquin Miller: Literary Frontiersman.* Stanford, Calif., 1937.

2750 PILKINGTON, William T. *My Blood's Country: Studies in Southwestern Literature.* Fort Worth, Tex., 1973. †

2751 PIZER, Donald. *The Novels of Frank Norris.* Bloomington, Ind., 1966.

2752 PORTER, Joseph C. "The End of the Trail: The American West of Dashiell Hammett and Raymond Chandler." *W Hist Q,* VI (1975), 411–424.

2753 ROBINSON, Cecil. *With the Ears of Strangers: The Mexican in American Literature.* Tucson, Ariz., 1963. †

2754 RUSK, Ralph Leslie. *The Literature of the Middle Western Frontier.* 2 vols. New York, 1925.

2755 SELLARS, Richard West. "The Interrelationship of Literature, History, and Geography in Western Writing." *W Hist Q,* IV (1973), 171–185.

2756 SHAMES, Priscilla. "The Treatment of the American Indian in Western American Fiction." See 457.

2757 SIMONSON, Harold P. *The Closed Frontier: Studies in American Literary Tragedy.* New York, 1970.

2758 SLOTE, Bernice, and Virginia FAULKNER, eds. *The Art of Willa Cather.* Lincoln, Neb., 1974. †

2759 SLOTKIN, Richard. *Regeneration Through Violence: The Mythology of the American Frontier, 1600–1860.* See 294.

2760 SMITH, Henry Nash. *Mark Twain: the Development of a Writer.* Cambridge, Mass., 1962. Especially Chapter III, which deals with *Roughing It.* †

2761 SMITH, Henry Nash. *Virgin Land: The American West as Symbol and Myth.* Cambridge, Mass., 1950. †

2762 SMITH, Henry Nash, ed., with assistance of Frederick ANDERSON. *Mark Twain of the Enterprise....* Berkeley, Calif., 1957.

2763 STARR, Kevin. *Americans and the California Dream, 1850–1915.* New York, 1973.

2764 STECKMESSER, Kent L. *The Western Hero in History and Legend.* Norman, Okla., 1965.

2765 Steck-vaughn. *Southwest Writers Series.* Austin, Tex., 1967–1970. More than thirty pamphlets were published in the series.

2766 STEGNER, Wallace. *The Sound of Mountain Water.* Garden City, N.Y., 1969. Collects Stegner's essays on Literature and conservation.

2767 STEWART, George R. *Bret Harte, Argonaut and Exile: Being an Account of....* Boston and New York, 1931.

2768 TAYLOR, J. Golden, ed. *Great Western Short Stories.* Palo Alto, Calif., 1967.

2769 TAYLOR, J. Golden, ed. *The Literature of the American West.* Boston, 1971. † Includes bibliographies.

2770 WALKER, Don D. "The Mountain Man as Literary Hero" *W Am Lit,* I (1966), 15–25.

2771 WALKER, Don D. "The Rise and Fall of Barney Tullus." *W Am Lit,* III (1968), 93–102.

2772 WALKER, Franklin. *Frank Norris: A Biography.* Garden City, N.Y., 1932.

2773 WALKER, Franklin. *Jack London and the Klondike: The Genesis of an American Writer.* San Marino, Calif., 1966.

2774 WALKER, Franklin. *A Literary History of Southern California.* Berkeley, Calif., 1950.

2775 WALKER, Franklin. *San Francisco's Literary Frontier.* New York, 1939. Repr. Seattle, Wash., 1970. †

2776 WALKER, Franklin. *The Seacoast of Bohemia: An Account of Early Carmel.* San Francisco, 1966. Enlarged ed. with no subtitle, Santa Barbara, Calif., and Salt Lake City, Utah, 1973. Includes Jack London, Mary Austin, Sinclair Lewis, Ambrose Bierce, Joaquin Miller, George Sterling, etc.

2777 WALKER, Robert H. "The Poets Interpret the Western Frontier." *Miss Val Hist Rev,* XLVII (1961), 619–635.

2778 WESTBROOK, Max. "Conservative, Liberal, and Western: Three Modes of American Realism." *S D Rev,* IV (Summer 1966), 3–19.

2779 WESTBROOK, Max. "The Practical Spirit: Sacrality and the American West." *W Am Lit,* III (1968), 193–205.

2780 WESTBROOK, Max. *Walter Van Tilburg Clark.* New York, 1969.

2781 WHITE, G. Edward. *The Eastern Establishment and the Western Experience: The West of Frederic Remington, Theodore Roosevelt, and Owen Wister.* New Haven, Conn., 1968.

2782 WOODRESS, James L. *Willa Cather: Her Life and Art.* New York, 1970. Repr. Lincoln, Neb., 1975. †

2783 "Writers and the West." *Am W,* X (November 1973), 4–39, 63.

XXXII. The Visual and Performing Arts

1. Art and Artists

2784 ADAMS, Ramon F., and Homer E. BRITZMAN. *Charles M. Russell: The Cowboy Artist.* Pasadena, Calif., 1948.

2785 ALTER, Judith. "Rufus F. Zogbaum and the Frontier West." *Mont: Mag W Hist,* XXIII (Autumn 1973), 42–53.

2786 BURNSIDE, Wesley M. *Maynard Dixon: Artist of the West.* Provo, Utah, 1973.

2787 DAWDY, Doris O. *Artists of the American West: A Biographical Dictionary.* Chicago, 1974

2788 DIPPIE, Brian W. "Charlie Russell's Lost West." *Am Her,* XXIV (April 1973), 4–21, 89.

2788A DYKES, Jefferson C. *Fifty Great Western Illustrators: A Bibliographic Checklist.* Flagstaff, Ariz., 1975.

2789 EWERS, John C. *Artists of the Old West.* Garden City, N.Y., 1965.

2790 FREEMAN, Martha D. "New Mexico in the Nineteenth Century: The Creation of an Artistic Tradition." *N M Hist Rev,* XLIX (1974), 5–26.

2791 HABERLY, Lloyd. *Pursuit of the Horizon: A Life of George Catlin, Painter and Recorder of the American Indian.* New York, 1948.

2792 HAMLIN, Edith. "Maynard Dixon, Artist of the West." *Calif Hist Q,* LIII (1974), 361–376. Profusely illustrated; text by his widow.

2793 HASSRICK, Peter H. *Frederic Remington: Paintings, Drawings, and Sculpture in the Amon Carter Museum and the Sid W. Richardson Foundation Collections.* New York, 1973.

2794 HASSRICK, Peter H. "Remington in the Southwest." *S W Hist Q,* LXXVI 1973), 297–314.

2795 MCCRACKEN, Harold. *The Charles M. Russell Book: The Life and Work of the Cowboy Artist.* Garden City, N.Y., 1957.

2796 MCCRACKEN, Harold. *The Frank Tenney Johnson Book: A Master Painter of the Old West.* Garden City, N.Y., 1974.

2797 MCCRACKEN, Harold. *Frederic Remington: Artist of the Old West.* Philadelphia, 1947.

2798 MCCRACKEN, Harold. *George Catlin and the Old Frontier.* New York, 1959.

2799 PINCKNEY, Pauline A. *Painting in Texas: The Nineteenth Century.* Austin, Tex., 1967.

2800 RUSSELL, Austin. *C. M. R.: Charles M. Russell, Cowboy Artist, A Biography.* New York, 1957.

2801 TAFT, Robert. *Artists and Illustrators of the Old West: 1850–1900.* New York, 1953.

2802 WILKINS, Thurman. *Thomas Moran: Artist of the Mountains.* Norman, Okla., 1966.

2803 YOST, Karl, and Frederic G. RENNER, comps. *A Bibliography of the Published Works of Charles M. Russell.* Lincoln, Neb., 1971.

2. Architecture

2804 BAIRD, Joseph A., Jr. *Time's Wondrous Changes: San Francisco Architecture, 1776–1915.* San Francisco, 1962.

2805 BANHAM, Reyner. *Los Angeles: The Architecture of Four Ecologies.* New York, 1971.

2805A BRETTELL, Richard A. *Historic Denver: The Architects and the Architecture, 1858–1893.* Denver, Colo., 1973.

2806 GARTH, Thomas R., Jr. "Early Architecture in the Northwest." *Pac N W Q,* XXXVIII (1947), 215–232.

2806A GREIFF, Constance M. *Lost America: From the Mississippi to the Pacific.* Princeton, N. J., 1972. Historic buildings that have been destroyed.

2807 HART, Arthur A. "Architectural Styles in Idaho: A Rich Harvest." *Idaho Yes,* XVI (Winter 1972–73), 2–9.

2808 KIRKER, Harold. "California Architecture and Its Relation to Contemporary Trends in Europe and America." *Calif Hist Q,* LI (1972), 289–305.

2809 KIRKER, Harold. *California's Architectural Frontier: Style and Tradition in the Nineteenth Century.* San Marino, Calif., 1960. Repr. New York, 1970; Salt Lake City, Utah, 1973. †

2810 KUBLER, George. *The Religious Architecture of New Mexico in the Colonial Period and Since the American Occupation.* Colorado Springs, Colo., 1940.

2811 MCCOY, Esther. *Five California Architects.* New York, 1960. †

2812 ROSS, Marion D. "Architecture in Oregon: 1845–1895." *Ore Hist Q,* LVII (1956), 33–64.

2812A SOBIN, Harris J. "From Vigas to Rafters: Architectural Evolution in Florence, Arizona." *J Ariz Hist,* XVI (1975), 357–382.

2812B STOEHR, C. Eric. *Bonanza Victorian: Architecture and Society in Colorado Mining Towns.* Albuquerque, N.M., 1975.

2813 VAUGHAN, Thomas, ed., and Virginia Guest FERRIDAY, assoc. ed. *Space, Style, and Structure: Building in Northwest America.* 2 vols. Portland, Ore., 1974.

2814 WINTER, Robert. "Architecture on the Frontier: The Mormon Experiment." *Pac Hist Rev,* XLIII (1974), 50–60.

3. Drama

2815 BRADY, Donal V. "The Theatre in Early El Paso, 1881–1905." *S W Stud,* IV (1966), 3–39.

2816 BRIGGS, Harold E. "Early Variety Theatres in the Trans-Mississippi West." *Mid-Am,* XXXIV (1952), 188–202.

2817 BRIGGS, Harold E., and Ernestine B. BRIGGS. "The Early Theatre on the Northern Plains." *Miss Val Hist Rev,* XXXVII (1950), 231–264.

2818 DAVIS, Ronald L. "Culture on the Frontier." *S W Rev,* LIII (1968), 383–403. Western drama.

2819 DAVIS, Ronald L. "They Played for Gold: Theatre on the Mining Frontier." *S W Rev,* LI (1966), 169–184.

2820 DIERDORFF, John. "Backstage with Frank Branch Riley, Regional Troubadour." *Ore Hist Q,* LXXIV (1973), 197–243.

2821 DRAPER, Benjamin P. "Colorado Theatres, 1859–1969." Doctoral dissertation, University of Denver, 1969.

2822 ELLIOTT, Eugene C. *A History of Variety-Vaudeville in Seattle from the Beginning to 1914.* Seattle, Wash., 1944.

2823 ERNST, Alice H. *Trouping in the Oregon Country: A History of Frontier Theatre.* Portland, Ore., 1961.

2824 GAGEY, Edmond M. *The San Francisco Stage: A History.* New York, 1950.

2825 GILLIARD, Fred. "Early Theatre in the Owyhees." *Idaho Yes,* XVII (1973), 9–15.

2826 GOHDES, Clarence, comp. *Literature and Theater of the States and Regions of the U.S.A.* See 2725.

2827 HINDMAN, Anne A. "The Myth of the Western Frontier in American Dance and Drama: 1930–1943." Doctoral dissertation, University of Georgia, 1972.

2828 HUME, Charles V. "First of the Gold Rush Theatres." *Calif Hist Soc Q*, XLVI (1967), 337–344.

2829 JOHNSON, Rue C. "Frontier Theatre: The Corinne Opera House." *Utah Hist Q*, XLII (1974), 285–295.

2830 MCCONNELL, Virginia. "A Gauge of Popular Taste in Early Colorado." *Colo Mag*, XLVI (1969), 338–350. Theatre.

2831 MACMINN, George R. *The Theater of the Golden Era in California.* Caldwell, Idaho, 1941.

2832 MAUGHAN, Ila Fisher. *Pioneer Theatre in the Desert.* Salt Lake City, Utah, 1961.

2833 RODECAPE, Lois F. "Celestial Drama in the Golden Hills: The Chinese Theatre in California, 1849–1869." *Calif Hist Soc Q*, XXIII (1944), 97–116.

2834 SALOUTOS, Theodore. "Alexander Pantages, Theatre Magnate of the West." *Pac N W Q*, LVII (1966), 137–147.

2835 SCHOBERLIN, Melvin. *From Candles to Footlights: A Biography of the Pike's Peak Theatre, 1859–1876.* Denver, Colo., 1941.

2836 VAN ORMAN, Richard A. "The Bard in the West." *W Hist Q*, V (1974), 29–38. Shakespeare on the frontier.

2837 WATSON, Margaret G. *Silver Theatre: Amusements of the Mining Frontier in Early Nevada, 1850 to 1864.* Glendale, Calif., 1964.

2838 WILLSON, Clair E. *Mimes and Miners: A Historical Study of the Theater in Tombstone* (Univ of Ariz Bull, VI, No. 7). Tucson, Ariz., 1935.

4. Music

2839 BLOOMFIELD, Arthur J. *The San Francisco Opera, 1923–1961.* New York, 1961.

2840 DAVIS, Ronald L. *A History of Opera in the American West.* Englewood Cliffs, N.J., 1965.

2841 HAHN, Henry. "Music of the Early North American West." *Pac Hist Rev*, XV (1971), 25–38.

2842 LINSCOME, Sanford A. "A History of Musical Development in Denver, Colorado, 1858–1908." Doctoral dissertation, University of Texas, Austin, 1970.

2842A PAREDES, Américo. *A Texas-Mexican Cancionero: Folksongs of the Lower Border.* Urbana, Ill., 1975.

2843 PUGH, Donald W. "Music in Frontier Houston, 1836–1876." Doctoral dissertation, University of Texas, Austin, 1970.

2844 RUNDELL, Walter, Jr. "The West as Operatic Setting." *Probing the American West.* Ed. K. Ross Toole, *et al.* Santa Fe, N.M., 1962.

2845 SANDERS, John. "Los Angeles Grand Opera Association: The Formative Years, 1924–1926." *S Calif Q*, LV (1973), 261–302.

2846 SPIESS, Lincoln B. "Church Music in Seventeenth-Century New Mexico." *N M Hist Rev*, XL (1965), 5–21.

2847 STEVENSON, Robert M. "Music in El Paso." *S W Stud*, No. 27 (1970), 3–40.

2848 SWAN, Howard. *Music in the Southwest, 1825–1950.* San Marino, Calif., 1952.

2848A WHITE, John I. *Get Along, Little Dogies: Songs and Songmakers of the American West.* Urbana, Ill., 1975.

2849 WINFREY, Dorman H. "Development of Music on the American Frontier." *Tex,* V (1967), 141–165.

XXXIII. Education

2850 ALLISON, Clinton B. "Frontier Schools: A Reflection of the Turner Hypothesis." Doctoral dissertation, University of Oklahoma, 1969.

2851 ALMACK, John C. "History of Oregon Normal Schools." *Q Ore Hist Soc,* XXI (1920), 95–169.

2852 BILLINGTON, Monroe. "Public School Integration in Oklahoma, 1954–1963." *Hist,* XXVI (1964), 521–537.

2853 BOLTON, Frederick E., and Thomas W. BIBB. *History of Education in Washington.* Washington, D.C., 1935.

2854 BRUDNOY, David. "Race and the San Francisco School Board Incident: Contemporary Evaluations." *Calif Hist Q,* L (1971), 295–312.

2855 BURNS, Edward M. *David Starr Jordan: Prophet of Freedom.* Stanford, Calif., 1953.

2856 CARR, William G. *John Swett, The Biography of an Educational Pioneer.* Santa Anna, Calif., 1933.

2857 CHAMPLIN, Ardath I. "Arthur L. Marsh and the Washington Education Association, 1921–1940." *Pac N W Q,* LX (1969), 127–134.

2858 CLOUD, Roy W. *Education in California: Leaders, Organizations, and Accomplishments of the First Hundred Years.* Stanford, Calif., 1952.

2859 CREMIN, Lawrence A. *The Transformation of the School: Progressivism in American Education, 1876–1957.* New York, 1961. †

2860 DALE, Everett E. "Teaching on the Prairie Plains, 1890–1900." *Miss Val Hist Rev,* XXXIII (1946), 293–307.

2861 DAVISON, Oscar W. "Early History of the Oklahoma Education Association." *Chron Okla,* XXIX (1951), 42–60.

2862 DUMKE, Glenn S. " Higher Education in California." *Calif Hist Soc Q,* XLII (1963), 99–110.

2863 EBY, Frederick. *The Development of Education in Texas.* New York, 1925.

2864 FERRIER, William W. *Ninety Years of Education in California, 1846–1936.* Berkeley, Calif., 1937.

2865 FURNESS, Edna L. "Image of the Schoolteacher in Western Literature." *Ariz Q,* XVIII (1962), 346–357.

2866 GARDNER, David P. *The California Oath Controversy.* Berkeley, Calif., 1967.

2867 HENDRICK, Irving, "California's Response to the 'New Education' in the 1930's." *Calif Hist Q,* LIII (1974), 25–40.

2868 HENDRICK, Irving. "The Impact of the Great Depression on Public School Support in California." *S Calif Q,* LIV (1972), 177–195.

2869 JAECKEL, Solomon P. "Edward Hyatt, 1858–1919: California Educator." *S Calif Q,* LII (1970), 33–55, 122–154, 248–274.

2870 MCGIFFERT, Michael, *The Higher Learning in Colorado, 1860–1940: An Historical Study.* Denver, Colo., 1964.

2871 MOFFITT, John C. *The History of Public Education in Utah.* Salt Lake City, Utah, 1946.

2872 NASH, Lee. "Harvey Scott's 'Cure for Drones': An Oregon Alternative to Public Higher Schools." *Pac N W Q,* LXIV (1973), 70–79.

2873 NUNIS, Doyce B., Jr. "Kate Douglas Wiggin: Pioneer in California Kindergarten Education." *Calif Hist Soc Q,* XLI (1962), 291–307.

2874 PARK, Joe, ed. *The Rise of American Education: An Annotated Bibliography.* Evanston, Ill., 1965. †

2875 RIDLEY, Jack. "Current Trends in Indian Education." See 451.

2876 RUDOLPH, Frederick. *The American College and University: A History.* New York, 1962. †

2877 SIAMPOS, Helen. "Early Education in Nebraska." *Neb Hist,* XXIX (1948), 113–133.

2878 STADTMAN, Verne A. *The University of California, 1868–1968.* New York, 1970.

2879 SZASZ, Margaret. *Education and the American Indian.* See 465.

2880 TYACK, David B. "Bureaucracy and the Common School: The Example of Portland, Oregon, 1851–1913." *Am Q,* XIX (1967), 475–498.

2881 TYACK, David B. "New Perspectives on the History of American Education." *The State of American History.* Ed. Herbert J. Bass. Chicago, 1971.

2882 TYACK, David B. *The One Best System: A History of American Urban Education.* Cambridge, Mass., 1974.

2883 TYACK, David B. "The Tribe and the Common School: Community Control in Rural Education." *Am Q,* XXIV (1972), 3–19.

2884 VEYSEY, Laurence R. *The Emergence of the American University.* Chicago, 1965. †

2885 WOODWARD, Robert C. "Education in Oregon in the Progressive Era: Liberal and Practical." Doctoral dissertation, University of Oregon, 1963.

XXXIV. Journalism

2886 ALTER, J. Cecil. *Early Utah Journalism: A Half Century of Forensic Warfare Waged by the West's Most Militant Press.* Salt Lake City, Utah, 1938.

2887 GURIAN, Jay. "Sweetwater Journalism and Western Myth." *Ann Wyo,* XXXVI (1964), 79–88.

2888 HALAAS, David F. "Frontier Journalism in Colorado." *Colo Mag,* XLIV (1967), 185–203.

2889 KNIGHT, Oliver. "*The Owyhee Avalance:* The Frontier Newspaper as a Catalyst in Social Change." *Pac N W Q,* LVIII (1967), 74–81.

2890 LYON, William H. *The Pioneer Editor In Missouri, 1808–1860.* Columbia, Mo., 1965.

2891 NASH, Lee M. "Refining a Frontier: The Cultural Interests and Activities of Harvey W. Scott." Doctoral dissertation, University of Oregon, 1961.

2892 NASH, Lee M. "Scott of the *Oregonian:* The Editor as Historian." *Ore Hist Q,* LXX (1969), 197–232.

2893 PRICE, Warren C. *Literature of Journalism: An Annotated Bibliography.* Minneapolis, Minn., 1959.

2894 SPLITTER, Henry W. "Newspapers of Los Angeles: The First Fifty Years, 1851–1900." *J W,* II (1963), 435–458.

2895 STRATTON, Porter A. *The Territorial Press of New Mexico, 1834–1912.* Albuquerque, N.M., 1969.

2896 TURNBULL, George S. *History of Oregon Newspapers.* Portland, Ore., 1939.

2897 WYMAN, Mark. "Frontier Journalism." *Idaho Yes,* XVII (Spring 1973), 30–36.

XXXV. Religion

2898 AHLSTROM, Sydney D. *A Religious History of the American People.* New Haven, Conn., 1972. †

2899 BELESS, James W., Jr. "Daniel S. Tuttle, Missionary Bishop of Utah." *Utah Hist Q,* XXVII (1959), 359–378.

2900 BENDER, Norman J. "The Crusade of the Blue Banner: Rocky Mountain Presbyterianism, 1870–1900." Doctoral dissertation, University of Colorado, 1971.

2901 BERGER, John A. *The Franciscan Missions of California.* New York, 1941.

2902 BERKHOFER, Robert F., Jr. *Salvation and the Savage: An Analysis of Protestant Missions and American Indian Response, 1787–1862.* Lexington, Ken., 1965. †

2903 BOREN, Carter E. *Religion on the Texas Frontier.* San Antonio, Tex., 1968. Disciples of Christ.

2904 BRECK, Allen duPont. *The Episcopal Church in Colorado, 1860–1963.* Denver, Colo., 1963.

2905 BURNS, Robert I. *The Jesuits and the Indian Wars of the Northwest.* New Haven, Conn., 1965.

2906 BURR, Nelson R., comp. *Religion in American Life.* New York, 1971. †

2907 DRURY, Clifford M. *Marcus and Narcissa Whitman and the Opening of Old Oregon.* 2 vols. Glendale, Calif., 1973.

2908 DRURY, Clifford M. "Protestant Missionaries in Oregon: A Bibliographic Survey." *Ore Hist Q,* L (1949), 209–221.

RELIGION

2909 EDMONDSON, William D. "Fundamentalist Sects of Los Angeles, 1900–1930." Doctoral dissertation, Claremont College, 1969.

2910 ELLIOTT, Errol T. *Quakers on the American Frontier.* Richmond, Ind., 1969.

2911 ENGLEHARDT, Zephyrin. *The Missions and Missionaries of California.* 4 vols. San Francisco, 1908–1915.

2912 GEIGER, Maynard J. *Franciscan Missionaries in Hispanic California, 1769–1848: A Biographical Dictionary.* San Marino, Calif., 1969.

2913 GEIGER, Maynard J. *The Life and Times of Fray Junípero Serra, O.F.M.; or the Man Who Never Turned Back, 1713–1784: A Biography.* Washington, D.C., 1959.

2914 GOODYKOONTZ, Colin B. *Home Missions on the American Frontier, with Particular Reference to the American Home Missionary Society.* Caldwell, Idaho, 1939.

2915 HANCHETT, William. "The Question of Religion and the Taming of California, 1849–1854." *Calif Hist Soc Q,* XXXII (1953), 49–56, 119–144.

2916 HINCKLEY, Ted C. *The Americanization of Alaska.* On Sheldon Jackson and missionary work in Alaska. See 54.

2917 JANZEN, Kenneth L. "The Transformation of the New England Religious Tradition in California, 1849–1869." Doctoral dissertation, Claremont Graduate School, 1964.

2918 JERVEY, Edward D. *The History of Methodism in Southern California and Arizona.* Nashville, Ten., 1960.

2919 JOHNSON, Charles A. *The Frontier Camp Meeting: Religion's Harvest Time.* Dallas, Tex., 1955.

2920 KESSELL, John L. "Friars versus Bureaucrats: The Mission as a Threatened Institution on the Arizona-Sonora Frontier, 1767–1842." *W Hist Q,* V (1974), 151–162.

2921 KESSELL, John L. *Mission of Sorrows: Jesuit Guevavi and the Pimas, 1691–1767.* Tucson, Ariz., 1970.

2922 LYONS, Letitia M. *Francis Norbet Blanchet and the Founding of the Oregon Missions (1838–1848).* Washington, D.C., 1940.

2923 LYTTLE, Charles H. *Freedom Moves West: A History of the Western Unitarian Conference, 1852–1952.* Boston, 1952.

2924 MCGLOIN, John B. *Jesuits by the Golden Gate: The Society of Jesus in San Francisco, 1849–1969.* San Francisco, 1972.

2925 MIYAKAWA, T. Scott. *Protestants and Pioneers: Individualism and Conformity on the American Frontier.* Chicago, 1964.

2926 MONTESANO, Philip M. "San Francisco Black Churches in the Early 1860's: Political Pressure Group." *Calif Hist Q,* LII (1973), 145–152.

2927 NEDRY, H. S. "The Friends Come to Oregon. . . ." *Ore Hist Q,* XLV (1944), 195–217, 306–325; XLVI (1945), 36–43.

2928 PETERS, Robert N. "From Sect to Church: A Study of the Permutation of Methodism on the Oregon Frontier." Doctoral dissertation, University of Washington, 1973. Covers 1834 to 1865.

2929 PETERS, Robert N. "Preachers in Politics: A Conflict Touching the Methodist Church in Oregon." *Pac N W Q,* LXIII (1972), 142–149.

2930 SCHECK, John F. "Transplanting a Tradition: Thomas Lamb Eliot and the Unitarian Conscience in the Pacific Northwest, 1865–1905." Doctoral dissertation, University of Oregon, 1969.

2931 SERVÍN, Manuel P. "The Secularization of the California Missions: A Reappraisal." *S Calif Q,* XLVII (1965), 133–149.

2932 SHANNON, James P. *Catholic Colonization on the Western Frontier.* New Haven, Conn., 1957.

2933 STECKLER, Gerard G. "Charles John Seghers, Missionary Bishop in the American Northwest." Doctoral dissertation, University of Washington, 1963.

2934 SWEET, William W. "The Churches as Moral Courts on the Frontier." *Church Hist,* II (1933), 3–21.

2935 SWEET, William W., ed. *Religion on the American Frontier.* 4 vols. New York and Chicago, 1931–1946. Includes volumes on Baptists, Presbyterians, Congregationalists, and Methodists.

2936 THOMAS, Lately. *Storming Heaven: The Lives and Turmoils of Minnie Kennedy and Aimee Semple McPherson.* New York, 1970. †

2937 TUTTLE, Daniel S. *Reminiscences of a Missionary Bishop.* New York, 1906.

2938 UNDERHILL, Ruth. *Red Man's Religion.* See 472.

2939 VOGHT, Martha. "Shamans and Padres: The Religion of the Southern California Mission Indians." *Pac Hist Rev,* XXXVI (1967), 363–373.

2940 VOLLMAR, Edward R. *The Catholic Church in America: An Historical Bibliography.* 2d ed. New York, 1963.

2941 WARDIN, Albert W., Jr. *Baptists in Oregon.* Portland, Ore., 1969.

2942 WEIGLE, Mary M. "*Los Hermanos Penitentes:* Historical and Ritual Aspects of Folk Religion in Northern New Mexico and Southern Colorado." Doctoral dissertation, University of Pennsylvania, 1971.

XXXVI. Western Characteristics

2943 "The American West as an Underdeveloped Region." *J Econ Hist,* XVI (December 1956). Contains eleven essays dealing with frontier West subjugation to vicissitudes of national booms and busts.

2944 BERKHOFER, Robert F., Jr. "Space, Time, Culture and the New Frontier." *Ag Hist,* XXXVIII (1964), 21–30. Followed by comments by Earl Pomeroy, pp. 31–33.

2945 BLOOM, Jo Tice. "Cumberland Gap Versus South Pass: The East or West in Frontier History." *W Hist Q,* III (1972), 153–167.

2946 CAUGHEY, John W. "The American West: Frontier and Region." *Ariz W,* I (1959), 7–12.

2947 CLARK, Thomas D. "Social and Cultural Continuity in American Frontiering." *People of the Plains and Mountains.* Ed. Ray A. Billington. Westport, Conn., 1973.

2948 DE VOTO, Bernard. "The West: A Plundered Province." *Harp,* CLIX (August 1934), 355–364.

2949 DE VOTO, Bernard. "The West Against Itself." *Harp,* CXCIV (January 1947), 1–13.

2950 DICK, Everett. "Water, a Frontier Problem." *Neb Hist,* XLIX (1968), 215–245.

2951 GASTIL, Raymond D. "The Pacific Northwest as a Cultural Region: A Symposium." *Pac N W Q,* LXIV (1973), 147–162. Includes comments by Norman Clark, Richard W. Etulain, and Otis A. Pease

2952 GRESSLEY, Gene M. "Colonialism: A Western Complaint." *Pac N W Q,* LIV (1963), 1–8.

2953 HANSEN, Klaus J. "The Millennium, the West, and Race in the Antebellum American Mind." *W Hist Q,* III (1972), 373–390.

2954 HOLLON, W. Eugene. *The Great American Desert: Then and Now.* New York, 1966. Repr. Lincoln, Neb., 1975. †

2955 IVES, Ronald L. "Geography and History in the Arid West." *Am W,* I (Spring 1964), 54–63.

2956 JOHANSEN, Dorothy O. "A Working Hypothesis for the Study of Migration." *Pac Hist Rev,* XXXVI (1967), 1–12.

2957 LAMAR, Howard R. "Historical Relevances and the American West." *Ventures,* VII (1968).

2958 MARKS, Barry. "The Concept of Myth in *Virgin Land.*" *Am Q,* V (1953), 71–76.

2958A MOTTRAM, Eric. " 'The Persuasive Lips': Men and Guns in America, the West." *J Am Stud,* X (1976), 53–84.

2959 PAUL, Rodman W. "Patterns of Culture in the American West." *Alas Rev,* III (1967–68), 137–150.

2960 POMEROY, Earl. "Toward a Reorientation of Western History: Continuity and Environment." *Miss Val Hist Rev,* XLI (1955), 579–600.

2961 POMEROY, Earl. "What Remains of the West." *Utah Hist Q,* XXXV (1967), 37–55.

2962 SMITH, Henry Nash. *Virgin Land: The American West as Symbol and Myth.* See 2761.

2963 SMITH, Henry Nash. "The West as an Image of the American Past." *U Kan City Rev,* XVIII (1951), 29–40.

2964 SORENSON, John L. "The West as a Network of Cultures." *Essays on the American West, 1972–1973.* Ed. Thomas G. Alexander. Provo, Utah, 1974.

2965 SPICER, Edward H. "Worlds Apart—Cultural Differences in the Modern Southwest." *Ariz Q,* XIII (1957), 197–237.

2966 STEGNER, Wallace. "History, Myth, and the Western Writer." *Am W,* IV (May 1967), 61–62, 76–79.

2967 STEGNER, Wallace. *The Sound of Mountain Water.* See 2766.

2968 STRATTON, David H. "The Dilemma of American Elbowroom." *Pac N W Q,* LVI (1965), 30–35.

2969 VEYSEY, Lawrence R. "Myth and Reality in Approaching American Regionalism." *Am Q,* XII (1960), 31–43.

2970 WEBB, Walter Prescott. "The American West, Perpetual Mirage." *Harp,* CCXIV (May 1957), 25–31.

2971 WEBB, Walter Prescott. "The West and the Desert" *Mont: Mag W Hist,* VIII (January 1958), 2–12.

2972 WELTER, Rush. "The Frontier West as Image of American Society, 1776–1860." *Pac N W Q,* LII (1961), 1–6.

2973 YOUNG, Mary. "The West and American Cultural Identity: Old Themes and New Variations." *W Hist Q,* I (1970), 137–160.

INDEX

Abajian, James de T., 2128
Abbott, Carl, 1819
Aberle, Sophie D., 353
Abernethy, Thomas P., 216, 217, 218, 219
Abler, Thomas S., 313
Abudu, Assibi O., 1026
Acuña, Rodolfo, 585, 875
Adams, Andy, 1131
Adams, Ephraim D., 586
Adams, Frank, 1373, 1374
Adams, James T., 23, 24
Adams, Kramer A., 1528
Adams, Ramon F., 25, 85, 1132, 2266, 2267, 2784
Ahlstrom, Sydney D., 2898
Albright, Robert E., 2354
Alden, John R., 220
Alenius, E. M. J., 1027
Alexander, Charles C., 2268
Alexander, Thomas G., 929, 1434, 1907, 2622
Allen, Harry C., 124
Allen, Howard W., 2421
Allen, James B., 929, 930, 930A, 968, 1820, 1821, 1956
Allen, John L., 766
Allen, Martha M., 2623
Allison, Clinton B., 2850
Almack, John C., 2851
Almaráz, Felix D., 825
Almquist, Alan J., 2249
Alter, J. Cecil, 484, 2886
Alter, Judith, 2785
Alvord, Clarence W., 221, 222
Ambler, Charles H., 587
Ambler, Thomas S., 313
Amerine, Maynard A., 1263
Anderson, Bern, 767
Anderson, Frederick, 2762
Anderson, George L., 1435, 1759, 1760, 1903
Anderson, Jack, 125
Anderson, Nels, 931
Anderson, Per Sveaas, 126
Andreano, Ralph L., 1617, 1618
Andrews, Charles M., 223
Andrews, Ralph W., 1529, 1530
Andrews, Thomas F., 588, 589, 1678, 1679, 2129

Andriot, John L., 26
Appleton, John B., 86
Arestad, Sverre, 2204, 2205
Arrington, Leonard J., 932, 933, 934, 935, 936, 937, 937A, 938, 1018, 1028, 1029, 1030, 1264, 1265, 1266, 1761, 1904, 1904A, 1905, 1906, 1907, 2046, 2422, 2624
Arroyo, Leobardo Luis (see Leobardo Arroyo, Luis)
Ashby, LeRoy, 2423
Astro, Richard, 2692
Athearn, Robert G., 40, 672, 673, 1762, 1763, 1764, 2355
Atherton, Lewis, 1031, 1032, 1134, 1822, 1823, 1908
Atkin, W.T., 485
Attebery, Louie W., 2693
Atwood, Wallace W., 27
Austin, Mary, 1229, 2694
Averbach, Alvin, 1824
Aydelotte, Frank, 1135
Ayres, Robert W., 1531

Babcock, Willoughby M., 486
Baden, Anne L., 1619
Bailey, Kenneth, 224
Bailey, Thomas A., 2047
Bain, Joe S., 1375, 1620
Baird, Joseph A., Jr., 2804
Bakeless, John E., 225, 768
Baker, Abner, 1909
Baker, Gladys, 1347
Bakewell, Dennis C., 2130
Bakken, Gordon M., 2356, 2357
Baldwin, Alice Blackwood, 2625
Baldwin, Donald N., 2529
Ball, Carleton, 1267
Ball, Larry D., 2269
Bancroft, Hubert H., 1, 826, 939, 2270
Banham, Reyner, 2805
Banning, Evelyn I., 2626
Bannon, John F., 827, 828, 830
Barber, William D., 226
Barker, Charles A., 2695
Barker, Eugene C., 590
Barnes, Donald M., 1957
Barnes, Robert J., 1621
Barnett, Paul S., 1910

INDEX

Barnhart, John D., 227
Barr, Alwyn, 2358
Barsness, Richard W., 1709
Barth, Gunther, 1825, 1826, 2048
Bartlett, Richard A., 127, 769, 770, 2530
Bartley, Ernest R., 1622
Baskauskas, Liucija, 2206
Bates, J. Leonard, 1623, 2424, 2531, 2532
Bauer, K. Jack, 591
Baur, John E., 1033
Bayard, Charles J., 1958
Beaglehole, J.C., 771
Beal, Merrill D., 41, 346, 674, 1765
Bean, Walton, 42, 2425, 2426
Beasley, Delilah L., 2131
Beaton, Kendall, 1624
Bechtol, Paul T., Jr., 1959
Beck, Warren A., 43
Becker, Carl, 128
Becker, George F., 1048
Beckham, Stephen Dow, 1532
Beckman, Alan C., 129
Beckwourth, James P., 487
Beers, Henry P., 675, 676, 677, 678
Beilharz, Edwin A., 829
Beless, James W., Jr., 2899
Bell, James C., Jr., 1680
Bell, William G., 2271
Beller, Jack, 2132
Belous, Russell E., 2133
Bemis, Samuel Flagg, 592
Bender, Averam B., 679
Bender, Norman J., 2900
Benge, Dennis E., 593
Bennett, M. K., 1268
Benson, Lee A., 130, 131, 132
Benson, Maxine, 80, 772
Bentley, Arthur F., 1269
Berge, Wendell, 1911
Berger, John A., 2901
Bergquist, James M., 1436
Berkhofer, Robert F., Jr., 133, 347, 348, 349, 2359, 2902, 2944
Berner, Richard C., 1533
Berthrong, Donald J., 350
Berton, Pierre, 1034
Berwanger, Eugene H., 2134, 2135
Betenson, Lula P., 2272
Bibb, Thomas W., 2853
Bicha, Karel D., 2427
Bieber, Ralph P., 2, 1035
Bill, Alfred H., 594

Billington, Monroe, 2852
Billington, Ray A., 3, 4, 5, 87, 134, 135, 136, 137, 138, 139, 140, 141, 142, 143, 144, 1437
Binkley, William C., 595, 596
Binns, Archie, 1827
Birney, Hoffman, 2273
Bittle, William E., 2136
Bitton, Davis, 940
Blackburn, George M., 2232, 2332
Blackford, Mansel G., 1912, 1913, 2428
Blackorby, Edward C., 2429
Blair, Alma R., 982A
Blake, Nelson M. 2627
Blankenship, Warren M., 2430
Blew, Robert W., 2274
Bloedel, Richard Henry, 2360
Blomkvist, E. E., 773
Bloom, Jo Tice, 2945
Bloom, John P., 6, 597, 2361, 2362
Bloomfield, Arthur J., 2839
Board, John C., 2628
Boatright, Mody C., 1625, 1626, 2696
Boehm, Eric, 88
Boening, Rose M., 1376
Bogue, Allan G., 1270, 1438, 2275
Bogue, Margaret B., 1438
Bohme, Frederick G., 2207, 2208
Bolino, August C., 1036
Bolkhovitinov, N. N., 145
Bolton, Frederick E., 2853
Bolton, Herbert E., 774, 775, 830, 831, 832, 833, 834, 835
Bond, Beverly W., Jr., 228
Bontemps, Arna, 2137
Boren, Carter E., 2903
Boskin, Joseph, 1828
Bosworth, Allan R., 2049
Bourne, Kenneth, 598
Bowen, William A., 1681
Bowers, William L., 1271
Box, Thadis W., 1136, 2533
Boyd, William H., 1766
Boyer, Paul S., 28
Boynton, Percy H., 2698
Brack, Gene M., 599, 600, 2241
Bradfute, Richard W., 1439
Brady, Donal V., 2815
Brammer, Clarence L., 2431
Branch, E. Douglas, 1137
Brandhorst, L. Carl, 1377
Brandon, William, 351
Branyan, Robert L., 1862
Brauer, Kinley J., 601

Brayer, Herbert O., 1138, 1440
Brebner, John B., 229, 602
Breck, Allen duPont, 2209, 2904
Brennan, John, 2432
Brettell, Richard A., 2805A
Brewster, William, 230
Bridenbaugh, Carl, 231
Briggs, Ernestine B., 2817
Briggs, Harold E., 44, 1230, 1231, 1272, 2816, 2817
Briggs, Jean L., 352
Brinckerhoff, Sidney R., 836
Brinley, John E., Jr., 1960
Brissenden, Paul F., 1961
Britzman, Homer E., 2784
Brodhead, Michael J., 2433
Brodie, Fawn M., 943
Brooks, Juanita, 944, 945, 946, 2210
Brophy, Robert J., 2699
Brophy, William A., 353
Brough, Charles H., 1378
Brown, Dee A., 680, 2629
Brown, E. K., 2700
Brown, Giles T., 1962
Brown, Harry J., 1232, 1233
Brown, Mrs. Hugh, 2629A
Brown, Mark H., 681
Brown, Richard D., 1441
Brown, Richard Maxwell, 2276, 2277, 2277A
Brudnoy, David, 2854
Brunton, Anne M., 876
Buchholtz, Curtis W., 2534
Buck, Elizabeth H., 232
Buck, Solon J., 232, 1273, 1274, 2434, 2435
Buley, R. C., 233
Bullock, Paul, 1829, 2138, 2436
Bunker, Robert, 573
Burbank, Garin, 2437
Burch, Albert, 1037
Burcham, L. T., 1139
Burg, B. Richard, 2278
Burgess, Sherwood D., 1535
Burke, John, 2630
Burke, Robert E., 2438
Burlingame, Merrill G., 45, 682
Burmeister, Charles A., 1140
Burnette, O. Lawrence, Jr., 146
Burns, Edward M., 2855
Burns, Robert I., 2905
Burnside, Wesley M., 2786
Burr, Nelson R., 2906
Burroughs, John R., 1141

Burt, Alfred L., 603
Burton, Robert E., 2439
Butcher, Edward, 1612
Butler, Lindley S., 234
Butler, Michael D., 2701
Butt, Paul D., 1914
Butterfield, Lyman H., 382

Caldwell, Norman W., 683, 684, 685
Calef, Wesley C., 1142
Camarillo, Albert M., 877
Cameron, Jenks, 1536
Camp, Charles L., 119, 493, 584, 819, 1708
Campbell, Howard L., 878
Cannon, Charles A., 947, 2631
Carlson, Alvar Ward, 1235
Carlson, Leland H., 1038
Carman, Ezra A., 1236
Carosso, Vincent P., 1275
Carpenter, Clifford D., 1143
Carpenter, Frederic I., 2702
Carpenter, John A., 686
Carpenter, Ronald H., 147
Carr, Ralph, 1442
Carr, William G., 2856
Carranco, Lynwood, 2050, 2279
Carriker, Robert O., 1915
Carroll, John A., 89
Carroll, John M., 687, 2139, 2140
Carroll, Peter N., 235
Carstensen, Vernon, 1443, 1916
Cart, Theodore W., 2535
Carter, Clarence E., 6, 2362
Carter, George E., 1144
Carter, Harvey L., 488
Caruso, John A., 236, 237, 238, 239
Cash, Joseph H., 1039, 1963
Castañeda, Carlos E., 837
Castillo, Edward D., 318
Catlin, George, 354
Caughey, John W., 7, 8, 46, 355, 1040, 1829A, 2280, 2536, 2946
Caughey, La Ree, 1829A
Cauley, T. J., 1145
Caves, Richard E., 1375
Cawelti, John G., 2281, 2702A, 2703
Chadwick, Robert A., 1041
Chaffee, Eugene B., 1830
Chambers, Clarke A., 1276
Chambers, William N., 604
Champlin, Ardath I., 2857
Chan, Loren B., 2439A

INDEX

Chaplin, Ralph, 1965
Chapman, Arthur, 1710
Chapman, Berlin B., 1444, 1831
Chapman, Charles E., 838
Chen, Wen-Hui Chang, 2051
Chittenden, Elizabeth F., 2632
Chittenden, Hiram M., 489, 1711
Chiu, Ping, 1966, 2052
Choate, Julian E., Jr., 1162
Choy, Philip P., 2053
Christensen, Harold T., 948, 2633
Chu, George, 2054
Clanton, O. Gene, 2440
Clapp, Earle H., 1537
Clapp or Clappe, Louise A. K.S., 2634
Clar, C. Raymond, 1538
Clark, Charles E., 240
Clark, Ira G., 1378A, 1767
Clark, James A., 1627, 1628
Clark, Norman H., 1539, 1832, 1967,
    2441
Clark, Thomas D., 241, 2947
Clarke, Dwight L., 690, 1917
Clawson, Marion, 1146, 1445, 1446,
    1447, 1448, 1449, 1450, 1509
Clay, John, 1147
Cleland, Robert G., 490, 1042, 1148
Clemens, Samuel L., 1043
Clendenen, Clarence C., 691, 692
Clepper, Henry E., 1540, 2537
Clifford, John, 2704
Clinch, Thomas A., 1768, 1968, 2442
Cline, Gloria Griffen, 491, 492, 776
Cline, Howard F., 839
Clinton, Katherine B., 1888
Cloud, Roy W., 2858
Clough, Wilson O., 2705
Clyman, James, 493
Cochran, John S., 1769
Cochran, Thomas C., 1770
Coffin, Arthur B., 2706
Coffman, Edward M., 693
Cohen, Jerry, 2141
Cohn, Edwin J., Jr., 1918
Cole, Arthur H., 1237
Cole, Robert L., 2443
Coleman, Roy V., 24
Coleman, William, 148
Coletta, Paolo E., 2444
Collier, John, 356
Collins, John R., 605
Colton, Ray C., 694
Coman, Edwin T., Jr., 1541
Commoner, Barry, 2538
Compton, Wilson M., 1542

Conkin, Paul K., 1379
Conkling, Margaret P., 1712
Conkling, Roscoe P., 1712
Conlin, Joseph R., 1969, 1970
Conn, Stetson, 2055
Connelly, Thomas L., 1713
Connor, L. G., 1238
Connor, Seymour V., 47, 606, 607,
    1451
Conot, Robert, 2142, 2282
Conrat, Maisie, 2056
Conrat, Richard, 2056
Conroy, Jack, 2137
Cook, Sherburne, 357
Cook, Warren L., 840
Cooley, Everett L., 90, 976, 2363
Cooley, Richard A., 2539, 2540
Coolidge, Mary R., 2057
Coombs, F. Alan, 2445
Cooper, Erwin, 1380
Copp, Nelson G., 880
Corkran, David H., 358, 359
Cornish, Dudley T., 695, 2143
Corwin, Arthur F., 881, 882
Cotroneo, Ross R., 1771
Cotterill, Robert S., 360
Coulter, C. Brewster, 1277, 1381, 1382,
    1383
Cowan, Charles S., 1543
Cowan, Ian McT., 494
Cowan, Richard O., 930, 949
Cowan, Robert E., 91
Cowan, Robert G., 91
Cowdrey, Albert E., 2541
Cox, John H., 1544, 1545
Cox, Thomas R., 1546, 2542, 2543
Coyner, David H., 495
Cracroft, Richard H., 950
Craig, Richard B., 883
Crane, Paul, 2058, 2283
Crane, Verner W., 242
Craven, Avery, 149, 150, 151
Craven, Wesley F., 243, 244
Crawley, Peter, 951
Creel, Cecil W., 1278
Cremin, Lawrence A., 2859
Croghan, George, 696
Crosby, Alfred W., Jr., 361
Cross, Ira B., 1971
Crouse, Nellis M., 496
Crowder, David L., 2211
Cunningham, Eugene, 2284
Curti, Merle, 152
Curtis, Edward S., 315
Custer, George Armstrong, 697

INDEX

Cuthbertson, Stuart, 497
Cutright, Paul R., 777
Cutter, Donald C., 778

Daggett, Stuart, 1772
Dahlie, Jorgen, 2212, 2213
Dale, Edward E., 153, 362, 1149, 1150, 2860
Dale, Harrison C., 779
Dana, Samuel T., 1547
Danhof, Clarence H., 1279
Daniel, James M., 841
Daniels, Roger, 2059, 2060, 2061, 2062, 2243, 2244
Danziger, Edmund J., Jr., 363
Darrah, William C., 780
Daum, Arnold R., 1675
Davidson, Gordon C., 498
Davies, J. Kenneth, 952, 1972, 1973
Davis, David B., 2707
Davis, J. Kenneth, 952
Davis, James E., 245
Davis, James H., 2285
Davis, Lenwood G., 2144, 2145
Davis, Richard C., 1548
Davis, Ronald L., 154, 2818, 2819, 2840
Davis, W. N., Jr., 9
Davison, Oscar W., 2861
Davison, Sol, 160, 161
Davison, Stanley R., 1384
Dawdy, Doris O., 2787
Day, David T., 1044
De Armond, R. N., 1045, 1833
Debo, Angie, 1834, 1835
Decker, Leslie E., 1452, 1453
DeGolyer, Everette L., 1629
DeGraaf, Lawrence B., 1836, 1837, 2146, 2147, 2148, 2245
DeGrazia, Alfred, 2446
Delmatier, Royce D., 2447
Deloria, Vine, 364
De Pillis, Mario S., 953
Derig, Betty, 2063
De Roos, Robert, 1385
De Rosier, Arthur H., Jr., 365
Dethloff, Henry C., 1280
Deutsch, Herman J., 2364
De Voto, Bernard, 246, 499, 500, 608, 781, 954, 2544, 2708, 2948, 2949
Dick, Everett, 247, 1281, 1454, 2636, 2950
Dierdorff, John, 2820
Dillingham, William B., 2709

Dillon, Richard, 782
Dimsdale, Thomas J., 2286
Dippie, Brian W., 366, 698, 2788
Dobie, J. Frank, 92, 2710
Dobyns, Henry F., 366A
Dockstader, Frederick J., 316, 367
Dodds, Gordon B., 1919, 2545, 2546, 2547, 2548, 2549, 2550
Dollar, Clyde D., 368
Donald, David, 2711
Dondore, Dorothy Anne, 2712
Donnelly, Joseph P., 501
Donnelly, Thomas C., 2448
Dorsett, Lyle W., 2214
Douglass, William A., 2215
Downes, Randolph C., 248, 369
Dozier, Edward P., 370
Dozier, Jack, 1455
Drache, Hiram M., 1282
Drago, Harry S., 1151, 2637
Draper, Benjamin P., 2821
Driver, Harold E., 317
Drotning, Philip T., 2149
Drucker, Philip, 371, 372
Drury, Clifford M., 2638, 2907, 2908
Dubofsky, Melvyn, 1974, 1975, 1976
Duckett, Margaret, 2713
Dué, John F., 1783
Duffus, Robert L., 1682
Dumke, Glenn S., 2862
Dunbar, Robert G., 1283, 1284, 1386
Dunbar, Seymour, 1714
Dunham, Harold H., 1456
Duniway, Abigail Scott, 2639
Dunn, Jacob P., Jr., 373
Dupree, A. Hunter, 783
Durham, G. Homer, 956
Durham, Philip, 1152, 2150
Durrell, Edward, 1744
Durrenberger, Robert W., 1387
Dusenberry, William, 1153
Dwyer, Robert J., 2216
Dykes, Jefferson C., 2788A
Dykstra, Robert R., 1154, 1285, 1838, 2287
Dysart, Jane, 841A, 2639A

Earl, Phillip I., 1977, 2217
Easton, Hamilton P., 1549
Eaton, Herbert, 1683
Eblen, Jack E., 2365, 2366
Eby, Frederick, 2863
Eccles, W. J., 249, 250
Edel, Leon, 2700

INDEX

Edmondson, William D., 2909
Edwards, Everett E., 155, 1155, 1286
Edwards, Glenn T., 699, 700
Edwards, Paul M., 982A
Eggenhofer, Nick, 1715
Elazar, Daniel J., 251, 1839
Elchibegoff, Ivan M., 1550
Elkins, Stanley, 156, 157
Ellet, Elizabeth F., 2640
Elliott, Errol T., 2910
Elliott, Eugene C., 2822
Elliott, Russell R., 48, 93, 1046, 1047, 1840, 1978
Ellis, David M., 252, 1457
Ellis, Elmer, 2449
Ellis, Richard N., 374, 701, 702
Ellison, Joseph, 2367
Ellison, William H., 2368
Ellsworth, S. George, 49, 2641
Emmett, Chris, 703, 704, 1156
Emmons, David M., 1458
Emmons, Samuel F., 1048
Englehardt, Zephyrin, 2911
Erdman, H. E., 1287, 1311
Erisman, Fred, 2551
Ernst, Alice H., 2823
Estergreen, M. Morgan, 502
Etulain, Richard W., 95, 2218, 2713A, 2714, 2715, 2716, 2717, 2718, 2719, 2720
Evans, Samuel L., 1288
Evans, Tony H., 2450
Evans, William B., 1049
Everhart, William C., 2552
Ewan, Joseph A., 784
Ewers, John C., 375, 376, 377, 378, 379, 497, 535, 2642, 2789

Fahey, John, 1050, 1773, 1841, 1979
Fahl, Ronald J., 1551, 2553, 2554
Farb, Peter, 380
Fargo, Lucile F., 1842
Farnham, Wallace D., 1774, 1775
Fatout, Paul, 1843
Faulk, Odie B., 50, 607, 609, 842, 1157, 1684, 1844, 2288
Faulkner, Virginia, 2758
Favour, Alpheus H., 503
Fearis, Donald F., 1980
Fedewa, Philip C., 1158
Fedorova, Svetlana, 51
Fehrenbach, T. R., 381
Fehrenbacher, Don E., 610

Fenton, William N., 382, 432
Ferrell, John R., 1388
Ferriday, Virginia Guest, 2813
Ferrier, William W., 2864
Fiedler, Leslie A., 2721
Field, Matthew C., 1685
Fierman, Floyd S., 1920, 1921, 1922
Fife, Alta, 957
Fife, Austin, 957
Fincher, Ernest B., 884
Fingerhut, Eugene R., 96
Fischer, Duane D., 1552
Fischer, LeRoy H., 2369
Fisher, James A., 2151, 2152, 2153
Fisher, Lloyd H., 1289
Fisher, Mary Frances K., 1290
Fisher, Raymond H., 504
Fite, Gilbert C., 1291, 1292, 1293, 1294, 1295, 1296, 2451
Flack, Dora, 2272
Flanders, Robert B., 958, 959, 960
Fleming, Donald, 2555
Fletcher, Marvin E., 704A, 2153A
Fletcher, Robert H., 1159
Flint, Timothy, 253
Flipper, Henry O., 705, 2154
Fodell, Beverly, 885, 1297, 1981
Fogel, Robert W., 1776, 1777
Fogelson, Robert M., 1845, 1846, 2155, 2289
Folmer, Henry, 254
Folsom, James K., 2722
Foner, Philip S., 1982
Forbes, Gerald, 1630
Forbes, Jack D., 158, 383, 2156
Ford, Worthington C., 1239
Foreman, Grant, 384, 385, 386
Foss, Philip O., 1160, 2556
Foster, Mark S., 1846A
Fowler, Arlen L., 706, 2157
Fowler, Harlan D., 1716
Fowler, Nolan, 611
Fowler, William W., 2643
Fox, Dixon R., 255
Fox, Feramorz Y., 937A, 961
Frakes, George E., 2246
France, Edward, 2158
Franklin, William E., 2159
Franklin, William E., Jr., 2370
Frantz, Joe B., 1161, 1162, 2290
Frazer, Robert W., 707
Frederick, James V., 1717
Fredman, L. E., 2371
Freeman, Martha D., 2790

INDEX

Freeman, Otis W., 1718
Freidel, Frank, 97
Freund, Rudolph, 159
Frey, Howard C., 1744
Friedheim, Robert L., 1983
Friend, Llerena, 612
Friis, Herman R., 785, 786
Frink, Maurice, 1163
Fritz, Emanuel, 1553
Fritz, Henry E., 387, 1164
Fritzsche, Bruno, 1923
Frome, Michael, 1554, 1555, 2557
Frost, Richard H., 1984
Fuchs, Victor R., 505
Fugate, Francis L., 1165
Fuller, John D. P., 613
Fuller, Wayne E., 1817
Furness, Edna L., 2865
Furniss, Norman F., 962
Fussell, Edwin, 2723

Gaboury, William J., 1985, 2452, 2453
Gagey, Edmond M., 2824
Galarza, Ernesto, 886
Galbraith, John S., 506, 507, 508
Gamble, Richard D., 708
Gamio, Manuel, 887, 888
Gannett, Henry, 1556
Ganoe, John T., 1389, 1390, 1459, 1460
Garber, Paul N., 614
Gard, Wayne, 1166, 1167, 2291
Gardner, David P., 2866
Gardner, Richard M., 889, 1461, 2292
Garnel, Donald, 1986
Garnett, Porter, 2293
Garnsey, Morris E., 1924
Garr, Daniel J., 843
Garrard, Lewis H., 509
Garrett, Julia K., 1847
Garth, Thomas R., Jr., 2806
Gartner, Lloyd P., 2237
Garvin, Roy, 2160
Gastil, Raymond D., 2951
Gaston, Edwin W., Jr., 2724
Gates, Charles M., 58, 510, 1332, 1925
Gates, Paul W., 256, 388, 1168, 1169,
    1298, 1299, 1462, 1463, 1464, 1465,
    1466, 1467, 1468, 1469, 1470, 1471,
    1472, 1473, 1474, 2294
Geiger, Maynard J., 2912, 2913
Geis, Gilbert L., 2136
Geiser, Samuel W., 787, 1300
Gentry, Curt, 1987

George, Henry, 1475
Georgetta, Clel., 1240
Ghent, W. J., 515, 1686
Gibb, George S., 1631
Gibbs, Helen M., 1541
Gibson, Arrell M., 98, 389, 390, 1051,
    1170
Gibson, Charles, 844
Gilbert, Benjamin F., 709
Gilbert, Edmund W., 788
Gilfillan, A. B., 1241
Gill, Frank B., 1719
Gilliard, Fred, 2825
Gilligan, James P., 1557
Gilmore, Gladys W., 890
Gilmore, Iris, 2194
Gilmore, N. Ray, 890
Gipson, Lawrence H., 257
Girdner, Audrie, 2064
Glaab, Charles N., 1848
Glad, Paul W., 2454
Glanz, Rudolph, 2219
Glasrud, Bruce A., 2161
Glass, Mary Ellen, 1391, 2455
Gluek, Alvin C., Jr., 511
Godfrey, Kenneth W., 963
Goe, Vernon, 1575, 1789
Goetzmann, William H., 512, 615, 710,
    789, 790, 791
Gohdes, Clarence, 2725, 2826
Gómez-Quiñones, Juan, 891, 892, 892A
Gonzalez, Nancie L., 893
Goode, Kenneth G., 2162
Goodrich, Carter, 160, 161
Goodwin, Cardinal L., 2372
Goodwin, Herbert M., 1778
Goodwyn, Frank, 52
Goodykoontz, Colin B., 2914
Gordon, Clarence W., 1171
Gordon, Margaret S., 1988
Gossett, Thomas F., 2247
Gould, Lewis L., 1407, 2295, 2373,
    2456, 2457
Gower, Calvin W., 2296, 2374
Graebner, Norman A., 616, 617, 618,
    1476
Graham, Stanley S., 711
Grassman, Curtis E., 2458
Graustein, Jeannette E., 792
Grebler, Leo, 894, 895
Greeley, William B., 1558, 1559
Green, Donald E., 1392
Greenleaf, Cameron, 1849
Greenleaf, Richard E., 1477

INDEX

Greever, William S., 1052, 1478, 1779, 1780
Gregg, Josiah, 513, 1687
Greiff, Constance M., 2806A
Gressley, Gene M., 162, 1172, 1173, 1393, 1632, 2375, 2952
Griffiths, David B., 2459, 2460, 2461
Grimes, Alan P., 2644
Grinnell, George Bird, 391
Griswold, Don L., 1053
Griswold, Jean H., 1053
Grodinsky, Julius, 1781
Grodzins, Morton, 2065
Grossman, James, 2726
Grover, David H., 1989, 2297
Gruening, Ernest, 53
Guest, Francis F., 1850
Guice, John D. W., 2376
Gunns, Albert F., 2298
Gunther, Erna, 392
Gurian, Jay, 1054, 2887
Guthrie, A. B., Jr., 10
Guzman, Ralph C., 895, 896, 2248

Haberly, Lloyd, 2791
Hafen, Ann W., 11
Hafen, LeRoy R., 2, 11, 514, 515, 1479, 1720, 1721
Hagan, William T., 393, 394, 395, 2645
Hahn, Henry, 2841
Haines, Francis D., Jr., 516
Hakola, John W., 1926
Halaas, David F., 2888
Halbouty, Michael T., 1628
Hale, Robert M., 2066
Haley, J. Evetts, 1174, 1175
Hall, James, 422
Hall, Linda, 1927
Haller, William, 258
Halvorson, Ora J., 1928
Hamilton, William B., 259
Hamlin, Edith, 2792
Hammond, George P., 846, 1688
Hammond, John Hayes, 1055
Hanchett, William, 2915
Hansen, Gary B., 1030
Hansen, Gladys C., 2067
Hansen, Klaus J., 964, 965, 2953
Hansen, William A., 619
Hardwicke, Robert E., 1633
Hargreaves, Mary W. M., 1301, 1302, 2646

Haring, Clarence H., 847
Harper, Norman D., 163, 164
Harris, Burton, 517
Harris, Chauncy D., 1851
Harris, Eleanor T., 547, 804
Harrison, John P., 662
Harstad, Peter T., 620
Hart, Arthur A., 2807
Harvey, James R., 2163
Harvey, Richard B., 2462
Haskett, Bert, 1242
Haslam, Gerald, 2727
Hassrick, Peter H., 2793, 2794
Hastings, Lansford Warren, 1689
Hata, Donald T., Jr., 2068
Hatcher, Averlyne M., 1176
Havins, T. R., 1177
Hawgood, John A., 621
Hayashi, Tetsumaro, 2692
Hayes, Carlton J. H., 165
Hays, Samuel P., 2558
Haywood, William D., 1990
Hazard, Lucy L., 2728
Heath, H. A., 1236
Heathcote, Lesley M., 1480
Hedges, James B., 1782
Heimert, Alan, 260
Heintz, William F., 2067
Heintzelman, Oliver H., 1303
Heizer, Robert F., 318, 396, 2249
Held, R. Burnell, 1450
Henderson, Lloyd R., 2463
Henderson, Richard B., 2464
Hendrick, Irving, 2867, 2868
Hendricks, George D., 2299
Hendrickson, James E., 2377
Hennings, Robert E., 2465, 2466
Henry, Robert S., 622, 1481
Hensel, Donald W., 2378
Hertzberg, Hazel W., 397
Hess, Leland E., 1852
Hewes, Leslie, 1303A
Hibbard, Benjamin, 1482
Hicks, Jimmie, 2300
Hicks, John D., 1853, 2467, 2509
Hidy, Muriel E., 1635
Hidy, Ralph W., 1560, 1561, 1634, 1635
Higgins, Ruth L., 261
High, James, 1056
Hill, Burton S., 1854
Hill, D. G., 2164
Hill, Edward E., 397A

INDEX

Hill, Forest G., 712
Hill, Frank E., 1561
Hill, Gertrude, 713
Hill, John A., 1244
Hill, Joseph J., 1690
Hill, Marvin S., 966, 967, 968
Hilton, George W., 1783
Hinckley, Ted C., 34, 1929, 2379, 2916
Hindman, Anne A., 2827
Hine, Robert V., 623, 1855
Hinton, Harwood P., 714, 1057
Hinton, Wayne K., 938
Hirschfelder, Arlene B., 319
Hirshson, Stanley P., 969, 1784
Hodge, Frederick W., 320
Hodgins, Francis E., Jr., 2729
Hoebel, E. Adamson, 418
Hoffman, Abraham, 897, 898
Hoffman, Daniel G., 1562
Hofstadter, Richard, 166, 167
Hogan, William R., 2380
Hogg, Thomas C., 2165
Holbrook, Stewart H., 1563, 1564, 1991
Holden, William C., 1179, 1304, 2301
Holder, Preston, 518
Holliday, Jaquelin S., 1058, 1243
Hollon, W. Eugene, 55, 793, 1483,
    2302, 2954
Holman, Frederick V., 519
Holmes, Beatrice H., 1394
Holmes, Jack D. L., 262, 848
Holmes, Jack E., 2468
Holmes, Kenneth L., 520
Homsher, Lola M., 100
Hoopes, Alban W., 398
Horgan, Paul, 56, 849, 850
Horr, David A., 321
Horsman, Reginald, 263, 399, 624
Hosmer, Helen, 1395
Hosokawa, Bill, 2069
Hough, Franklin B., 1565
Hough, John, 1180
Hough, Merrill, 1992
House, Kay S., 2730
Houston, James D., 2070
Houston, Jeanne Wakatsuki, 2070
Howard, James K., 1856
Howard, Joseph K., 57
Howard, Richard P., 970
Howd, Cloice R., 1566
Howes, Edward H., 1688
Hsu, Frances L. K., 2071
Hudson, Charles M., 400

Hudson, Estelle, 2220
Hughes, Willis B., 715
Hughson, Oliver G., 1567
Hultz, Fred, 1244
Hume, Charles V., 2828
Hundley, Norris, Jr., 400A, 899, 1396,
    1397, 1398, 1399, 2072
Hungerford, Edward, 1722
Hunsaker, Kenneth B., 971, 2731
Hunt, Aurora, 716
Hunt, William R., 1059
Hunter, Louis C., 1723
Hunter, Milton R., 972
Huntting, Marshall T., 1060
Hurt, Peyton, 2381
Husband, Michael B., 1691
Hussey, John A., 521
Hutchins, James S., 717
Hutchinson, C. Alan, 851
Hutchinson, William H., 1568, 1636
Hutchison, Claude B., 1305
Huth, Hans, 2559
Hutton, Harold, 2303
Hyde, George E., 401, 402
Hyman, Harold M., 1569, 1993

Ichihashi, Yamato, 2073
Icolari, Dan, 325
Iga, Mamoru, 2074
Inman, Colonel Henry, 1692
Innis, Harold A., 522, 523, 524, 525
Irving, Washington, 526, 527, 794
Ise, John, 1306, 1571, 1637, 2560
Israel, Fred L., 2469
Ives, Ronald L., 2955
Ivins, Stanley S., 973
Iwata, Masakazu, 1307, 2075

Jackson, Donald, 795, 796, 797, 798
Jackson, Helen Hunt, 403
Jackson, Richard H., 974, 1400
Jackson, W. Turrentine, 1061, 1062,
    1063, 1064, 1181, 1182, 1724, 1725,
    1726, 1727, 1857, 1929A, 2382
Jacobs, Melvin C., 625
Jacobs, Wilbur R., 168, 169, 170, 171,
    404, 405, 406, 2561
Jacobson, Larry K., 2734
Jacobstein, J. Myron, 1401
Jaeckel, Solomon P., 2869
James, Alfred P., 264

INDEX

James, Edward T., 28
James, George Wharton, 1402
James, James A., 265
James, Janet W., 28
Janzen, Kenneth L., 2917
Jarrett, Henry, 2562
Jellison, Charles A., 266
Jenkins, Myra E., 1484
Jensen, Billie Barnes, 2647
Jensen, Joan M., 2166
Jensen, Ronald J., 625A
Jensen, Vernon H., 1065, 1572, 1994, 1995, 1996, 2304
Jervey, Edward D., 2918
Jody, Marilyn, 2735
Johannsen, Robert W., 626, 627, 2383
Johansen, Dorothy O., 58, 628, 1719, 1728, 1729, 2384, 2956
John, Elizabeth A. H., 406A
Johnson, Allen, 29
Johnson, Arthur M., 1638, 1639, 1785
Johnson, Charles A., 2919
Johnson, Claudius O., 2470
Johnson, Ralph W., 2563
Johnson, Rue C., 2829
Johnson, Steven L., 322A
Johnson, Virginia W., 718
Jonas, Frank H., 2471, 2472
Jones, Charles O., 2564
Jones, Everett L., 1152, 2150
Jones, Holway R., 2565
Jones, Lamar B., 1308
Jones, Oakah L., Jr., 852, 853
Jones, Wilbur D., 629, 630
Jordan, Lois B., 900
Jordan, Philip D., 2305, 2306, 2307
Jordan, Terry G., 2221
Jorgensen, Joseph G., 407
Josephson, Hannah, 2648
Josephy, Alvin M., Jr., 408, 409, 719
Judah, Charles, 655
Judd, Gerrit P., 101
Juricek, John T., 172

Kachi, Teruko O., 2076
Kagan, Hilde H., 30
Kane, Elizabeth Wood, 976, 2649
Kane, Lucile M., 528
Kane, Murray, 173
Kaplan, Justin, 2736
Kaplan, L. S., 174
Kaplan, Louis, 102
Kaplan, Mirth T., 2385

Kappler, Charles J., 323
Karlin, Jules A., 2077, 2078, 2309, 2472A
Karolides, Nicholas J., 2737
Katz, William L., 2167
Kay, Margarita A., 2650
Keleher, William A., 2310
Kelley, Robert L., 1066
Kellogg, Louise P., 267
Kelly, Lawrence C., 410, 411
Kelsay, Laura E., 324
Kelsey, Harry E., Jr., 1929G
Kemble, John Haskell, 1786
Kenny, Judith Keyes, 1245
Kenny, William R., 1067
Kensel, W. Hudson, 1068
Kernek, Sterling, 175
Kerr, William T., Jr., 2473
Kessell, John L., 2920, 2921
Kesselman, Steven, 176
Kibbe, Pauline R., 901
Kibby, Leo P., 720
Kikuchi, Charles, 2079
King, C. Richard, 2651
King, James C., 631
King, James T., 721, 722
Kinney, Jay P., 412
Kirker, Harold, 2808, 2809
Kirkland, Herbert D., 111, 1573
Kitagawa, Daisuke, 2080
Kitano, Harry H. L., 2081, 2243
Kizer, Benjamin H., 2652
Klein, Barry T., 325
Kleinsorge, Paul L., 1404
Kliewer, Waldo O., 1859
Klingaman, David C., 267A
Klose, Nelson, 1309
Kluckhohn, Clyde, 413
Knapp, F. A., Jr., 632
Knapp, Joseph G., 1310
Knight, Oliver, 1860, 1930, 2889
Knight, Robert E. L., 1997
Knowles, Ruth S., 1640
Knowlton, Clark S., 1485
Knowlton, Evelyn H., 1631
Knowlton, Ezra C., 1787
Koepplin, Leslie W., 2474
Kolko, Gabriel, 1788
Konvitz, Milton R., 2082
Koontz, Louis K., 268
Kortum, Karl, 1574
Kraemer, Erich, 1311
Kraenzel, Carl F., 59
Kroeber, Alfred L., 326, 327

INDEX

Kroeber, Clifton B., 215
Kroeber, Theodora, 414
Kubler, George, 2810
Kuehl, Warren F., 103
Kung, Shien-woo, 2083
Kupper, Winifred, 1246
Kushner, Howard I., 632A

Labbe, John T., 1575, 1789
Lacy, James M., 2653
LaFarge, Oliver, 1861
Lain, Bobby Dave, 2386
Lake, Stuart N., 2311
Lamar, Howard R., 5, 12, 31, 177, 1486, 2387, 2388, 2957
Lambert, C. Roger, 1183, 1184, 1185
Lambert, Neal E., 950
Lange, Dorothea, 1312
Langford, Nathaniel P., 2312
Langum, David J., 2313
LaPiere, Richard T., 2222
Lapp, Rudolph M., 1069, 1070, 2168, 2169, 2170
Larpenteur, Charles, 529
Larrowe, Charles P., 1998
Larsen, Lawrence H., 1862
Larson, Gustive O., 977, 2389
Larson, Henrietta M., 1641
Larson, Robert W., 902, 2251, 2314, 2390, 2475
Larson, T. A., 60, 2058, 2283, 2476, 2654, 2655, 2656, 2657, 2658, 2658A, 2659, 2660
Laslett, John H. M., 1999
Lass, William E., 1731, 1732
Laut, Agnes C., 530
Lavender, David, 60A, 61, 62, 531, 532, 633, 1071, 1693, 1790, 1931
Lawson, Murray G., 533
Lea, Tom, 1186
Leach, Douglas E., 269, 270, 415
Leacock, Eleanor B., 416
Leader, Leonard J., 1863
Leary, William M., Jr., 2477
Leavitt, Francis H., 1733
Leckie, William H., 723, 724, 2171
Leder, Hans H., 2223
LeDuc, Thomas, 1487, 1488, 2566
Lee, Everett S., 178
Lee, Lawrence B., 978, 1405, 1489, 1490, 1491
Lee, Robert Edson, 2738
Lee, Rose Hum, 2084

Lehmann, Valgene W., 1247
Lehmer, Donald J., 855
Leighton, Alexander H., 2085
Leighton, Dorothea, 413
Lenon, Robert, 1130A
Lent, D. Geneva, 534
Leobardo Arroyo, Luis, 892A
Leonard, Glen M., 930A
Leonard, Thomas C., 725
Leonard, William E., 1313
Leonard, William N., 1791
Leonard, Zenas, 535
Lerner, Robert E., 179
Levi, Steven C., 2315
Levine, Stuart, 417
Levinson, Robert E., 1932, 2224, 2225
LeWarne, Charles P., 2000
Lewis, Howard T., 1314
Lewis, Marvin, 1072
Lewis, Merrill E., 180
Lewis, Oscar, 1073, 1792
Lillard, Richard G., 1074
Lilley, William, III, 1406, 1407
Limbaugh, Ronald H., 2391
Linford, Orma, 979
Lingenfelter, Richard E., 1075, 2001, 2316
Link, Arthur S., 2477
Linscome, Sanford A., 2842
Lippincott, Isaac, 536
Lisca, Peter, 2739
Littlefield, Daniel F., Jr., 2684
Littlefield, Henry M., 181
Llewellyn, Karl N., 418
Lloyd, John W., 1315
Locklear, William R., 2086
Loewy, Jean, 2661
Loftis, Anne, 2064, 2087, 2252
Logan, Leonard M., 1642
Lonsdale, David L., 2002, 2003
Lord, Eliot, 1076
Lotchin, Roger W., 1864
Lower, Richard C., 2478
Lowie, Robert H., 419
Lowitt, Richard, 2479
Lucas, Henry S., 2226
Lucia, Ellis, 1576
Luckingham, Bradford, 1865
Luebke, Frederick C., 2227
Lurie, Nancy Oestreich, 416, 417, 420, 421
Luttig, John C., 537
Lyman, George D., 1077
Lyman, Stanford M., 2088, 2089

INDEX

Lyon, E. Wilson, 634
Lyon, T. Edgar, 980
Lyon, William H., 182, 2890
Lyons, Letitia M., 2922
Lythgoe, Dennis L., 981, 2172
Lyttle, Charles H., 2923

Maas, Arthur, 1408
McAfee, Ward M., 1793, 1794
McCague, James, 1795
McCallum, Frances T., 1187, 1316
McCallum, Henry D., 1187, 1316
McCarthy, G. Michael, 2479A, 2480, 2567
McClellan, Robert, 2090
McClelland, Peter D., 1492
McClintock, James H., 982
McClintock, Thomas C., 1317, 2481
McCloskey, Michael, 2568
McComb, David G., 1866
McConnell, Grant, 1577, 2569
McConnell, Virginia, 2830
McCoy, Donald R., 2482
McCoy, Esther, 2811
McCoy, Joseph G., 1188
McCracken, Harold, 2795, 2796, 2797, 2798
McCrum, Blanche P., 106
McCulloch, Walter F., 1578
McDermott, John F., 271, 272, 800, 856
MacDonald, Norbert, 1867, 1933, 1934
McGeary, M. Nelson, 2570
McGiffert, Michael, 2870
McGloin, John B., 2924
McHenry, Robert, 2571
McHugh, Tom, 2571A
MacKay, Douglas, 538
McKenna, Marian, 2483
McKenney, Thomas L., 422
McKenzie, R. D., 2091
McKiernan, F. Mark, 982A
McKinley, Charles, 2572
McKitrick, Eric, 156, 157
McLaughlin, R. P., 1643
McLear, Patrick E., 1889
McLeod, Alexander, 2092
McLoughlin, William G., 423
MacMinn, George R., 2831
MacMullen, Jerry, 1734
McMurrin, Sterling M., 983
McMurry, Donald L., 2004
McNelis, Sarah, 1078

McNickle, D'Arcy, 424
McNiff, William J., 984
McNitt, Frank, 425
McPhee, John A., 2573
McReynolds, Edwin C., 63
McWilliams, Carey, 903, 1318, 1319, 2005, 2006, 2093
Maginnis, Paul M., 183
Mahnken, Norbert R., 1189
Major, Mabel, 2740
Majors, Alexander, 1735
Malin, James C., 1320, 1321, 1322
Malone, Dumas, 29
Malone, Michael P., 63A, 2484, 2485
Malone, Rose Mary, 104
Mann, Ralph E., 1079, 1868, 1869
Manning, Thomas G., 801
Mardock, Robert W., 426
Margolis, Julius, 1375
Marken, Jack W., 328
Marks, Barry, 2958
Marley, Bert W., 2392
Marquis, Arnold, 329
Marsden, Michael T., 2720
Marshall, S. L. A., 726
Martin, Albro, 1795A, 1934A
Martin, Calvin, 426A
Martin, Douglas D., 427
Martin, Robert L., 1870
Martin, Walter T., 1871
Martin, William E., 1338
Martínez, John R., 904
Mason, David T., 1579
Mason, Philip P., 1736
Mathews, John J., 428, 1644
Mathews, Lois K., 273
Mattes, Merrill J., 1694, 1695, 1696
Matthews, Fred H., 2094
Mattison, Ray H., 539, 540, 727, 1190
Maudslay, Robert, 1248
Maughan, Ila Fisher, 2832
Mauss, Armand L., 985
May, Dean L., 937A
Mead, Elwood, 1409, 1410
Mead, Walter J., 1580
Meany, Edmond S., Jr., 1581
Meers, John R., 1323
Meier, Matt S., 905, 906
Meinig, D. W., 13, 64, 64A, 65, 986, 1324, 1325, 1326
Meisel, Max, 802
Meldrum, George W., 2253
Melendy, H. Brett, 1582, 1583, 2095
Melton, William Ray, 1584

INDEX

Melville, J. Keith, 987
Mercer, Asa S., 2317
Mercer, Lloyd J., 1493
Meriam, Lewis, 429
Merk, Frederick, 541, 542, 635, 636, 637, 638, 639, 640
Merk, Lois Bannister, 639, 640
Merrens, H. Roy, 274
Merriam, H. G., 2254
Merriam, Paul G., 1872, 1872A
Mersky, Roy M., 1401
Messing, John, 1494
Metz, Leon C., 2318
Metzgar, Joseph V., 907, 2255
Meyer, Albert J., 1327
Meyer, Arthur B., 1540
Meyer, Roy W., 430, 2741
Miles, Edwin A., 641
Miller, Nyle H., 105, 2319
Miller, Orlando W., 1328
Miller, Perry, 275
Miller, Ronald L., 1935
Miller, Stuart C., 2096
Miller, Thomas L., 1495, 1496
Miller, William H., 1329
Miller, Zane L., 1873
Millis, H. A., 2097
Mills, Randall V., 1737
Milton, John R., 2742, 2743, 2744
Miner, H. Craig, 1645
Minto, John, 1236, 1249
Mintz, Warren, 1330
Mittelbach, Frank G., 1874
Miyakawa, T. Scott, 2925
Miyamoto, S. Frank, 2098
Modell, John, 2099, 2100, 2662
Moeller, Beverly B., 1411
Moffitt, John C., 2871
Mohr, Walter H., 431
Moloney, Francis X., 543
Monaghan, Jay, 728, 729, 1697
Montesano, Philip M., 2173, 2174, 2926
Montgomery, James W., 2663
Montgomery, Richard G., 544
Mood, Fulmer, 184, 185
Moody, Eric N., 2486
Moody, Ralph, 1738
Moore, Arthur K., 276
Moore, Joan W., 895, 908, 1874
Moore, Marjorie (see Brown, Mrs. Hugh)
Moore, R. Laurence, 66
Moore, Richard R., 1646
Moore, Waddy W., 2320

Moorhead, Max L., 1698
Morgan, Arthur E., 1412
Morgan, Dale L., 545, 546, 547, 803, 804, 988, 1699, 1700, 1875, 2393
Morgan, George T., 1585, 1586, 1587
Morgan, Lewis H., 432
Morgan, Murray, 1876
Morgan, Neil, 14
Morrell, W. P., 1080
Morris, John R., 2487
Morris, Richard B., 32
Morrisey, Richard J., 1191
Mortensen, A. Russell, 991
Mosk, Sanford A., 1192, 1497
Mothershead, Harmon R., 1193, 2175
Mottram, Eric, 2958A
Mowry, George, 2488
Moynihan, Ruth Barnes, 2664
Mugridge, Donald H., 106
Mulder, William, 989, 990, 991
Muller, William G., 2176
Mullin, Robert N., 2321
Munns, E. N., 1588, 1589
Murdock, George Peter, 330
Murphy, George G. S., 186
Murphy, Paul L., 1413
Murphy, William S., 2141
Murray, Keith A., 548, 730, 2489
Murray, Robert A., 731, 1081
Myer, Dillon S., 2101
Myers, Lee, 732
Myers, Rex C., 1796
Myres, Sandra L., 1194, 1195

Nadeau, Remi, 1877, 1878
Nance, Joseph M., 642
Nankivell, John H., 2177
Nardroff, Ellen von, 187
Nasatir, Abraham P., 549, 857, 858
Nash, A. E. Keir, 2178
Nash, Gary B., 277, 433
Nash, Gerald D., 15, 1498, 1499, 1500, 1501, 1647, 1648, 1936, 1937, 1938, 2007
Nash, Lee M., 2872, 2891, 2892
Nash, Roderick, 2575, 2576, 2577, 2578
Navarro, Joseph P., 909, 910
Nedry, H. S., 2927
Neil, William M., 2394, 2395
Nelson, Harold L., 733
Nelson, Lowry, 992, 1331, 1879
Nesbit, Robert C., 1332, 1797, 1880, 2102, 2322

INDEX

Nettels, Curtis, 188
Nevins, Allan, 734, 805, 1561
Newcomb, William W., Jr., 434
Newell, F. H., 1415
Nibley, Preston, 993
Nichols, Claude W., Jr., 1590, 2008
Nichols, Roger L., 435, 736, 737, 806, 1880A
Nichols, Roy F., 2396
Nimmo, Joseph, Jr., 1196
Nissen, Karen M., 318
Nixon, Herman C., 189
Nogales, Luis G., 911
Noggle, Burl, 859, 1649
Nordhauser, Norman, 1650
Nordin, Dennis S., 1333, 1334
Nordstrom, Carl, 189A
Norquest, Carrol, 912, 2009
North, Douglass C., 1939, 1940
North, Hart H., 2103, 2104
Northrop, Stuart A., 1082
Norton, Thomas E., 550
Nostrand, Richard L., 860
Nugent, Walter T. K., 2490, 2491
Nunis, Doyce B., Jr., 551, 552, 1083, 1880B, 2323, 2873
Nye, Russel B., 2492, 2745

O'Callaghan, Jerry A., 1503, 1504, 1591
O'Connor, Richard, 1651, 1798, 2324, 2746
O'Dea, Thomas F., 994, 995
Oehler, Charles M., 738
Ogden, Adele, 1941, 1942
Ogle, Ralph H., 436, 739
Oglesby, Richard E., 553, 554, 2579
Okimoto, Daniel K., 2105
Okubo, Miné, 2106
Olin, Spencer C., Jr., 2107, 2228, 2244, 2493
Oliphant, J. Orin, 1197, 1198
Oliva, Leo E., 740
Olmsted, Roger, 1574, 2256
Olsen, Barton C., 2325
Olsen, Michael L., 1335, 1336
Olson, James C., 67, 437
O'Meara, Walter, 555, 2665
O'Riordan, Timothy, 2580
Ormsby, Waterman L., 1739
Orsi, Richard J., 1337
Ortiz, Alfonso, 438
Osgood, Ernest S., 1199, 2326

Ostrander, Gilman M., 68, 190, 2494
Oswalt, Wendell H., 439
Otis, D. S., 440
Ottoson, Howard W., 1505, 1506
Ourada, Patricia K., 2108
Overton, Richard C., 1799, 1800, 1801
Oviatt, Alton B., 1944
Owen, Edgar W., 1651A
Owens, Kenneth N., 2397, 2398, 2399
Owsley, Frank L., 278

Paden, Irene D., 1702
Padfield, Harland, 1338
Page, Evelyn, 279
Paher, Stanley W., 1083A
Palmer, Frederick A., 2711
Palmer, Hans C., 2229
Palmer, William R., 1945
Papanikolas, Helen Z., 2010, 2230
Paredes, Américo, 2842A
Parish, William J., 1946
Park, Joe, 2874
Parker, Watson, 1084
Parkman, Francis, 280, 281, 282, 1703
Parman, Donald L., 440A
Parsons, A. B., 1085
Parsons, Stanley B., 2495
Past, Raymond E., 2747
Patterson, George J., 2231
Patterson, James T., 2496, 2497
Pattie, James Ohio, 557
Paul, Rodman W., 861, 996, 1043, 1086, 1087, 1088, 1089, 1090, 1099, 1119, 1339, 1340, 1341, 2109, 2110, 2327, 2328, 2329, 2666, 2667, 2667A, 2959
Paullin, Charles O., 34
Pawar, Sheelwant B., 2011
Paxson, Frederic L., 16, 191, 1803
Paylore, Patricia, 1342
Peake, Ora B., 441, 1200
Pearce, Roy Harvey, 442
Pearce, T. M., 192, 2740, 2748
Pearce, William M., 1201
Pearson, Jim B., 1507
Pearson, John E., 1881
Pease, Theodore C., 283
Peattie, Donald C., 1592
Peckham, Howard H., 284, 285, 443
Peffer, E. Louise, 1508
Pelling, Henry, 2012
Pelzer, Louis, 1202
Penick, James L., 2582

Penny, J. Russell, 1509
Perrigo, Lynn, 69, 1091, 1882, 2330
Perry, Louis B., 2013
Perry, Richard S., 2013
Peters, Robert N., 2928, 2929
Peterson, Charles S., 997, 998, 1593
Peterson, F. Ross, 69A, 2498
Peterson, Levi S., 1203
Peterson, Martin S., 2749
Peterson, Richard H., 193, 1092, 1093
Peterson, Robert L., 1049
Pettit, Arthur G., 2179
Peyton, Green, 70
Philbrick, Francis S., 286
Phillips, George H., 444
Phillips, Paul C., 287, 558
Pierce, Richard A., 1950
Pierson, George W., 194, 195, 196
Pilkington, William T., 2750
Pilson, Victor, 1828
Pinchot, Gifford, 1594, 2583, 2584
Pinckney, Pauline A., 2799
Pinkett, Harold T., 2585
Pino, Frank, 913
Pitt, Leonard, 862, 2257
Pizer, Donald, 2751
Pletcher, David M., 643
Polenberg, Richard, 2586, 2587
Poll, Richard D., 999, 1000, 2400
Pollack, Norman, 2500
Pomeroy, Earl, 17, 18, 19, 71, 1883, 1884, 2401, 2402, 2960, 2961
Pomfret, John E., 288
Porter, Joseph C., 2752
Porter, Kenneth W., 559, 560, 1641, 2180, 2181
Post, Robert C., 1804
Poulton, Helen J., 35, 93
Powell, Donald M., 107
Prassel, Frank R., 2331
Pratt, Julius W., 644, 645
Pressly, Thomas J., 1343
Price, Glenn W., 646
Price, Monroe E., 332
Price, Warren C., 2893
Priest, Loring B., 331, 445
Prucha, Francis Paul, 440, 446, 447, 448, 741, 742, 743
Pugh, Donald W., 2843
Pulling, Hazel A., 1204
Pursinger, Marvin G., 2111
Puter, Stephen A. D., 1595
Putnam, Jackson K., 196A, 2501

Quiett, Glenn C., 1805
Quinn, Larry D., 1947, 2112, 2258

Rader, Benjamin G., 1596, 2014
Rakestraw, Lawrence, 1250, 1510, 1597, 2588, 2589, 2590, 2591, 2592
Ramsey, Bobby Gene, 807
Ramsey, Robert W., 289
Randall, Ruth Painter, 2668
Rasmussen, Wayne D., 1344, 1345, 1346, 1347
Ray, Arthur J., 449
Rayback, Joseph G., 2015
Redwood, Boverton, 1653
Reese, James V., 2016
Reid, Agnes J., 2669
Reiger, John F., 2593
Reinhardt, Richard, 2594
Reisler, Mark, 914, 914A
Renner, Frederic G., 2803
Renner, G. K., 1205
Renshaw, Patrick, 2017
Reps, John W., 1885
Resh, Richard W., 620
Rhodehamel, Josephine D., 2670
Ricards, Sherman L., 2232, 2332
Rice, Lawrence D., 2182
Rice, Otis K., 290, 290A
Rich, Edwin E., 561, 562, 563
Rich, Russell R., 1001
Richards, Kent D., 2403
Richardson, Elmo R., 2595, 2596, 2597, 2598, 2599, 2600
Richardson, Rupert N., 450
Richey, Elinor, 2670A, 2671
Rickard, Thomas A., 1094
Rickey, Don, 744
Ricks, Joel E., 1002
Ridge, Martin, 1948
Ridley, Jack, 451, 2875
Riegel, Robert E., 1806
Risch, Erna, 745
Rischin, Moses, 2259, 2260
Rister, Carl C., 746, 1511, 1654
Rittenhouse, Jack D., 1704
Rivera, Feliciano, 905, 906
Rives, George L., 647
Robbins, Lynn A., 2672
Robbins, Roy M., 1512
Robbins, William G., 1886
Roberts, Brigham H., 1003, 1004
Roberts, Gary L., 2333
Roberts, Harold, 1655

INDEX

Roberts, Paul H., 1598
Robinson, Cecil, 915, 2753
Robinson, Elwyn B., 72
Robinson, Robert M., 2018
Robinson, William W., 1513, 1887
Rocq, Margaret M., 108
Rodecape, Lois F., 2833
Rodgers, Andrew D., 111, 1599
Roeder, Richard B., 63A, 2502
Rogers, Earl M., 1348
Rogin, Leo, 1349
Rogin, Michael P., 2503
Rohrbough, Malcolm J., 1514
Rolle, Andrew F., 73, 2233
Rollins, Philip Ashton, 1206
Romig, Robert L., 1095
Rosa, Joseph G., 2334, 2335
Rose, Alice, 2504
Roske, Ralph J., 1096
Ross, Alexander, 564
Ross, Marion D., 2812
Ross, Nancy Wilson, 2673
Ross, William M., 1656
Rostad, Lee, 1251
Rostow, Eugene V., 1657, 2113
Rothman, David J., 2404
Rowe, John, 1097
Rowell, Edward J., 1366
Rowley, William D., 2505
Rowse, A. L., 2234
Royce, Charles C., 332A
Royce, Sarah, 2674
Rudolph, Frederick, 2876
Ruetten, Richard T., 2506, 2507
Rundell, Walter, Jr., 109, 197, 1658, 1659, 2844
Rusk, Ralph Leslie, 2754
Russel, Robert R., 1807
Russell, Austin, 2800
Russell, Carl P., 565, 566
Russell, Nelson V., 291
Rutledge, Peter J., 1600
Ruxton, George F., 567

Sacconaghi, Charles D., 747
Sage, Leland L., 74
Sageser, A. Bower, 1417
Sakoda, James M., 2114
Sale, Roger, 1887A
Salmond, John A., 2601
Saloutos, Theodore, 1207, 1350, 1351, 1515, 2508, 2509, 2834
Samora, Julian, 916, 917
Sanchez, George I., 918

Sanders, Douglas E., 313
Sanders, John, 2845
Sandmeyer, Elmer C., 2115
Sanford, Mollie D., 2674A
Sargent, Charles S., 1601
Satz, Ronald N., 452
Sauer, Carl O., 292, 863
Saum, Lewis O., 453, 568
Saunders, Lyle, 110
Saunderson, Mont H., 2602
Savage, W. Sherman, 748, 1098, 2182A, 2183, 2184, 2185, 2186
Savage, William W., 1208
Sawyer, Byrd W., 1252
Saxton, Alexander P., 2019, 2020, 2116, 2336, 2510
Scamehorn, H. Lee, 1808, 1948A
Schafer, Joseph, 198, 199
Schaffer, Ronald, 2675, 2675A
Schapsmeier, Edward L., 1351A
Schapsmeier, Frederick H., 1351A
Scheck, John F., 2930
Scheffer, Victor B., 2603
Scheiber, Harry N., 200
Schell, Herbert S., 75
Scherer, James A. B., 2337
Schiff, Ashley L., 1602
Schlebecker, John T., 1209, 1210, 1352, 1353, 1354
Schmalz, Bruce L., 1418
Schmeckebier, Laurence F., 454
Schmidt, Louis B., 648, 1355
Schmitt, Peter J., 2604
Schnell, J. Christopher, 649, 1888, 1889
Schoberlin, Melvin, 2835
Schoen, Harold, 2187
Schoenberger, Dale T., 2188
Scholes, Frances V., 864, 865
Schonfeld, Robert G., 1419
Schoolcraft, Henry R., 455
Schrepfer, Susan R., 1603
Schroeder, John H., 650
Schruben, Francis W., 1660, 1661, 2511
Schubert, Frank N., 2189
Schwartz, Harry, 1356
Schwarzman, Richard C., 1662
Scofield, William H., 1343
Scott, George W., 2512
Scruggs, Otey M., 919, 920, 921, 922, 2021, 2022
Seager, Robert, II, 2117
Sellars, Richard West, 2755
Sellers, Charles G., 651
Servín, Manuel, 923, 924, 2931
Settle, Mary L., 1740, 1741, 1742, 1743

INDEX

Settle, Raymond W., 1740, 1741, 1742, 1743
Severin, Timothy, 293
Seymour, Flora W., 456
Shames, Priscilla, 457, 2756
Shannon, Fred A., 82, 201, 1211, 1357, 1516
Shannon, James P., 2932
Sharp, Paul F., 76, 652, 1604, 1949
Sharrow, Walter G., 653
Shaw, R. M., 1253
Sheehan, Bernard W., 458, 459
Sheffy, Lester F., 1212
Sheldon, Addison E., 1517
Shelton, Emily J., 2676
Shepherd, William R. E., 1254
Shepperson, Wilbur S., 2235
Sherwood, Morgan B., 77, 808, 809
Shideler, James H., 1213, 1358, 1358A, 1605
Shinn, Charles H., 1099, 1100, 2405
Shirk, George A., 749
Shover, John L., 2503
Shumway, George, 1744
Siampos, Helen, 2877
Siegel, Stanley, 2406
Sievers, Michael, 750
Simler, Norman J., 202
Simmons, Marc, 866
Simmons, Ozzie G., 925
Simms, D. Harper, 1359
Simonson, Harold P., 203, 2757
Sims, Robert C., 2023
Singletary, Otis, 654
Skaggs, Jimmy M., 1214
Slobodek, Mitchell, 2024
Sloss, Frank H., 1950
Slote, Bernice, 2758
Slotkin, Richard, 294, 2338, 2759
Smith, A. Robert, 2513
Smith, Alice E., 1951
Smith, Bradford, 2118
Smith, Charles W., 111
Smith, David C., 1606
Smith, Duane A., 80, 1101, 1102, 1103, 1104, 1890
Smith, Dwight L., 112, 333
Smith, Frank E., 2605
Smith, George W., 655
Smith, Gibbs M., 2025
Smith, Grant H., 1105
Smith, Helena H., 2339
Smith, Henry Nash, 810, 2760, 2761, 2762, 2962, 2963
Smith, Joseph, 1005, 1006

Smith, Justin H., 656, 657
Smith, Page, 2677
Smith, Robert W., 1106, 2026, 2340
Smith, T. Lynn, 2190
Smurr, J. W., 558, 2191, 2341, 2407
Smythe, William E., 1420
Snell, Joseph W., 2319
Snider, Luther C., 1663
Snodgrass, Marjorie P., 334
Snoke, Elizabeth R., 658
Sobin, Harris J., 2812A
Socolofsky, Homer, 1518
Solberg, Curtis B., 2246
Sonnichsen, C. L., 460, 1107, 1215, 2342
Sorenson, John L., 2964
Sosin, Jack M., 295
Spence, Clark C., 1108, 1109, 1422, 1951A, 2408, 2409
Spence, Mary Lee, 798
Spencer, Betty G., 1607
Spicer, Edward H., 461, 462, 463, 2119, 2965
Spiess, Lincoln B., 2846
Splitter, Henry W., 2894
Spoehr, Luther W., 2120, 2193, 2261
Sprague, Marshall, 77A, 1109A
Sprague, William F., 2678
Spratt, John S., 1664
Spring, Agnes W., 1745
Spritzer, Donald E., 2514
Stadtman, Verne A., 2878
Stanger, Frank M., 1608
Stanton, William, 811
Starr, Kevin, 2763
Stauss, Joseph H., 464
Steck, Francis B., 867
Steckler, Gerard G., 2933
Steckmesser, Kent L., 2343, 2764
Stedman, Murray S., Jr., 2515
Stedman, Susan W., 2515
Steer, Henry B., 1609
Stegner, Wallace E., 812, 1007, 1008, 1705, 2606, 2766, 2966, 2967
Stein, Walter J., 1360
Steinel, Alvin T., 1361
Stelter, Gilbert A., 1891, 1892
Stenberg, Richard R., 659, 660
Stenhouse, T. B. H., 1009
Stensland, Anna L., 335
Stephenson, W. A., 1423
Stern, Norton B., 2236
Stevens, Horace, 1595
Stevens, Wayne E., 569

INDEX

Stevenson, Robert M., 2847
Stewart, Edgar I., 752
Stewart, George R., 36, 1706, 1707, 2344, 2767
Stewart, William J., 1519
Stimson, Grace H., 2027
Stoehr, C. Eric, 2812B
Stone, Harry W., 2028
Stout, Joseph A. Jr., 609, 661, 1216, 2607
Stoutenburgh, John L., 336
Stover, John F., 1809, 1810
Stowe, Noel J., 1520
Stratton, David H., 1665, 2516, 2968
Stratton, Porter A., 2895
Streeter, Thomas W., 116
Strickland, Rennard, 464A
Strickland, Rex W., 204
Strong, Douglas H., 2608, 2609
Strong, Edward K., Jr., 2121, 2122
Stuart, Robert, 813
Sudweeks, Leslie L., 1362
Suggs, George G., 1110, 2029, 2030
Sully, Langdon, 753
Summerhayes, Martha, 2679
Sundborg, George, 1363, 1424
Sunder, John E., 570, 571, 572
Sung, Betty Lee, 2123
Supple, Barry E., 1785
Susman, Warren I., 205
Sutton, Imre, 336A, 1425
Swadesh, Frances L., 117, 868
Swain, Donald C., 1426, 2610, 2611, 2612, 2613
Swan, Howard, 2848
Swanson, Edward B., 1666
Swanson, Merwin, 95
Swanton, John R., 337
Sweedlun, Verne S., 1364
Sweet, William W., 2934, 2935
Swierenga, Robert P., 1521
Swisher, Carl B., 2410
Sypolt, Charles M., 1255
Szasz, Margaret, 465, 2879

Taft, Philip, 2031, 2032, 2033
Taft, Robert, 2801
Taggart, Stephen G., 1010
Tait, Samuel W., Jr., 1667
Talmadge, Marian, 2194
Tanner, Annie C., 1011, 2680
Tarcay, Eileen, 1012
Tattersall, James N., 1610, 1952

Taylor, Frank J., 1671
Taylor, Graham D., 466
Taylor, J. Golden, 2768, 2769
Taylor, Morris F., 1746, 2345
Taylor, Paul S., 926, 927, 1312, 1365, 1366, 1367, 2034, 2035
Taylor, Philip A. M., 1013, 1014, 1015, 1016, 1017, 1018
Telling, Irving, Jr., 1893
Terrell, Donna M., 2681
Terrell, John U., 2681
Thaxter, B. A., 814
Thomas, Dorothy S., 2124
Thomas, George, 1019, 1427, 1428
Thomas, Lately, 2936
Thompson, Erwin N., 2195
Thompson, John T., 1429, 2614
Thompson, Kenneth, 2615
Thompson, Laura, 467
Thompson, Richard A., 2125
Thompson, Robert L., 1818
Thompson, Thomas G., 1111, 1112
Thomson, George, 2346
Thorp, Raymond W., 573
Thrapp, Dan L., 754
Throckmorton, Arthur L., 1953
Thurman, Sue Bailey, 2196
Thwaites, Reuben G., 20, 815, 816
Tinsley, James A., 2517
Tobie, Harvey E., 574, 2036
Tobin, Gregory M., 82
Todd, Arthur C., 1113
Todd, Edgeley W., 575
Todes, Charlotte, 1611
Toll, William, 206, 2197
Tolson, Arthur, 2198
Tompkins, Walker A., 1668
Tooker, Richard H., 1600
Toole, K. Ross, 45, 78, 79, 1114, 1115, 1116, 1612
Tourville, Elsie A., 118
Towne, Charles W., 1217, 1256
Townley, John M., 1117, 1118
Trask, David S., 2518
Traxler, Ralph N., Jr., 1811
Trennert, Robert A., Jr., 468
Tressman, Ruth, 1218, 2682
Trimble, William J., 1119, 2347
Trottman, Nelson, 1812
Trulio, Beverly, 2683
Turnbull, George S., 2896
Turner, Albert B., 2126
Turner, Frederick Jackson, 21, 207, 208, 296

INDEX

Turner, Wallace, 1020
Tuttle, Daniel S., 2937
Tyack, David B., 2880, 2881, 2882, 2883
Tyler, David B., 817
Tyler, Robert L., 1613, 2037, 2348
Tyler, S. Lyman, 468A, 469
Tyson, Carl, 2519

Ubbelohde, Carl, 80
Udall, Stewart L., 2616
Ulibarri, George S., 662
Ulibarri, Richard O., 869
Underhill, Lonnie E., 2684
Underhill, Ruth M., 470, 471, 472, 2938
Unrau, William E., 472A
Utley, Robert M., 473, 474, 475, 756, 757, 758, 1814

Vagners, Juris, 1669
Vail, R. W. G., 297
Valentine, Alan C., 2349
Van Alstyne, Richard W., 663, 664
Vance, Harold, 1629
Van Deusen, John G., 2201
Vande Vere, Emmett K., 1431
Vandiver, Frank E., 21A
Van Doren, Charles, 2571
Van Every, Dale, 298, 299, 300, 301
VanHise, Charles R., 2618
Van Orman, Richard A., 123, 1894, 1895, 2836
Van Zandt, Franklin K., 39
Vasey, Tom, 1367
Vaughan, Alden T., 302, 476
Vaughan, Thomas, 2813
Vecoli, Rudolph J., 2262
Vedder, Richard K., 267A
Vevier, Charles, 665
Veysey, Laurence R., 2884, 2969
Victor, Frances Fuller, 577
Vigil, Ralph H., 870
Vigness, David M., 666
Vinson, J. Chal, 630
Voegelin, C. F., 343
Voegelin, F. M., 343
Voelker, Frederick E., 578
Voeltz, Herman C., 1432, 2038
Voght, Martha, 2939
Vollmar, Edward R., 2940
Vorspan, Max, 2237

Wade, Richard C., 303, 1896, 1897
Wagner, Henry R., 119, 818, 819, 871, 1708
Wagner, Jack R., 1120A
Wagoner, J. J., 1220, 2411
Waldron, Gladys H., 2263
Walker, Arthur L., 1121
Walker, Don D., 579, 1221, 1222, 2770, 2771
Walker, Franklin, 2772, 2773, 2774, 2775, 2776
Walker, Henry P., 1746A, 1747, 1748
Walker, Robert H., 2777
Wallace, Andrew, 1849
Wallace, Anthony F. C., 477, 478
Wallace, Edward S., 820
Wallace, William S., 120
Wallis, Wilson D., 2238
Walsh, James P., 2520
Walter, Paul A. F., 1954
Walters, Donald E., 2521
Wandesforde-Smith, Geoffrey, 2540
Ward, James R., 2350
Wardin, Albert W., Jr., 2941
Warne, William E., 2618A
Warner, Charles A., 1670
Warner, Donald F., 667
Warren, Sidney, 81
Washburn, Wilcomb E., 304, 344, 382, 479, 479A, 480, 481
Waters, Frank, 1122
Waters, Lawrence L., 1815
Watkins, T. H., 1123, 1522, 2039
Watson, Charles S., Jr., 1522
Watson, Margaret G., 2837
Wayne, George H., 2201A
Weaver, Sally M., 313
Webb, Walter P., 22, 82, 305, 306, 1223, 1368, 1433, 2351, 2970, 2971
Weber, David J., 580, 872, 872A
Weber, Francis J., 121
Weems, John E., 668
Weigle, Mary M., 2942
Weigley, Russell F., 759
Weinberg, Albert K., 669
Weinstein, Allen, 2522
Weinstein, Robert A., 1614
Weisel, George F., 581
Weiss, Stuart L., 2523
Wells, Merle W., 41, 1124, 2040, 2412, 2413, 2414, 2524
Welter, Rush, 209, 210, 307, 2972
Welty, Earl M., 1671
Welty, Raymond L., 760

INDEX

Wentworth, Edward N., 1217, 1256, 1258, 1259
Werner, M. R., 1021
Wertenbaker, Thomas J., 308
Wesley, Edgar B., 761
West, Elliott, 1898
West, John O., 2352
West, Ray B., Jr., 1022, 1899
Westbrook, Harriette J., 582
Westbrook, Max, 2778, 2779, 2780
Westermeier, Clifford P., 1224, 1225
Westphall, Victor, 1523, 1524, 2415
Whalen, William J., 1023
Wharton, David, 1125
Wheat, Carl I., 821, 1126
Wheeler, Kenneth W., 1900
Whipple, Mary A., 396
Whitaker, Arthur P., 309, 310, 873
Whitaker, James W., 1369
White, Charles L., 1260
White, G. Edward, 2781
White, Gerald T., 1672, 1673, 1674
White, Jean B., 2685
White, John H., Jr., 1816
White, John I., 2848A
White, Lonnie J., 762, 2416
Whitten, Woodrow S., 2041
Wickens, James F., 2525
Wickson, Edward J., 1370, 1371
Wik, Reynold M., 1372
Wilcox, Virginia L., 122
Wilkins, Thurman, 822, 2802
Williams, Blaine T., 2686
Williams, David A., 2417, 2418
Williams, Donald A., 2619
Williams, Mary F., 2353
Williams, R. Hal., 1525, 2419
Williams, William A., 211
Williamson, Harold F., 1675, 1676
Willson, Clair E., 2838
Wilson, Dorothy C., 2687
Wilson, Elinor, 583, 2202
Wilson, Iris H., 823
Wilson, James A., 1226, 1227, 1228
Wilson, William H., 1901
Wiltsee, Ernest A., 1749
Winfrey, Dorman H., 2849
Winkenwerder, Hugo, 1615

Winn, Charles C., 2042
Winter, Robert, 2814
Winters, Robert K., 1616
Winther, Oscar O., 83, 123, 669A, 1750, 1751, 1752, 1753, 1754, 1755, 1756, 1902, 1955, 2239
Wissler, Clark, 482
Wolf, Jerome, 2043
Wolfe, Linne M., 2620
Wollenberg, Charles, 928, 2044, 2256, 2264, 2265
Wood, Raymond F., 2670
Wood, Richard G., 763, 824
Woodress, James L., 2782
Woodward, Robert C., 2526, 2527, 2885
Woolfolk, George R., 212, 2203
Worcester, Donald E., 873A
Working, D. W., 1361
Wright, Benjamin F., Jr., 213, 214
Wright, Chester W., 1261
Wright, J. Leitch, Jr., 670, 874
Wright, James E., 2528
Wright, Louis B., 311, 312
Wright, Muriel H., 345
Wright, William, 1127
Wyllys, Rufus K., 84, 2240
Wyman, Mark, 1128, 1129, 2045, 2897
Wyman, Walker D., 215, 1757, 1758
Wynne, R. E., 2127

Yavno, Max, 1290
Yee, J. E., 2621
Yonce, Frederick J., 1526, 1527
Yost, Karl, 2803
Young, Karl, 1024
Young, Kimball, 1025
Young, Mary, 2973
Young, Otis E., Jr., 764, 765, 1130, 1130A
Yount, George C., 584

Zellner, Arnold, 186
Zimmermann, Erich W., 1677
Zolla, Elémire, 483
Zwelling, Shomer S., 671

NOTES